Demand-Driven Supply Chain Management

Transformational performance improvement

Simon Eagle

KoganPage

First published in Great Britain and the United States in 2017 by Kogan Page Limited

2nd Floor, 45 Gee Street	c/o Martin P Hill Consulting	4737/23 Ansari Road
London	122 W 27th St, 10th Floor	Daryaganj
EC1V 3RS	New York, NY 10001	New Delhi 110002
United Kingdom	USA	India

www.koganpage.com

© Simon Eagle, 2017

The right of Simon Eagle to be identified as the author of this work has been asserted by him in accordance with the Copyright, Designs and Patents Act 1988.

ISBN   978 0 7494 7997 8
E-ISBN   978 0 7494 7998 5

British Library Cataloguing-in-Publication Data

A CIP record for this book is available from the British Library.

Library of Congress Cataloging-in-Publication Data

Names: Eagle, Simon, author.
Title: Demand-driven supply chain management : transformational performance
   improvement / Simon Eagle.
Description: 1st Edition. | New York : Kogan Page Ltd, [2017] | Includes
   bibliographical references and index.
Identifiers: LCCN 2017001571 (print) | LCCN 2017009074 (ebook) |
   ISBN 9780749479978 (alk. paper) | ISBN 9780749479985 (ebook)
Subjects: LCSH: Business logistics. | Materials management.
Classification: LCC HD38.5 .E24 2017 (print) | LCC HD38.5 (ebook) |
   DDC 658.5—dc23

Typeset by Integra Software Services, Pondicherry
Print production managed by Jellyfish
Printed and bound by CPI Group (UK) Ltd, Croydon, CR0 4YY

Praise for *Demand-Driven Supply Chain Management*

'Demand-Driven SCM is powerful and practical. I hope these ideas continue to gain traction in industry and that the concept of "Demand-Driven" quickly becomes the norm.' **Martin Christopher, Emeritus Professor of Marketing and Logistics, Cranfield School of Management**

'This work helps cement the Demand-Driven methodology in the mainstream by dramatically strengthening the case for change with clear logic and common sense. Simon Eagle has been a huge advocate for the Demand-Driven movement and this book is a very welcome contribution to the body of knowledge!' **Carol Ptak and Chad Smith, Co-founders, Demand Driven Institute**

'The circumstances and environments for which the current and universally used forecast push MPS/MRP model was designed are totally different to those of today's highly uncertain world. In this book, Simon Eagle makes a very strong case for the urgent need for migrating to Demand-Driven models in supply chain management. You will find a comprehensive description of the knowledge frontier in this fundamental area, including the basic equations that should drive it, seldom known by people working in the field. Applying these concepts with rigour will give any company a substantial competitive advantage and a clear path for sustainable growth. A must-read for any industry professional in any area, at any level in any industry.' **David Poveda, Owner and Director, Flowing Consultoría, Colombia**

'Thank you to Simon Eagle for this in-depth work that contributes significantly to clearly explaining the what, how and why of Demand-Driven MRP. For example, how forecasts *should* be used to transform supply chain and operations performance. Thank you also for the very interesting appendix on the story behind DDMRP.' **Caroline Mondon, Directrice Générale, Fapics, and author, *The Missing Links: A demand driven supply chain detective novel***

CONTENTS

ACKNOWLEDGEMENTS

With thanks to Wendy, Katie, Oliver and Lucy for their forbearance and frequent reminders that Demand-Driven SCM is 'how we always restock the fridge!'

Many thanks also to Chad Smith and Carol Ptak, co-founders of the Demand Driven Institute for their contribution, and leadership, publicity and support in showing how commercial supply chain management should be practised in the 21st century.

LIST OF ABBREVIATIONS

5S	sort, set in order, shine, standardize/systemize, sustain (work place management)
APICS	American Production and Inventory Control Society
APIOBPCS	automatic pipeline inventory and order-based production control system
APS	advanced planning system
ATO	assemble to order
BOD	bill of distribution
BOM	bill of materials
CAS	complex adaptive system
CCC	core commercial cycle
CDDL	Certified Demand Driven Leader
CDDP	Certified Demand Driven Planner
CI	continuous improvement
CoV	coefficient of variation
CPFR	collaborative planning, forecasting and replenishment
CPG	consumer packaged goods
DDI	Demand Driven Institute
DDMRP	Demand-Driven Materials Requirements Planning
DFM	design for manufacture
DRP	distribution requirements planning
ERP	enterprise resource planning
ETO	engineer to order
FG	finished goods
GAAP	generally accepted accounting principles
IBP	Integrated Business Planning
ISCEA	International Supply Chain Education Alliance
IT	information tecŸology
JIT	just in time
KPI	key performance indicator
MEIO	multi-echelon inventory optimization
MOQ	minimum order quantity

MPS	master production schedule
MRP	materials requirements planning
MRPII	manufacturing resource planning
MTO	make to order
MTS	make to stock
OEE	overall equipment effectiveness
OTIF	on time in full
PCE	process-cycle efficiency
POS	point of sale
ROC	reorder cycle
ROI	return on investment
ROP	reorder point
RM	raw materials
S&OP	sales and operations planning
SaaS	Software as a Service
SCM	supply chain management
SFTP	secure file transfer protocol
SKU	stock-keeping unit
SMED	single-minute exchange of die (quick machine-changeover tecŸique)
3PL	third-party logistics
ToC	Theory of Constraints
TPM	total productive (preventative) maintenance
TPS	Toyota Production System
TQM	total quality management
VMI	vendor managed inventory
VUCA	volatile, uncertain, complex, ambiguous
VUT	variability, utilization, time
WIP	work in progress

'In science, novelty emerges only with difficulty, manifested by resistance, against a background provided by expectation.'

'Because it demands large-scale paradigm destruction and major shifts in the problems and tecŸiques of normal science, the emergence of new theories is generally preceded by a period of pronounced professional insecurity.'

Thomas S KuŸ, *The Structure of Scientific Revolutions*, 1962

'... most companies in Britain today base production on long-term sales forecasts, which are only altered at infrequent intervals. Because it is not given to human beings to foretell the future, they usually end up with a warehouse full of slow-moving products, and none of the products that they could sell if they had them.'

'MRP generates excessive stocks because it is based on sales forecasts for long periods into the future, which are always inaccurate.'

Professor Jack Burbidge, *Five Golden Rules to Avoid Bankruptcy*, 1983

'The definition of insanity is doing the same thing over and over again, but expecting different results.'

Albert Einstein (reputedly)

'Our doubts are traitors, and make us lose the good we oft might win, by fearing to attempt.'

William Shakespeare, *Measure for Measure*, Act 1, Scene 4

'Heaven help you if your competitors do this before you do.'

Carol Ptak, 2014

Introduction and summaries

01

What this book is about

The book has a single, unrelenting and proven message: driving replenishment execution through materials requirements planning (MRP)-dependent demand network with today's high levels of forecast inaccuracy inevitably leads to unbalanced inventories that cause supply chain and production instability, or variability, as schedules frequently have to be amended to prevent service issues. This leads to the development of excessive inventories, excessive lead times and necessitates the use of unplanned capacity. However, adoption of the Demand-Driven Supply Chain Management (SCM) approach, especially in 'make to stock' supply chains, allows planned service levels to be achieved from half the average inventories, with far higher overall equipment effectiveness (OEE) and significantly shorter lead times.

Over the last 80 years supply chain management (SCM) has evolved from being of interest to only, perhaps, economists with a simple transactions-cost focus (eg 'The Nature of the Firm', written by Ronald Coase in 1937: perhaps the earliest form of 'make or buy' analysis), to one in which the chief supply chain officer is increasingly taking his or her seat on the board of numerous FTSE100/Fortune 500 companies. SCM is now studied around the world as a core subject in Business and MBA degrees and in its own right, with a significant community of specialists, researchers and professors.

Yet despite this growth in profile and the large numbers of people worldwide who now work in SCM, many would struggle to describe exactly what it is and how it differs from, say, procurement, manufacturing or operations, logistics and customer service.

Maybe SCM is simply a term that encompasses all of these. In which case it is an excellent descriptor of one of the three core activities in any enterprise: supply (the others being innovation and marketing). And, if so, SCM is indeed of immense importance and deserves a high corporate profile, which makes it all the more surprising that the core principles of SCM are, with few exceptions, poorly practised across industry and little properly understood by those who work in it.

Those core principles are simply those of material flow and queuing. After all, what is supply chain management if it isn't about managing flows of materials through multiple value-adding conversion processes (ie manufacturing machines) and warehouses, which are all too frequently not moving but are static inventories queuing up and waiting to be processed or sold?

And, surprisingly, it is the materials requirements planning (MRP) engine and its use of inaccurate sales forecasts to drive replenishment (at the heart of all those expensive, but ubiquitous enterprise resource planning (ERP) and advanced planning system (APS) software systems in most company supply chains) that is actually making those inventory queues longer. This causes poor service levels and ensures that capacity utilization is significantly lower than desired or planned.

The reason is simple and should be well known: all forecasts are wrong so forecast-driven replenishment causes the wrong quantity of stuff to be bought/made/shipped to the wrong places at the wrong time, which means that inventories become unbalanced, service threats appear and schedule changes have to be made to head them off. This uses up unplanned capacity, and schedule interruptions cause lead times to be extended (MRP assumes they are static!). This creates further service threats and so the cycle continuously repeats itself, despite the use of so-called 'safety stocks' (which actually contribute to the problem), leading to the typical supply chain of today: one that is highly bloated with excessive capacity, inventories and lead times, still suffering service misses and staffed by planners who spend all their time firefighting after formulating master production schedules (MPSs) that are inaccurate as soon as they are completed.

The alternative to forecast-driven replenishment is Demand-Driven SCM, which can be applied in any form of supply chain – be it make to order (MTO) or make to stock (MTS); short and simple or global and complex; and whether demand is stable, volatile, seasonal or trending. And when Demand-Driven SCM is adopted in place of 'forecast push MPS/MRP' the benefits are always transformational, including the achievement of planned service levels from up to 50 per cent less average inventory, lower costs from higher OEE and significantly shorter lead times.

This book explains why Demand-Driven SCM is the correct process for managing supply chains, how it works and how it can be inexpensively phased into your company with no risk.

Who should read this book?

Anyone with an interest in SCM ranging from chief executives and academics through to supply planners and students.

Chief executives and board members

Maybe you are concerned about your company's cash-flow performance and its ability to meet demand as you attempt to penetrate new global markets? Perhaps you are threatened by competitors who seem to have lower costs or can apparently operate with lower margins? This book will demonstrate that it is almost certain that your company can significantly improve its competitiveness in terms of service, cash flow and margin without any high cost investment (or disinvestment!). If you don't follow this path, and others do, might your company suffer a competitive disadvantage?

Manufacturing and operations

Demand-Driven SCM will ensure that your production schedules become stable, predictable and efficient. No longer will you have to make unplanned and time-consuming machine changeovers to prevent the appearance of back orders; your levels of unplanned overtime will diminish significantly and your OEE will start to climb rapidly. Factory-floor stability will also enable you to focus upon continuous improvement without interruption from planners wanting to head off the latest back-order threat. (NB Demand-Driven SCM does not require you to manufacture in smaller batches.)

Supply chain leaders

No doubt you are fed up with the annual challenge of improving both service and inventory performance when you know that neither are really under your control. No matter how much effort has been put into improving forecast accuracy, the needle hardly moves and your sales and marketing colleagues seem oblivious to the difficulty of changing schedules at short notice in response to promotions and for products that are in short supply. And when it comes to inventory performance, how can that be improved when demand is becoming ever more volatile and you need more, not less, safety stock? Demand-Driven SCM will enable your supply chain to achieve its planned service levels while also significantly increasing its inventory turn, and your planning team will be able to focus upon real value-add activities instead of expediting and firefighting.

Marketing and sales

You will be able to sell and promote virtually what and when you like, without service problems, and without having to spend inordinate amounts of time on promotions planning and forecasting. For the purposes of supply planning and good customer service, all you will be expected to do is provide early warning of significant demand events, such as extreme and exceptional promotions, and contribute to quantifying seasonal demand patterns.

Finance

Less stock, more cash, predictable cash flows, higher margins, capital expenditure delay! Does that sound attractive?

Procurement

If you know that a key to unlocking significant cost reduction is via collaborating more effectively with suppliers, but have found it extremely difficult to achieve successfully, then Demand-Driven SCM will help achieve this goal. Your supply schedules will stabilize and become accurate and your suppliers will be able to both reduce their lead times and become more efficient – and some of that cost reduction should accrue to you, their customer.

Demand planners

The focus of your role will change. You will, of course, still have to continue forecasting at the item level – but no longer will achieving high levels of time-phased accuracy (eg weekly or monthly) be your goal. Easily achievable levels of average forecast accuracy, over three or four periods at the item level, will be all that is required. In fact, your forecasting software will be able to do it automatically if it is tuned correctly and 'naive' forecasting tecŸiques that incorporate trend and seasonality are perfectly adequate. What you will be focusing on is working with your sales colleagues and customers and getting early visibility of significant demand events (such as extreme and exceptional promotions) and communicating them, by exception, to supply planners. You will also need to be aware of, and to roughly quantify, demand patterns for products that are experiencing significant trend, seasonality and step changes.

Supply planners

If you enjoy a daily crisis and the challenge of using your, no doubt, excellent spreadsheet skills to quickly cut new supply plans and prevent all those imminent back orders, then Demand-Driven SCM may not be very welcome. However, if you have always felt that there must be a better way to run a supply chain and you would like to spend more time generating real business value for your company and learning new ways of working – that will contribute to your continuous professional development, expertise and value in the job market – then this book is for you!

Academics

Most of the content of this book will not be news, but you may be surprised how little of what you take for granted – regarding supply chain dynamics, replenishment methodologies and the impact of variability upon supply chain flow – is currently so little practised in industry.

Students

On your course you will no doubt be learning about the 'bullwhip' effect, how there is a supposed trade-off between service and inventory, and the fundamentals of Lean and MRP. This book takes all that a lot further (though not in a complicated way), reverses some of the conventional wisdoms and, when fully grasped, you will know considerably more about it than most people who work in industry. That will make you a potentially very valuable asset – but be careful when you take up employment:

> It ought to be remembered that there is nothing more difficult to take in hand, more perilous to conduct, or more uncertain in its success, than to take the lead in the introduction of a new order of things. Because the innovator has for enemies all those who have done well under the old conditions, and lukewarm defenders in those who may do well under the new. This coolness arises partly from fear of the opponents, who have the laws on their side, and partly from the incredulity of men, who do not readily believe in new things until they have had a long experience of them.
>
> (Machiavelli, *The Prince*)

How the book is structured

Understanding Demand-Driven SCM can be difficult to grasp and counter-intuitive for many people. That is maybe because they have worked all their lives within a 'forecast push MPS/MRP' environment and it appears, intuitively, to make eminent sense: 'plan to make what we think we are going to sell and build in some safety stock in case we guess wrongly'. Unfortunately, this apparent logic is, and always has been, false – as you will learn.

Recognizing that different people learn in different ways and not everyone has the time to read and learn from an entire text-book-style narrative, the book contains, in addition to the core content, many comprehensive stand-alone articles that explain and demonstrate why supply chains behave the way they do, and how Demand-Driven SCM can put management back in control and significantly improve performance. Some of these articles cover similar material but from different angles and perspectives, and reading them will, hopefully, overcome the subject's counter-intuitive nature. These articles are also designed to enable readers who are short on time to get a full grasp of the book's main theme from an approach to the subject that particularly resonates with them.

The paradigm shift occurring in SCM

In the natural sciences, paradigms are: 'universally recognized scientific achievements that, for a time, provide model problems and solutions for a community of practitioners' and occasionally paradigm shifts occur: 'Successive transition from one paradigm to another via revolution is the usual developmental pattern of mature science.'[1]

Within the 'science' that is SCM, genuine revolution is quietly under way that will transform the way in which manufacturing and distribution supply chains are run. And because this is occurring in a commercial environment, those companies that adopt the new paradigm early will enjoy a significant competitive advantage, which is perhaps why there is relatively little overt publicity from them. The nature of this shift is the growth in understanding and adoption of the Demand-Driven SCM process and its replacement of traditional 'forecast push' enterprise resource planning (ERP), distribution requirements planning (DRP), materials requirements planning (MRP) and advanced planning systems (APS).

Demand-Driven SCM can be applied in all supply chain configurations (eg distributors and manufacturers, both 'make to stock' and 'make to order', in fact anywhere stock is planned to be held – even at external locations such as suppliers or customers), irrespective of the demand pattern, and is not a new or a highly expensive 'black box' IT solution. It is an 'end to end' supply chain replenishment process with an impregnable rationale[2] that is being implemented by increasing numbers of companies with leaders who have recognized that this way of working can now be robustly adopted across supply chains (and complex networks) using low-cost 'Software as a Service' (SaaS).

The rationale for Demand-Driven SCM is based on what supply chains really are: flows of materials through several 'conversion' processes (eg production machines and warehouses) that are prone to develop into inventory queues due to variability. Remarkably, these delays and queues usually account for around 95 per cent of a product's total lead time,[3] and these lead times are continuously changing in line with load. Queues represent static stock (tied-up cash) while long and variable lead times negatively impact responsiveness and service. Both can only be reduced by the existence of expensive spare capacity or through reducing flow variability.

Obvious ways to reduce variability, on the supply side, include preventing machine breakdowns and quality issues, quick changeovers and other Lean activities such as standard work, 5S, design for manufacture, etc.[4]

Less obvious, though far easier and quicker to implement, is ceasing to use the inevitably inaccurate item-level forecast to directly drive replenishment through ERP/DRP/MRP/APS. It creates excessive but unbalanced stock levels with service issues and leads to all that high-cost 'firefighting', schedule changing and expediting that is the other significant source of supply chain variability.

The Demand-Driven SCM process involves the deliberate positioning of multiple independent, but planned, inventory locations in the supply chain (including within the factory, if appropriate), the setting of appropriate stock targets (reflecting average demand levels and local variability with adjustments for any seasonality, trend and events) and their optimally sequenced, stable replenishment in response to actual demand. This prevents forecast error-induced variability being blown up the supply chain, and the inventory buffers break traditional MRP's erroneous use of dependent demand

(and fixed lead times), thereby preventing residual variability being cascaded up the supply chain. Given that lead times vary with load and, in MTS environments, the execution driving forecasts are badly wrong for most products, traditional supply chains suffer very severely from such variability and all the consequent unplanned cost-generating buffers (ie time, capacity and inventory) due to the high level of consequent service-chasing expediting and firefighting.

Why should the supply chain management paradigm be shifting now, around 50 years since Forrester, Burbidge, Little and Kingman laid the necessary conceptual framework in 1961?[5] One reason is that Carol Ptak, the past president of the American Production and Inventory Control Society (APICS), and Chad Smith, who co-authored *Orlicky's Material Requirements Planning* (McGraw Hill, 2011; third edition) have launched the Demand Driven Institute, an educational organization that now has affiliates worldwide.

Another reason is that the existence of SaaS allows the Demand-Driven SCM process to be both quickly and easily simulated and enables fast, inexpensive and low-risk pilots before implementation – without high-expenditure 'entry barriers'. An additional benefit of SaaS is that it can overlay multiple ERP systems and, therefore, support the use of Demand-Driven collaborative replenishment and planning across separate organizations, be they affiliates within the same company or those with a supplier/customer relationship.

But perhaps the most persuasive reason for why the Demand-Driven approach is starting to diffuse through industry is that it is so very effective due to its minimization of supply chain variability. Typical supply chain and operations performance improvements are:

1 achieve planned service levels, with

2 reductions in average inventories of between 30 per cent to 50 per cent;

3 with reductions in costs of around 20 per cent due to avoidance of unplanned overtime and higher levels of capacity utilization;

4 planned lead-time reductions of up to 85 per cent;

5 without expediting and firefighting or any focus upon achieving high levels of forecast accuracy.

And these types of performance improvements also contribute immensely to corporate performance, so this revolution could be quick as well as permanent – and very painful for those companies that ignore it!

It is no wonder that Martin Christopher recently said of Demand-Driven SCM:

> I think the approach that Carol [Carol Ptak, co-founder of the Demand Driven Institute] was advocating is powerful and practical. I hope that these ideas continue to gain traction in industry and that the concept of 'Demand-Driven' quickly becomes the norm.[6]

What every CEO really needs to know about SCM

All chief executive officers (CEOs) should be aware of the recent comment by Carol Ptak, APICS's past president and co-founder of the Demand Driven Institute:

> Heaven help you if your competitors do this before you.

Oddly, the 'top' strategy and management consultancies fail ever to mention 'this'. They are more likely to advise the need for CEOs, for instance, to actively manage functional supply chain trade-offs within their company such as the following:

1 Supply chain versus sales: sales-orientated discounting and promotions generating unsustainable demand volatility for operations and the supply chain.

2 Supply chain versus service: do all customers really need the same level of service, be it in the form of high 'on time in full' or delivery lead time? Both incur significant cost in the form of inventory and transport and neither might be cost-effective, or even required, by certain customer groups.

3 Supply chain versus product proliferation: uncontrolled and unfettered stock-keeping unit (SKU) proliferation in search of incremental sales incurs significant costs in the form of inventories and production capacity due to short production runs. Detailed

analysis will often reveal that many products are actually losing money and that a significant proportion are contributing negligibly to revenue.

Other advice often includes:

- Differentiate your supply chain and align it with corporate strategies.
- Create a modern, end-to-end supply chain organization.
- Set supply chain performance standards for the entire organization.

SCM is indeed important to corporate performance (eg reaching markets, service, cash flow, cost) and it is becoming ever more difficult to manage, let alone improve, because of increasing levels of competitiveness and demand volatility, shortening product life cycles and market fragmentation, in addition to globalization of markets and offshoring with the consequent growth of lead times and complexity.

So such advice is entirely sensible but omits an immensely significant activity that most CEOs should urgently undertake in order to start drastically improving supply chain, operations and corporate performance – and that makes those trade-offs far less of an issue. The activity is to simply ask why the company's supply chain and operations are still being driven by an increasingly inaccurate forecast[7] through an ERP/MRP or APS system when there is a proven,[2] simple and low-cost alternative available that can deliver:

- sustainable achievement of planned service levels, irrespective of demand patterns, with
- reductions in average inventory of between 30 per cent to 50 per cent, and
- cost improvements of around 20 per cent, and
- planning lead-time reductions of up to 85 per cent
- all without the expensive and continuous 'firefighting', expediting and frustration that is seen in most operations and supply planning organizations.

The alternative is to become 'Demand-Driven' instead of 'forecast-driven'.

Demand-Driven SCM can be applied in all supply chain configurations (eg 'make to stock', 'make to order', etc) and is not a new or a highly expensive 'black box' IT solution. It is an 'end to end' supply chain replenishment process with an impregnable rationale[2] that is being quietly implemented by increasing numbers of companies with leaders who have recognized that this way of working can now be robustly adopted across complex networks using low-cost SaaS.

The rationale for 'Demand-Driven SCM' is based on what supply chains really are: flows of materials through several 'conversion' processes that are sources of flow variability, which cause delays and queues. Remarkably, these delays and queues usually account for around 95 per cent of a product's total lead time, and these lead times are continuously changing in line with load. Queues represent static stock (tied-up cash) and diminish both responsiveness and flexibility, while variable lead times negatively impact availability and service. Both can only be reduced by the existence of expensive spare capacity or through reducing variability.

Obvious ways to reduce variability, on the supply side, include preventing machine breakdowns and quality issues and other Lean activities such as total productive maintenance (TPM), total quality management (TQM), standard work, quick changeovers, 5S, design for manufacture (DFM), etc.

Less obvious is ceasing to use the inevitably inaccurate item-level forecast to directly drive replenishment through ERP/DRP/MRP/APS. It creates excessive but unbalanced stock levels with service issues and leads to all that rescheduling, expediting and 'firefighting' as planners struggle to respond to MRP's avalanche of unprioritized exception messages. Interrupting supply schedules to prevent back orders generates supply chain variability, it amplifies as it cascades up the supply chain (ie the bullwhip effect) and disrupts smooth and efficient material flow.

Deliberately positioning planned inventory locations within the supply chain and replacing the forecast[7] with actual demand as the prime driver of 'end to end' supply chain replenishment is the quickest, easiest and most cost-effective method available for improving flow, generating operational stability and significantly improving corporate performance: service, cost and inventory – do you really want to wait until competitors get there before you?

If you would like your chief supply chain officer to know more about the how and why of Demand-Driven SCM and how it will transform operational performance, perhaps ask them to read this book and then ask him/her what (s)he is waiting for.

An executive summary

As demand patterns become more volatile and supply chains grow in complexity and length, so companies are spending ever more significant sums on tecŸologies to improve their forecast accuracy and using 'real time' and 'super fast' ERP/SCM software. At first this might seem a sensible and obvious response, but is it? How much improvement in forecast accuracy is actually possible? And how quickly can supply chains respond to new demand information anyway?

Significantly reducing forecast mix error of, say, 30 per cent by 30 per cent still leaves it at 21 per cent wrong! And if replenishment is driven with such levels of error (and bear in mind that the majority lower volume/higher variability SKUs in a portfolio achieve accuracy levels well below 60 per cent) then service issues will inevitably appear as inventories become unbalanced – unless expensive and capacity hungry/lead-time-increasing schedule changes are made (see Figure 1.1).

This forecast error is one of the key causes of poor supply chain and operations performance, through its creation of supply chain variability and unplanned cost-generating buffers: lead-time delays, use of unplanned capacity and unbalanced/inflated inventories. It is brought about by the MPS- and MRP-dependent demand network transmitting and amplifying forecast error-induced variability up the supply chain. This happens as planners inevitably amend some of their production and supply schedules in response to the avalanche of MRP exception messages that are triggered whenever safety stock usage is predicted.

So improvements in forecast accuracy, though limited and expensive, are always welcome but not sufficient. How does 'real time' or 'super fast'-enabled ERP/SCM software help?

The issue here is how quickly the supply chain can efficiently respond to real-time information. Nearly all APS- or ERP-driven supply chains

Figure 1.1 The inevitable picture of unbalanced and excessive on-hand
inventories as a consequence of inaccurate forecast-driven MPS/
MRP replenishment execution

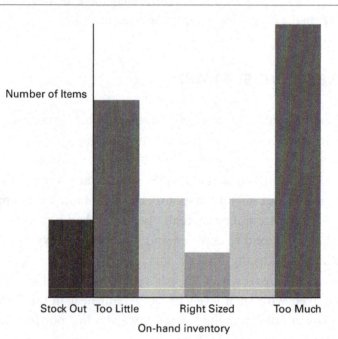

used by companies to service customers ex-stock, use a forecast and
plan to a finished goods safety stock. Upstream of this stock position,
supply is driven by the net forecast using a fully dependent demand
network and an assumption of fixed lead times (which, in fact, they
are not as they flex with the level of capacity utilization, which is a
fundamental weakness of MRP).

Assuming there is no intervention, and supply is executed to meet
the forecast, finished goods inventory will inevitably be unbalanced,
and service issues will develop due to the SKU level forecast error.
Real-time information about, say, unforecasted demand or supply
issues, are all very well but what is the planner supposed to do with
it? If (s)he uses up unplanned capacity to interrupt the supply schedules, then unless catch-up is possible with further spare capacity, the
lead times of the interrupted products will be extended, product will
arrive late and more service issues will be threatened.

Due to the inevitable frequency with which supply lead time 'on
time in full' is missed and service issues experienced or threatened,

planned MRP lead times and safety stocks often end up getting increased by planners, but to no avail because the logic of MRP, and its exception messages, relentlessly drives the same repeating vicious circle. And using forecast push MPS/MRP with a 'super fast' calculating engine effectively just delivers the wrong supply plans more quickly.

This is why *all* forecast-driven MPS/MRP supply chains *always* suffer from unbalanced but excessive inventories, artificially long lead times, underuse of capacity (too many unplanned schedule amendments and changeovers) and planners spending all their time firefighting and expediting instead of planning.

Is there an alternative to the forecast-driven MRP supply chain with, or without, so-called real-time capability?

How about supply chains and factories that:

- sense demand and autonomously respond delivering consistently high planned service levels;
- require up to 50 per cent lower 'end to end' average inventories;
- have stable, efficient and uninterrupted production sequences/ cycles;
- are not under pressure to be impossibly flexible yet still deliver matchless service and higher OEE;
- place orders upon suppliers that are stable and very rarely changed or expedited;
- do not require high levels of forecast accuracy;
- do not involve firefighting and expediting, which are replaced by a focus upon continuous improvement, exception management and value-add planning.

The process that meets this specification is Demand-Driven SCM. Its key features are:

1 Separation of planning from execution: forecasts are not used for directly driving replenishment but are used for getting forward visibility of required aggregate levels of capacity, inventory projections and the likely financials, through sales and operations planning (S&OP).

2 Multiple independent inventory locations: carefully positioned (but not everywhere), planned and maintained in the supply chain and, if appropriate, in the factory, to absorb both demand- and supply-side variability, improve responsiveness and decouple replenishment activities. It is counter-intuitive, but these planned multiple independent inventory buffers cushion demand and supply variability, prevent the need for schedule amendments and, thereby, actually *reduce* aggregate inventories, lead times and the need to use 'catch-up' capacity.

3 Replenishment timing: the timing of replenishment at each inventory position follows its own optimal, stable and predetermined sequence/cycle with the quantity bought/made/shipped simply being that required to replenish up to the planned stock targets[8] and rounded for order quantity policies.

4 Demand-Driven: replenishment at every inventory position therefore follows actual demand and the planned inventory buffers are always able to meet day-to-day demand and its variations, with really extreme and exceptional events being managed through planning (ie anticipation and appropriate stock build).

The result is that throughout the Demand-Driven Supply Chain, including the factories, replenishment activities occur independently of each other, in their most efficient sequence/cycle, in line with end-customer demand and meet planned service levels with right-sized inventories. In effect, demand is 'sensed' at the furthest downstream inventory position through inventory consumption and this is reflected in upstream replenishments as quickly as the predetermined cycles of replenishment/order quantities allow. Theoretically a batch size of one across all replenishment activities would deliver perfectly synchronized end-to-end' supply chain flow!

Batching, however, is inevitable and the bigger they are, of course, the more inventory will be found in the Demand-Driven Supply Chain. But these levels are always significantly lower than that found in 'like for like' forecast push MPS/MRP-driven supply chains because replenishment is aligned with demand and the independent inventory positions absorb any residual variability, thereby preventing the need for capacity-hungry unplanned schedule interventions and the consequent increases in planning lead times and unplanned growth in inventory. In addition, OEE will be higher because the Demand-Driven factory no longer suffers the high levels of non-productive and expensive unplanned service-saving changeovers and expedites that are so prevalent in forecast push MPS/MRP environments.

In order for a supply chain/factory to efficiently and autonomously respond to demand, various maintenance activities are required as follows:

- Capacity planning: use of the forecast to plan and manage capacities (machines, labour, warehouse space, etc)/financials, through an S&OP process.

- Buffer target maintenance: review and adjustment of the planned buffer inventory targets, in line with persistent changes in demand (eg trend, seasonality) is usually a monthly process and is part of the S&OP cycle. This process requires upstream buffer inventory targets to be aligned with any such changes downstream (and at customers as appropriate) to ensure that the rate of supply is aligned up and down the supply chain, thereby preventing the negative impact of demand latency (ie the frequently observed tendency of factory production to be significantly out of phase, both in terms of timing and quantity, with the market – commonly known as bullwhip).

- Event management: clearly, autonomous response of supply to demand is only viable if demand levels are within certain limits. If significant abnormal demands occur (ie extreme and exceptional 'spikes'), they must be planned for with an advance stock build or, if unanticipated and processed as an order, an order rationing process implemented until supply can catch up. Similarly, in the case of inadequate capacity availability during high-season demand periods then an advance stock build will be necessary. In both cases, of course, the item-level forecast is used to help calculate the necessary advance stock build and there is a need for active collaboration between supply planning, demand planning and, ideally, with customers. Such intervention is, however, by exception; autonomous supply chain response to demand is the rule leaving planners time to more effectively deal with such events.[9]

With the recent emergence of Demand-Driven SaaS systems, all these activities can now be supported across the end-to-end supply chain (and, if desired, the extended or collaborative supply chain). Such systems support the forecast-driven S&OP, planned buffer target sizing and maintenance, event management and the generation of execution transactions through legacy ERP transaction systems.

Summary

Increasing expenditure upon forecasting and 'real-time' tecŸologies can achieve relatively little in today's volatile markets and complex supply chains. It is the elimination of unnecessary supply chain variability that creates unplanned cost-generating buffers (inventory, time and capacity), and allowing the supply chain to autonomously respond to demand that is the most effective way forward to achieve step-change improvements in factory and supply chain performance.

Demand-Driven SCM does not use the inevitably inaccurate forecast to directly drive replenishment through MRP's dependent demand network. Instead it deliberately positions, and maintains, multiple *independent* inventory buffers in the supply chain and factory that are each replenished in their own stable and efficient sequence and in line with demand. This eliminates forecast error-induced variability (and natural process variability) being amplified and propagated up and down the supply chain through service-chasing expediting and firefighting.

As a result, such Demand-Driven supply chains reliably and consistently deliver:

1 planned service levels, with

2 average inventory reductions of up to 50 per cent, and

3 significantly higher levels of capacity utilization or overall equipment effectiveness (OEE), and

4 planning lead-time reductions of up to 85 per cent,

5 without any expediting or firefighting and focus upon achieving high levels of forecast accuracy.

Through 'sensing' demand via consumption of inventory, Demand-Driven supply chains respond autonomously to all demand patterns, leaving planners to manage S&OP, exceptional event management, inventory buffer maintenance and other value-add activities such as continuous improvement and collaboration with customers and suppliers.

Counter-intuitively, Demand-Driven Supply Chains deliver their greatest benefit in the most volatile and complex supply chains because these are so much more difficult and costly (and stressful) to manage with forecasts due to the inevitably higher level of forecast error-induced variability. But even in simple supply chains, with relatively stable demand, the benefits can be significant just through eliminating the impact of inaccurate forecasts.

And because Demand-Driven SaaS systems are inexpensive and paid for on a 'pay as you go' basis, the entry barriers are very low – 'proof of principle' simulations can be undertaken within two weeks and full pilots can be up and running within two months: can you afford not to investigate further?

A summary for the non-specialist

The vast majority of fast-moving consumer goods, life-science and other manufacturing and distribution supply chains today are being managed using a wholly ineffective process through very expensive enterprise requirements planning (ERP)/materials requirements planning (MRP) or advanced planning system (APS) software systems. The process uses forecasts of future demand to tell suppliers and factories what, when and how much to supply, make and move – but, because the forecasts are always wrong (and for most products the forecasts are more than 50 per cent wrong!), the wrong quantities are sourced/made/shipped to the wrong places so stock levels are very poorly balanced and customers do not get the service they want. To try to avoid such problems these companies spend an inordinate amount of time expediting materials and products through their factories and supply chains, which is very expensive, wastes huge amounts of capacity, causes stocks to be far higher than needed and, very often, fails to solve the service problem – and, if it does, the cost and cash-flow implications are enormous.

But there is an alternative called Demand-Driven SCM, which, when it replaces the forecast-driven method, allows companies to achieve their planned service levels from, unbelievably, up to half the average level of stock with no expediting, no wasted capacity and with no requirement for highly accurate forecasts.

Demand-Driven SCM simply involves positioning the right quantities of stock where they are needed up and down the supply chain and topping them up, as they are consumed, in a stable and repetitive sequence. In this way materials and products are pulled through the supply chain using a simple 'make to replace' and 'ship to replace' mechanism in line with actual demand, without any need for expensive and disruptive intervention and expediting. And the great thing about Demand-Driven SCM is that it works with any demand pattern, even those with lots of promotional activity – bar those exceptional and highly extreme events that, instead, can be anticipated and managed with an advance stock build.

Large and complex companies still need traditional transaction systems to manage their supply chains but, aided by a new wave of specialist software, Demand-Driven SCM is now beginning to be adopted by a rapidly increasing number of well-known companies that have recognized, and experienced, the transformational impact that this remarkably simple way of working delivers.

Notes

1 KuŸ, TS (1962) *The Structure of Scientific Revolutions*, University of Chicago Press, Chicago

2 See the section 'Can SCM be deductive?' in Chapter 3. The theoretical underpinning of Demand-Driven began in 1961 with the development of supply chain dynamics and progress in queuing theory by Forrester and Burbidge, and Little and Kingman, respectively. More recently, WJ Hopp and ML Spearman (1996), *Factory Physics*, has made further significant contributions, while at the same time, and in the same terms, explaining why the tools of Lean and Six Sigma are so effective. It is also worth noting that the importance of flow to effective supply chain

management was also emphasized by one of the key 'fathers' of MRP, George Plossl, and Eli Goldratt, founder of the Theory of Constraints

3 Perfect flow is when value-add time/lead-time = 100 per cent

4 Hopp and Spearman (2004) describe Lean as 'fundamentally about minimizing the cost of buffering variability', in 'To pull or not to pull: what is the question?', *Manufacturing & Service Operations Management*, 6 (2), pp 133–48

5 The theoretical underpinning of Demand-Driven SCM began in 1961 with the development of supply chain dynamics and progress in queuing theory by Forrester and Burbidge, and Little and Kingman, respectively

6 Personal communication

7 'World class' forecast mix accuracy across a product portfolio is around 80 per cent (despite great strides in demand planning over the last 10 years such as Bayesian forecasting), which means, due to 'pareto', that the majority of your SKU forecasts (ie those of low and medium volume with medium and high levels of demand variability) will be no better than 60 per cent accurate and most significantly worse. With increasing demand volatility due to competitive promotions, emerging markets, channel fragmentation and SKU proliferation etc, there is no prospect of significant improvements in forecast accuracy despite expensive new tecŸologies such as 'demand sensing' (and why should inevitably inaccurate forecasts be used at all for replenishment execution when demand is, by definition, always 100 per cent accurate?). Demand-Driven SCM does continue to use forecasts but only for capacity planning and S&OP, and inventory buffer sizing for which high item level, time-phased forecast accuracy is not required. This allows demand planners and sales teams to concentrate properly upon exceptional and extreme event management. And such real events become very much the exception: the Demand-Driven SCM process is surprisingly resilient and easily able to absorb the variability associated with 'volatile' and promotions-intensive markets such as consumer-packaged goods (CPG)

8 Order quantity = (stock target + future events + backorder + today's orders) − (stock in warehouse + stock on order) rounded for order quantity policies

9 Companies that think they are in a highly volatile demand environment due to regular promotions are always surprised at how resilient the Demand-Driven Supply Chain is at successfully servicing promotions-led demand patterns. A promotion has to be very exceptional and extreme to require an advance stock build

What is Demand-Driven SCM?

02

Demand-Driven SCM: agility thru' stability

In a supply chain context the expression 'agility thru' stability' might appear to be something of an oxymoron. After all, 'agility' is usually associated with a supply chain's ability to respond quickly to changing demand patterns through amending its schedules at short notice. It is very different to the common understanding of stability as being visibility of future firm schedules (often two weeks in consumer packaged goods (CPG) but sometimes four weeks or longer in life science) that can be planned for with a high degree of reliability.

How, then, can 'agility' be achieved with, let alone through, 'stability'?

To appreciate how, the definitions of these words need to be clarified in terms that are accurate (but often misunderstood) in a supply chain context:

- *Stability* is the various supply chain value-add activities working to their own efficient and predictable *sequence* with minimal unplanned changes and interruptions.

The benefits of stability are that costs can be minimized through working to a *sequence* that maximizes changeover efficiencies and can be relied upon so that, for instance, people, materials, machines, etc can be prepared as necessary and work to their greatest efficiency. To achieve such stability, there needs to be a minimum of interruptions, be they due to lack of components, quality issues, machine breakdowns or changes to the schedule to prevent service threats.

On the other hand:

- *Agility* is the ability of a supply chain to be autonomously responsive to real demand, and its variability, with buffers that are of the right size and in the form that best serves both the company and its customers – and is 'designed in'.

  The essence of 'agility' is in the use of the terms:

  - '*Autonomously responsive*': responding to changing demands immediately and without prior thought and preparation.

  - '*Buffers that are of the right size and in the right form*': buffers are always associated with variability unless the supply chain is so flexible that it is able to meet demand exactly while operating at 100 per cent utilization without customers either being kept waiting or supplied ex-stock. The aggregate of these buffers (capacity, time and stock) should be minimized in terms of their cost generation and be in the form that 'delights' the customer.

  - '*Designed in*': it is in how the supply chain is planned, operated and improved upon (ie continuous improvement to achieve flexibility and flow) that delivers planned and high service levels with ever decreasing levels of buffer.

In most 'make to stock' (MTS) supply chains (ie those using short-term, item-level, time-phased forecasts to drive execution with a master production schedule), efforts to achieve stability are usually through the holding of 'safety stock' and use of time fences that freeze schedules over the internal manufacturing lead time (followed by a limited degree of mix flexibility out to the cumulative lead time). Despite significant time and effort being put into achieving high forecast accuracy, however, pressure to break these time fences is often immense.

When one considers that world-class portfolio mix forecast accuracy is just 80 per cent (ie 20 per cent wrong and hiding the fact that the majority of SKUs – those with medium to small volumes and medium to high variability – will be achieving errors of 40 per cent +) it is not surprising that finished goods inventories tend to be severely unbalanced and prone to service threats, which generate the capacity-hungry and schedule-changing 'hot lists' via MRP's 'exception messages'[1] (see Figures 2.1 and 2.2). In addition, the manufacturing lead-time lengths that the frozen time fence is supposed to protect are always significantly longer than strictly necessary (ie the actual manufacturing 'value-add' time) due to the need to add significant queue-time buffer into the planning parameter.

Figure 2.1   The inevitable picture of unbalanced and excessive on-hand inventories as a consequence of inaccurate forecast-driven MPS/ MRP replenishment execution

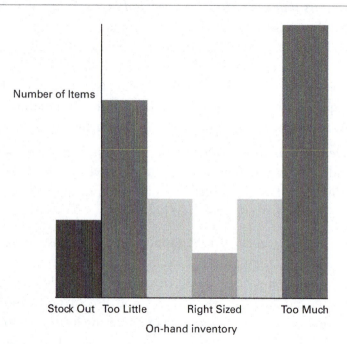

Figure 2.2   The impact upon production of inaccurate forecast-driven MPS/MRP replenishment

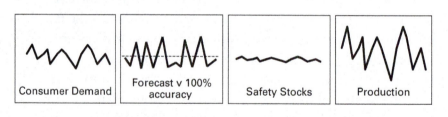

Already it can be seen that the desire for stability inevitably causes the supply chain to generate use of unplanned buffer (lead time, inventory and use of unplanned capacity) due to the variability induced by the inaccurate forecasts.[2] Given this, how can meeting customers' unpredictable demands be met without creating these excessive and cost-generating buffers (ie agility)?

One answer, of course, is to implement Lean, which through its tool kit (eg TQM, TPM, quick changeovers, standard work, DFM, etc) continuously drives supply chain reliability and flexibility.[3]

The other answer is via implementation of the Demand-Driven supply chain, which is, in effect, simply enterprise(s)-wide pull, and can be defined as:

> A segmented supply chain execution process featuring multiple deliberately planned and positioned, but independent/decoupled, inventory locations that are each replenished, in an efficient and stable sequence, to a calculated and maintained stock target, in line with real demand – not the forecast [which is used for S&OP, planned inventory buffer sizing and event management].[4]

The key definitions are:

- *Segmented*: using the most appropriate replenishment tecŸique for each item/location's demand profile (volume and variability – see below) and by avoiding use of the inaccurate forecast (or netted forecast) to directly drive replenishment except for really exceptional events (also see below).

- *Multiple deliberately planned and positioned, but independent/ decoupled, inventory locations*: these recognize that some variability is inevitable (eg all value-add process lead times suffer natural variation as well as responding to load, especially when capacity utilization is high). These inventory positions minimize response lead times and both absorb and prevent their variation being propagated/amplified up and down the supply chain through MRP's 'dependent demand' network.

- *Replenished to a calculated and maintained stock target in line with real demand*: each inventory position is sized, and maintained, according to average demand, and its variability, over the local replenishment lead time and order interval with appropriately calculated adjustments for trend, seasonality and known planned events. Inventory at every position is replaced, in a predictable cycle, as it is consumed by downstream demand or consumption and the supply chain thereby *autonomously* responds to, and meets, real demand without the need for variability-creating, service-chasing interventions that generate those performance-destroying unplanned buffers of capacity, time and inventory.

- *Efficient and stable sequence*: replenishment has an optimal sequence and cycle, which is always followed,[5] respecting minimum order quantities (MOQs), and never interrupted,[6] so operations can be level loaded to extremely high levels of capacity utilization without 'stress'.

The appropriate replenishment tecŸiques and when they should be used are as illustrated below:

Figure 2.3   Demand volume and variability analysis for replenishment
technique selection

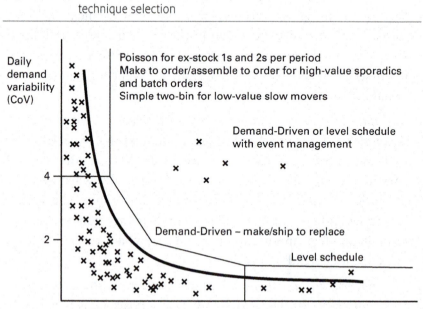

1 High volume/low variability: 'level schedule' or 'rate based',[7] usually a small number of items but can often account for more than 50 per cent of total output.

2 Low volume/low to high variability: depending upon the circumstances the appropriate tecŸique might be assemble to order (ATO), make/buy to order (MTO), a simple two-bin system for low-value items or poisson-based for higher-value sporadic 1s and 2s per period (eg spare parts supply).

3 Medium volume/medium variability: replenish against demand/consumption, up to a managed stock target in a stable and optimal sequence.

4 High volume/high variability: use of 1 or 3 but with either ATO response to extreme and exceptional events or their anticipation, and advance stock build, using a forecast. But real events that need planning for, or reacting to, are very much less common than might be expected in, say, a highly promotions-intensive marketplace, because the autonomous Demand-Driven response to stock targets are surprisingly resilient.

These item-level tecŸiques can be different at different levels within the supply chain (ie raw materials, sub-assemblies, finished products) depending upon the local pattern of demand volume/variability. And they can just as easily apply across the extended collaborative supply chain as within a single company's supply chain.[8] For instance, a supplier with visibility of downstream stock versus target at a customer might replenish against that consumption, while using level schedule for upstream material supply.

The evidence that Demand-Driven SCM delivers 'agility with stability' and significantly minimizes the cost-generating buffers can be seen from its results.

Typical supply chain performance improvements are:

- achievement of consistently high planned service levels;
- reductions in average inventory of between 30 per cent to 50 per cent;
- increases in OEE enabling cost reductions of around 20 per cent;
- planning lead-time reductions of up to 85 per cent;

- stable, predictable replenishment orders upon suppliers that allow shorter supply lead times and greater upstream efficiency that can convert, subject to negotiation, into significant procurement cost savings;

- without any expediting or firefighting and focus upon high levels of forecast accuracy.

The reason that Demand-Driven SCM is so effective is that it enables the supply chain to flow by eliminating the forecast error-induced variability and minimizing any that is residual – thereby also minimizing the cost-generating buffers of stock, time and capacity.[9]

And the reason why we can talk about 'agility thru' stability' is that it is the stable and reliable production sequences driven by relatively stable demand (ie compared to the volatile forecast), along with the multiple independent and variability-absorbing inventory positions, that allow planned service levels to be met autonomously through flow with minimal unplanned buffers (Figure 2.4).

Demand-Driven SCM is a major change in the way that most companies manage their supply chain, but tecŸical implementation is relatively simple. Robust, functionality rich and globally tested SaaS that supports the critical processes of demand segmentation and positioning, sizing and maintaining of the independent inventory positions is now available; they also support the various 'work to' lists generation and continuous exception-based monitoring of flow. In addition, these systems support forecast-driven simulations through the relevant replenishment rules, inventory parameters, bill of materials (BOM) and routings, so the planner can understand future inventory and capacity requirements, which of course form the basis of S&OP decision making.

Figure 2.4   Efficient and stable production enabled by Demand-Driven SCM

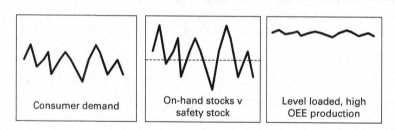

| Consumer demand | On-hand stocks v safety stock | Level loaded, high OEE production |

The SaaS model also facilitates quick simulations comparing your supply chain's historical performance versus that which Demand-Driven SCM would have delivered, as well as low-cost, fast pilots prior to a revenue-expensed implementation and roll out. These systems operate through legacy transaction systems and can be implemented piecemeal across complex supply chains so 'barriers to entry' are very low.

A rapidly growing number of CPG, life science and industrial companies are quietly piloting and implementing Demand-Driven supply – quietly because they know that 'agility thru' stability' will give them a significant competitive advantage!

No wonder that Professor Martin Christopher (Cranfield University) said of Demand-Driven SCM:

> I think that the approach that Carol (ie Carol Ptak, co-founder of the Demand Driven Institute) was advocating is powerful and practical. I hope that these ideas continue to gain traction in industry and that the concept of 'demand driven' quickly becomes the norm.[10]

Ever heard of Kaikaku?

Nor me until I came across it described by Aleksander Sosnowski as a:

> Significantly less known improvement approach, translated as radical change – a major transformation. Kaikaku changes the landscape fast and strongly… It is like fast-forward Kaizen bundled and made at once. Radical change is radical, it is not to please the current state – it is to question the so far unquestioned. It becomes apparent that Kaikaku calls for change management competencies, robust risk management but it also means making bold managerial decisions in a VUCA (volatile, uncertain, complex, ambiguous) environment. It means leaving your comfort zone, resigning from safety into risk taking. You jump on another wave. You move from follower into a leader.[11]

Understandably, many in senior management positions might want to shy away from Kaikaku – all that talk of 'leaving your comfort zone', 'resigning from safety into risk taking', and 'radical change'.

How about Kaikaku without risk?

How about introducing a significant step-change improvement into supply chain and operations processes that is risk free and guaranteed to deliver performance improvements such as:

- consistent delivery of planned service levels;
- up to 50 per cent less average inventory;
- requiring up to 20 per cent less capacity (read OEE improvement and cost reduction);
- and without firefighting, unplanned schedule changes and production instability or focus upon high levels of forecast accuracy?

Does such a risk-free Kaikaku opportunity really exist?

In terms of the process having an impregnable rationale and a 100 per cent track record then the answer is a resounding 'yes'.

And in terms of the process being something that can be introduced inexpensively and gradually, so that it continuously generates results, credibility and support, then again, the answer is 'yes'.

And if you are worried that Kaikaku is something a bit left field and weird, don't worry – some very major companies are adopting it but keeping quiet because they know it will deliver them a competitive advantage.

Want to learn more? Take a look at the section on 'Demand-Driven SCM: agility thru' stability' earlier in this chapter.

What Demand-Driven SCM is not

Demand-Driven SCM is not just 'make to order' (MTO) and it has nothing to do with attempts to increase forecast accuracy, as supply is not driven directly by the forecast. Instead, supply is driven by inventory-buffered 'make to replace' and 'ship to replace' mechanisms and supply is effectively pulled through the supply chain and factories by customer demand in the same way that water flowing in a river is pulled along by gravity.

Nor is Demand-Driven SCM anything to do with what supply chain tecҰology vendors refer to as supply chain optimization.

Optimization is discussed in greater detail later but, suffice to say at this stage, Demand-Driven SCM is all about contributing to the elimination of supply chain variability in pursuit of flow – and no greater performance efficiency can be achieved.

And finally, the Demand-Driven Supply Chain does not need any form of tecŸology-supported 'real-time' visibility of inventory, demand or capacity, nor any form of so-called 'real-time response' capability. Such tecŸology may well be needed in the management of nuclear power stations, certain chemical plants and power stations where real-time control of flow and events is important. But in discrete and most process-manufacturing environments, where real-time process flow management is not necessary, traditional low-cost daily batch transactions are perfectly adequate to support Demand-Driven SCM.

Banishing the myths surrounding Demand-Driven SCM

With the recent emergence of the Demand-Driven SCM approach to planning and replenishment (see the section 'Demand-Driven SCM: agility thru' stability'), its adoption by some of the world's most admired companies and its record of delivering transformational supply chain performance improvements, it is inevitably starting to ruffle the feathers of those whose vested interest is in traditional ways of running supply chains. Their response is to either dishonestly co-opt the Demand-Driven terminology for themselves or attempt to position Demand-Driven as a minor niche in an attempt to prevent it undermining their own entrenched view (ie revenue stream) of how supply chains should be managed.

The key myths that are being bandied about by those who wish to muddy the waters are as follows:

The myths

Demand-Driven SCM is just MTO The belief that Demand-Driven SCM is just 'make to order' is generally held by those who still, erroneously, think that 'pull' in a Lean context is about responding directly to customer orders. In fact MTO *is* a form of Demand-Driven SCM but is clearly not appropriate where customers require response times that are less than that of the supply lead time, as is the case with fast-moving products that require ex-stock supply. As described earlier in 'Demand-Driven SCM: agility thru' stability', Demand-Driven SCM's greatest impact is in such ex-stock supply chains where the forecast is used to size the buffers (and for event management and S&OP) but replenishment is driven by demand.

In many customer-facing MTO companies both forms of Demand-Driven SCM co-exist – a time-buffered MTO version for the finished assembly and the stock-buffered version that ensures the upstream components, materials and sub-assemblies are available as and when required. This design might also be known as 'assemble to order' (ATO).

The decoupling point Students of supply chain management usually learn quite early in their course about the supply chain decoupling point, where customer demand meets forecast-driven supply. It is often emphasized that the further upstream the decoupling point can be located the better because it maximizes the extent of the supply chain that is driven by what customers actually want (ie their orders). This is actually an overly simplistic view as it ignores the practical fact that customers do not always want to wait for availability and the economics of supply are such that it is often immensely more efficient to meet demand from a finished stock instead of responding to high-frequency customer orders, particularly for standardized products. In fact, supply chains should consist of numerous such decoupled or independent Demand-Driven inventory positions, not just the one decoupling point, to prevent the transmission of performance-eroding variability.

It is often thought that replenishment of a decoupling point, described earlier as 'forecast-driven supply' implies a 'forecast push' process. As we have seen, however, in the section 'Demand-Driven SCM: agility thru' stability', making to stock is far more effectively undertaken using a Demand-Driven SCM or 'pull' process.

The conventional "good/bad" dichotomy between 'make to order' and 'make to stock' at the decoupling point is wrong – both are good as long as supply is driven by demand. They really only differ in terms of the mix of the planned buffers being used to enable response to customer order variability: time in the case of MTO and inventory in the case of MTS.

Demand-Driven SCM is only for material replenishment This is one of those myths that contains its own fatal illogicality. Demand-Driven SCM is certainly very suitable for managing the replenishment of materials that are stocked upstream to support an ATO or MTS final assembly. Such materials are an inventory buffer that, when used in MTO supply chains, allows for a faster response in the form of ATO. And in MTS the rationale for using a Demand-Driven buffer for materials can be equally applied to planned sub-assemblies and finished goods. In fact the benefit is usually much greater because of the schedule stability and efficiency that it brings to the factory.

Demand-Driven is not suitable for driving production Allied to the above, this suggestion seems to be based on the idea that somehow production activities are so complex that equally complex algorithms are necessary to 'optimize' performance. In fact, most of the difficulty involved in managing fast-moving and apparently complex supply chains – such as those that are capacity constrained, have shared work centres and deep BOMs and involve promotional demand patterns – is self-inflicted. It is caused by inevitably inaccurate forecasts being used to drive execution and all the consequent nervousness and variability that this generates through the MRP-dependent demand network. No matter how complicated the production process, material flow always follows the queuing theory principles that justify the use of Demand-Driven SCM. In fact, the greater the complexity and volatility of the demand and supply environment the stronger is the case for using Demand-Driven SCM to eliminate variability and its costs.

Demand-Driven is about demand sensing/shaping and real-time response This is the key message from certain supply chain tecŸology providers that have a vested interest in selling overly complex (and expensive) software and who seek to improve the performance of the 'forecast push MPS/MRP' supply chain model that they have been selling for around 40 years. Demand-Driven SCM is a completely different approach to supply chain management, which harnesses the fundamental principles of flow by explicitly minimizing the destructive impact of supply chain variability. This is in contrast to the ubiquitous 'forecast push MPS/MRP' approach that actively generates variability through its use of inevitably incorrect forecasts for driving execution, and the propagation and amplification of that variability through its dependent demand network. No amount of expenditure upon sophisticated forecasting tecŸology (eg demand sensing), price discount-driven demand shaping or real-time response capability can compensate for the fact that the 'forecast push MPS/MRP' engine inside such 'advanced planning systems' or super-fast ERP systems is fundamentally flawed. These tecŸologies might marginally improve the performance of such 'forecast push MPS/MRP' supply chains but the increment comes at an enormous cost and is significantly less than that offered by the Demand-Driven SCM approach that enables the supply chain to autonomously flow.

Demand-Driven SCM is multiple echelon inventory optimization The idea and mathematics behind multiple echelon inventory optimization (MEIO) is that in a multi-echelon supply chain less aggregate stock needs to be held, by relocating it from the customer-facing echelon and positioning it upstream. While this might appear to be similar to Demand-Driven SCM it isn't because the replenishment is still forecast-driven through a dependent demand network and the logic of the forecast push MPS/MRP process is still to avoid use of the buffer through generation and response to exception messages. Whereas the MEIO static aggregate safety stock calculations may be correct, the dynamic reality continues to be high levels of supply chain variability and unplanned buffer due to the forecast error and its propagation up the supply chain. Supply chains are dynamic 'complex adaptive systems' that, as such, cannot be optimized in a static sense – only continuously improved upon.[12]

Demand-Driven value networks This is a frequently used terminology to describe a vision of how supply chains should ideally be managed. It typically consists of:

- A culture that develops and acquires talent to encourage new learning and improvement that also shares standardized and proven best practices.

- An S&OP process that links execution with strategy to support actively made trade-offs across demand, supply and product networks.

- The use of sensing and shaping processes to improve management of demand and the ability to translate that demand into supply that delivers a profitable and sustainable value chain.

- End-to-end, multiple enterprise-wide alignment and synchronization of demand, supply and product cycles.

- Metrics that drive joint value for all supply chain stakeholders.

- A tecYology architecture that enables collaborative relationships, end-to-end supply chain visibility, end-to-end responsiveness and data-driven decision making to maximize value and mitigate risk.

Most of this is very sensible, if somewhat general, but note the reference to the need for demand sensing and shaping and the complete lack of any reference to the key element of what defines a real Demand-Driven supply chain: its use of multiple planned but independent/decoupled inventory buffers that are replenished in line with demand, not the forecast.

Demand-Driven SCM defined

Demand-Driven SCM is a segmented supply chain planning and execution process featuring multiple deliberately planned and positioned, but independent/decoupled, inventory locations that are each replenished, in an efficient and stable sequence, to a calculated and maintained stock target, in line with real demand/consumption – not the forecast (which is used for S&OP, event management and inventory target sizing).

Segmented

Demand patterns cover an enormous spectrum from sporadic ones and twos to many thousands per period. The nature of demand at the extremes tends to determine the type of supply chain response. For instance, at one end of the spectrum there is 'engineer to order' (ETO) because customers are prepared to wait for their product to be designed, made and delivered and the orders are too occasional and bespoke to warrant any other form of supply response. On the other hand, manufacturers of fast-moving products such as CPG and life science use 'make to stock' (MTS) because their product is standardized, demand is continuous and reliable, and customers (and the competitive environment) demand immediate supply. In between ETO and MTS are other supply response mechanisms such as 'make to order' (MTO) and 'assemble to order' (ATO) and across the ETO, MTO, ATO, MTS spectrum, the order-to-delivery lead time becomes progressively shorter as planned inventories reduce the order-to-ship response time.

At present, large numbers of manufacturers and distributors of standardized products requiring an ex-stock service are using just one single method to drive their supply chain: 'forecast push MPS/MRP'. Later we will discuss in more depth the problems inherent in this form of replenishment but let's first just focus on the issue of forecast accuracy.

When demand volumes are high and stable, as they usually are for mature products (and often for generic upstream finished product sub-assemblies and components or raw materials), forecast accuracy can be very high. Such items usually account for a majority share of output but just a small percentage of the SKU range. The rest of the portfolio is composed of lower-volume items and products that are far more variable in their demand patterns and, therefore, impossible to forecast accurately. World-class forecast mix accuracy is around 80 per cent and that is achieved only because the few high-volume items that achieve around 95+ per cent skew the measure from the 60 per cent and below that is achieved by the majority.

Instead of the 'one size fits all' approach taken by 'forecast push MPS/MRP', which is inappropriate for most items in a portfolio due to inevitable forecast inaccuracy, Demand-Driven SCM uses replenishment tecŸiques that are appropriate, and effective, for particular demand patterns. Instead of using an inaccurate forecast-driven MPS (from which netted demand through MRP calculations translates into supply plans of even greater inaccuracy), Demand-Driven SCM uses the most appropriate tecŸique at each separate inventory position.

The relevant replenishment tecŸiques and when they should be used are as illustrated in Figure 2.5:

Figure 2.5 Demand volume and variability analysis for replenishment technique selection

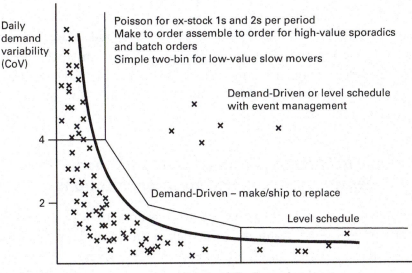

1 High volume/low variability: 'level schedule' or 'rate-based', ideally using heijunka or mixed-model scheduling so that demand upon upstream supply is not volatile.

2 Low volume/low to high variability: depending upon the circumstances the appropriate tecŸique might be ATO or MTO for otherwise disruptive large-volume batch orders or high-cost items, two-bin for low-value slow movers or poisson-based for higher-value sporadic demands of 1s and 2s per period.

3 Medium volume/medium variability: replenish against demand/consumption, up to a managed buffer stock target in a stable and optimal sequence.

4 High volume/high variability: use 1 or 3 but with either ATO response to events or their anticipation, and advance stock build, using a forecast. But real events that need planning for, or reacting to, are very much less common than might be expected in, say, a highly promotions-intensive marketplace, because the autonomous Demand-Driven response to stock targets is very resilient.

These item-level tecŸiques can be different at different levels within the supply chain, depending upon the local pattern of demand volume/variability. And they can just as easily apply across the extended collaborative supply chain as within a single company's supply chain. For instance, a supplier might respond to a customer via ATO or, assuming it has visibility of downstream stock versus target, replenish against consumption (which can also eliminate lumpy order patterns), while using level schedule for upstream material supply.

Multiple deliberately planned and positioned, but independent/decoupled inventory locations

Within any supply chain you will see stock waiting to be processed or sold. Apart from the planned safety stock in the finished goods warehouse, these are unplanned stock positions – the stock is effectively 'work in progress' awaiting processing or, if in the customer-facing warehouse, waiting to be sold.

Why does this unplanned static stock exist?

If it were just due to insufficient processing capacities such queues of stock would grow without limit. Queues of work in progress, however, will be found to exist even when the average rate of stock arrivals at a processing work centre is below that of the work centre's average capacity. This is because there is always an element of cycle stock due to batching, despite the average rates of supply and demand being aligned and the queue will be longer if stock batches arrive early at a processing work centre, or at the warehouse, before the preceding batch has been completely processed or sold. Sometimes processing of a batch might be deliberately delayed to allow a higher-priority item to be processed first – this, of course, happens a lot in forecast-driven supply chains because the forecasts are all wrong and expediting is necessary. In addition, of course, if there is a problem with the operation of a processing work centre, some processing capacity will be permanently lost but stock batches will still continue to arrive and join the queue. And a machine breakdown also might starve a downstream processing machine of material to process, which wastes further capacity.

In all these examples we are seeing work-in-progress queues not because of a capacity shortage per se but because of variability in the arrival patterns of stock at work stations and variability in the amount of capacity that they have available (ie their processing rate). The same happens to stock in finished goods warehouses because the supply variability is vastly different, due to batching, to that of the demand variability (which explains the cycle stock) and a planned safety stock also has to be held to cover the risk of the supply-and-demand variability occasionally causing a stock out.

As we will see later, inventory queue length is directly related to the levels of supply chain variability (ie variability in the rate of stock arrivals and processing/demand rates) and the queues grow exponentially when there are higher levels of capacity utilization.

One might reasonably ask, if there are bound to be variability-generated inventories in a supply chain, why does Demand-Driven SCM involve the deliberate positioning of independent/decoupled stock locations in the supply chain – surely that just adds to the inventory problem?

Well, no – unless we are receiving materials, making product and shipping it to customers in a continuous stream (ie perfect flow) we are adding value in cycles (which is a form of variability) and cycles require us to make enough at each stage to service demand over the off-cycle period. This is why we make in batches. So cycle stock is inevitably going to be found between value-add processes and in the finished goods (FG) warehouse. In forecast push MPS/MRP supply chains the raw materials (RM), work in progress (WIP) and FG inventories are always higher than they should be because *multiple* batches queue up between value add processes, and in the warehouse, because of:

1 Forecast error-induced variability: the schedules are frequently changed to prevent service issues, so stock arrivals at work centres are accelerated and delayed leading to greater variability, congestion and delay.

2 Supply variability: natural variability in processing rates, and events such as machine breakdowns, quality release delays and waiting for 'hot list' batches, cause capacity to be lost and further queue development.

This is the variability that causes supply chains to become congested with excessive levels of stock, which causes queues/lead times to grow and eventually requires unplanned capacity (overtime) to ensure catch-up to prevent further service issues. And if capacity-wasting schedule changes are not happening in an inaccurate 'forecast push MPS/MRP'-driven supply chain, then either service levels will be impacted or very large amounts of finished goods buffer have to be in place instead.

But Demand-Driven SCM's multiple independent/decoupled inventory positions are not replenished through an inaccurate forecast (or netted forecast) – they are replenished in line with actual demand, or consumption, which is always, by definition, correct thereby eliminating the forecast error-induced interruptions and variability that necessitates all that inventory, queue time and use of unplanned capacity. The planned inventory buffers also act to absorb local supply variability that would otherwise cause loss of capacity and supply delays to be passed on through the supply chain. With these 'supply variability cushions' in place, late arrivals and processing delays will be prevented from disrupting downstream activities, and lost capacity due to material shortages can be avoided. Thus natural supply chain variability is absorbed and materials are able to flow much faster, and average inventories are much lower, than in an MRP 100 per cent-dependent demand supply chain.

Replenished to a calculated, and maintained, stock target in line with real demand/consumption

The inventory positions that serve to decouple the value-add activities are sized according to simple reorder point or reorder cycle rules.

They consist of a level of planned cycle stock and an 'on order' quantity to cover the supply lead time (Figure 2.6). The planned cycle stock exists to meet downstream demand between new stock arrivals (eg when the supplying work centre is busy doing something else) and in reorder cycle it must therefore be sized to reflect average demand over the planned order interval. If the order quantity is fixed, as with reorder point, the order interval varies depending upon the rate of sale and the size of the fixed order quantity.

Figure 2.6 The Demand-Driven SCM inventory buffer target components

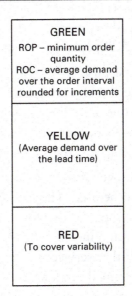

In both reorder point and reorder cycle, if the order quantity exceeds demand over the replenishment lead time there can only be a maximum of one outstanding order at any point in time. Conversely, the smaller the order quantity relative to demand over the lead time, the larger the number of possible outstanding orders, the greater the frequency of stock deliveries and the faster the on-hand stock turn.

In addition to the planned cycle stock, there also needs to be an additional level of planned stock in case the actual demand between planned replenishments and the over-the-supply lead time is higher than expected, or because the arrival is late. This is the variability buffer.

Assuming that the stock targets are calculated correctly with respect to average demand and its variability and the order intervals and supply lead times are adhered to, there will be no stock outs (except those statistically expected due to the level of service that is planned). It might reasonably be asked why this rarely happens under 'forecast push MPS/MRP', which also uses a lead time, order interval and variability buffer called the safety stock. The answer is threefold:

1 Stock target quantities based upon an *average* of the forecast over the order interval and lead time are inevitably far more accurate and reliable than the short-period time-phased forecasts that a 'forecast push MPS/MRP' process depends upon.

2 Safety stocks in forecast push MPS/MRP are often rule of thumb and inaccurate (eg x weeks of forecast) and tend not to be monitored and adjusted very frequently, whereas management of Demand-Driven SCM stock targets becomes a core activity of planning.

3 The logic of 'forecast push MPS/MRP' generates an exception report whenever it calculates, using the inaccurate forecast, that the safety stock is going to be used. These tempt planners to expedite and interfere with the schedules to avoid service issues, which uses up unplanned capacity and increases the lead times of other products, which leads to further service threats and a self-perpetuating vicious circle of unplanned buffer generation. Demand-Driven SCM does not generate such exception messages – the process is designed to actually use the variability buffer, and the lack of schedule interference, combined with 'roughly right' stock targets, ensures that materials are allowed to autonomously flow in line with actual demand.

An important feature of the Demand-Driven Supply Chain is that, based upon the calculated inventory buffer targets, the planner knows that on-hand inventories are capped at the variability buffer level plus the full order quantity. In fact, across a range of products, such an aggregate is highly unlikely to ever be reached because there will inevitably be many different order cycles and lead times, while demand variability will mean that for some items their variability buffer has been consumed and for others it hasn't. Thus a reasonable estimate of total average on-hand inventory is the aggregate of variability buffers plus half the order quantities.

Due to this 'inventory cap' feature of Demand-Driven SCM it becomes possible to reliably calculate future inventory levels, based upon the forecast, knowing that the estimate is robust. This is in contrast to estimating inventory levels when using forecast push MPS/MRP, where there is no inventory cap and inventory levels can go out of control due to forecast inaccuracy and the development of *unplanned* inventory buffer.

Efficient and stable sequence

In many factories, efficiencies can be achieved if materials are sequenced through machines in a manner that minimizes changeover times. Schedule sequences that can be relied upon without need for service-saving interruptions also maximize utilization of available capacity and increase it through 'economies of repetition' and the learning curve. Demand-Driven Manufacturing schedules are stable, repetitive and in their most efficient sequence with the quantities being made varying according to the consumption (or sales) of each item (with appropriate rounding for order quantity policies). And because these schedules are buffered by the correct levels of inventory and never have to be changed, very high levels of production efficiency and planned service levels will be achieved. This is the meaning of 'agility thru' stability'.

Not the forecast

It is incorrect, as is sometimes thought, that forecasts are not needed to run a Demand-Driven Supply Chain. Although it is true that short-term forecasts are not used to directly drive replenishment schedules, forecasts are used for:

- *Inventory buffer sizing*: whether the inventory buffers (ie the lead time element and, in reorder cycle (ROC), that of the order interval) are sized using a historical average or an average from the extrapolated forecast (or a blend), we are undoubtedly using a form of forecast! However, we do not need high accuracy of future time-phased forecasts, we just need to get the average over multiple periods roughly right and this is very easy to achieve. The reason a 'roughly right' average can deliver planned service levels is because it is the ability of the materials to autonomously flow in line with actual demand patterns, subject to minimum order quantities, that allows the Demand-Driven Supply Chain to meet customer demand – it does not rely upon an inevitably inaccurate advance guess of the quantities of what will be ordered and when.

- *Sales and Operations Planning (S&OP)*: forecasts must be used in conjunction with BOMs and routings to ensure supply chain capacities can be set up in advance to allow the materials to flow adequately. Again, however, high levels of SKU-level forecast accuracy are not required as adequate accuracy is only needed at an appropriate aggregate level over the long term, which is again quite easy to achieve.

- *Event management*: with the welcome reduction in focus upon high levels of item-level time-phased forecast accuracy, not to mention the elimination of continuous firefighting and expediting, Demand-Driven supply-and-demand planners are able to focus effectively upon the real events that planned variability buffer inventory cannot accommodate. These include demand spikes that need to be predicted and built for in advance. If promotions are a fact of life, the historical volatile demand patterns will allow adequate variability buffers to be calculated so it is only the really *exceptional and extreme* promotions that need to be planned for in this way (see Figures 2.7a and 2.7b). Other events that require active use of the forecast for planning execution activities include new product launches and seasonality in combination with capacity constraints (that therefore requires an advanced stock build) and, on the supply side, plant closures etc.

Figure 2.7a   Consistently high-demand volatility that will not disrupt a Demand-Driven Supply Chain

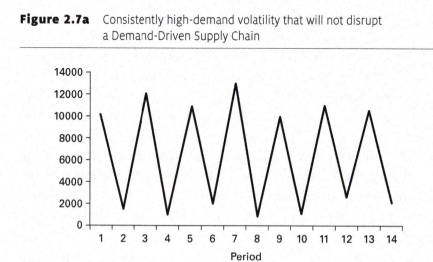

Figure 2.7b The same demand pattern but with an abnormal demand spike that should be anticipated and built for – event management

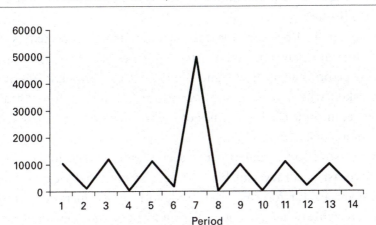

Forget the forecast accuracy KPI

Should we forecast?

Of course, but we should be very careful how we use them.

Almost all companies that supply customers 'ex-stock' (eg CPG, life science, distributors, etc) have a significant investment in demand planning or forecasting. This usually takes the form of specialist software and people dedicated to generating accurate short-term item-level forecasts – in monthly or weekly buckets – for the purpose of driving replenishment execution through DRP/MRP/ERP/APS. In many cases, the demand planning team are 'specialists' and different to the supply planning team, who use the forecasts to generate the supply plans for execution by operations and/or supply.

The key performance metric for demand planning is, of course, 'forecast accuracy' and this is usually measured using some form of aggregated absolute forecast mix error as a percentage of the total forecast across a portfolio for a given time bucket (usually monthly) with an appropriate lead time offset. Measured in this way, consistent forecast accuracy of 80 per cent is generally considered 'world class' and is extremely rare.

The rationale for setting store by such a 'forecast accuracy' KPI is obvious: in a 'forecast push' replenishment environment, it is the forecast of future demand that is used to drive the supply activities that will ensure the right levels of stock are located in the right locations to meet that demand and achieve the desired level of 'on time in full' (OTIF) service.

Of course 100 per cent forecast accuracy is not expected as it is impossible and, anyway, safety stock is held to buffer against the forecast error. But as all demand planners know, the first questions to be asked when service issues occur are around the forecast and, of course, in some cases extremes of demand can be identified as the cause of a stock out.

So far so good – the process seems entirely sensible: reasonable forecast accuracy can be achieved, safety stocks can be used to compensate for forecast error and, so long as operations/supply deliver roughly what is required, roughly on time, desired service levels will be achieved and stock turns will be as expected given average order quantities. Right?

Wrong!!

Why using forecasts to drive replenishment doesn't work

There are two key reasons why desired supply chain performance cannot be achieved using this 'forecast push' process and the root cause for both is 'variability'.

Forecast error The 80 per cent level of world-class portfolio mix accuracy actually hides a huge amount of inaccuracy; 80 per cent is only achieved due to the weighting of the relatively few high-volume/low-variability demand pattern SKUs that can enable forecast accuracies of 90 per cent +. Due to 'pareto', the majority of SKUs in any portfolio are of medium and low variability, for which forecast accuracies of 60 per cent and below are the norm. Driving supply with inaccurate forecasts inevitably leads to unbalanced and excessive stocks. (See Figures 2.8 and 2.9.)

Most companies spend far too little time on managing their safety stock levels accurately and very rarely use a properly calculated and maintained 'forecast error with offset' algorithm. And even if they did, the entire logic behind DRP/MRP/APS generates exception messages whenever the forward inventory balance does not calculate to safety stock – which it nearly always doesn't. If the exception messages are responded to, the forecast error is simply 'bounced' up the supply chain in the form of supply schedule adjustments that disrupt flow and generate variability. (See Figure 2.10.)

Of course, the avalanche of unprioritized exception messages can be ignored but the consequence is a risk of service or inventory issues that might have to be responded to sooner or later, anyway, with the same result. And for most planners, ignoring all exception messages simply is not an option due to their need to avoid possible back orders.

Figure 2.8 Typical range of forecast mix accuracies across a product range

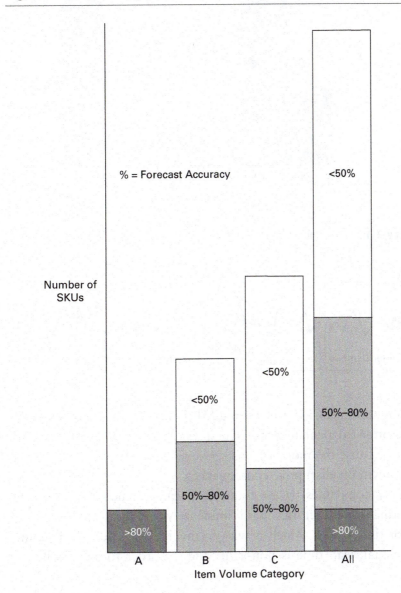

Figure 2.9   The inevitable picture of unbalanced and excessive on-hand inventories as a consequence of inaccurate forecast-driven MPS/MRP replenishment execution

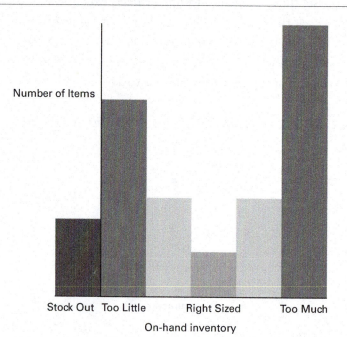

Number of Items

Stock Out   Too Little   Right Sized   Too Much

On-hand inventory

Figure 2.10   The impact upon production of inaccurate forecast-driven MPS/MRP replenishment

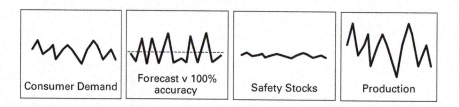

| Consumer Demand | Forecast v 100% accuracy | Safety Stocks | Production |

So those products, identified using MRP data dropped into a spreadsheet (often to calculate stock cover days versus the forecast) that seem likely to cause the more serious service issues, are pulled forward – with inevitably disruptive consequences.

Many companies try to minimize frequent schedule changes by buffering their factories with immensely exaggerated lead times and/or time fences, which is why so much of a product's planning, and actual, lead time is non-value-add. In order to avoid schedule interruptions this approach requires extremely high levels of finished goods buffer, yet the logic of MRP will still generate exception messages and rarely are they all ignored. (See the section 'Should planners ignore MRP's exception messages?' in Chapter 3).

And all of this applies in materials supply just as much as it does in manufacturing. Whether the materials are components, raw materials or finished goods (as in wholesalers and distributors) it is, of course, the suppliers that are asked to expedite deliveries due to their customers' 'overselling', which is why they usually quote excessively long lead times (to give them some protection) and their costs (and prices?) are higher than necessary because of the excess capacity or inventory they also often hold to enable them to respond.

Fixed lead times and dependent demand A fundamental assumption of MRP is that lead times are fixed but this is wrong. Lead times are directly proportional to levels of variability, increase in line with 'load' and do so in an exponential manner when capacity utilization is high. This can be graphically illustrated as follows:

Figure 2.11 Demonstration of how increasing levels of supply chain variability and capacity utilization increase lead times and inventory

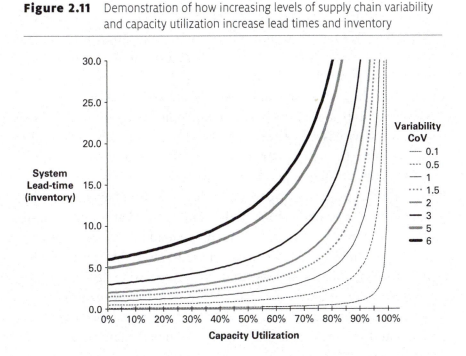

There is even a mathematical equation that quantifies these relationships and in its most simple form it tells us that:

---

average waiting time in a **Q**ueue = **V**ariability (of arrivals and process time) x 1/(1 − **U**tilization) x average processing **T**ime[13]

or

Q = VUT

And because MRP uses dependent demand, any extension in a lead time ripples out across the supply chain and disrupts flow, particularly as, in such an environment, delays accumulate but gains do not (gains can only be made with additional or spare capacity).

Variability

As we have seen, inaccurate forecasts, blown through MRP, result in service-saving schedule changes/expediting and consequent unplanned factory machine changeovers that inevitably impact the planned schedules of other products and their lead times. Even if the forecasts were 100 per cent accurate, however, natural process variability and sensitivity to load would still lead to fluctuating lead times with knock-on effects that result in congestion and further waves of variability throughout the supply chain – particularly if capacity utilization is high. The inevitable result is excessive lead times, excessive levels of unbalanced stock, use of unplanned overtime and, often, continuing service issues. And as discussed, companies that buy products also suffer from these issues in the form of excessively long lead times, expediting charges and high supply prices to cover the inevitable variability buffer, and its costs, that their suppliers have to absorb.

All of this can be understood in the context of what supply chains really are – flows of materials through value-add processes that are prone to turn into queues whenever there is variability, particularly in the presence of high-capacity utilization. The variability inevitably generates a mix of unplanned buffers: time (ie longer-than-planned lead times that can cause the customer to wait), unplanned capacity (ie chop and change the schedule with unplanned changeovers) and excessive levels of inventory.

If the supply chain is not flexible enough to respond perfectly to real demand then these buffers are inevitable and MRP's erroneous assumption of fixed lead times and dependent demand directly propagate and amplify the variability. The frequently seen user response, MRP system lead time inflation to compensate, only makes the situation worse – not least by causing more work to be released to the factory floor, thereby further increasing planned capacity utilization.

The aggregate buffer in forecast push MRP supply chains is always unbalanced, and, far more than that, necessary, because of the variability injected by the forecast error and its amplification by dependent demand.

What can be done? Supply chains will always suffer from variability to some extent, but it can be minimized. One method is via implementation of Lean, which is: 'fundamentally about minimizing the cost of buffering variability'.[14]

Activities such as TPM, TQM, standard work, single-minute exchange of die (SMED) and batch-size reduction all contribute to flexibility and reliability that reduces 'supply side' variation.

Another well-known Lean tool is pull, and Demand-Driven SCM is simply a cross-enterprise(s) version of pull that allows the entire 'end-to-end' supply chain to flow in line with real demand.

The essence of Demand-Driven SCM is the deliberate positioning of multiple planned, but independent/decoupled, inventory locations up and down the supply chain that are each replenished, in an efficient and stable sequence, to a carefully calculated, and maintained, stock target (reflecting average demand, variability and replenishment frequency) in line with demand (Figure 2.12).

The result is that the supply chain is able to autonomously respond to demand,[15] while the inventory positions decouple the 'value-add' activities thereby preventing residual variability from being propagated and amplified across it. And because replenishment is driven by demand (effectively using a 'make/ship to replace' mechanism), not the forecast, it is always accurate so the inventories are right sized, service-saving schedule interruptions are eliminated, the variability buffer is actually used and the planned lead times adhered to (and they can actually be a lot shorter than planned as the level of variability-generated queuing in the lead time will be reduced). (See Figure 2.13.)

Figure 2.12 Demand-Driven SCM – strategically positioned inventory buffers prevent variability transmission and replenishment is driven by demand

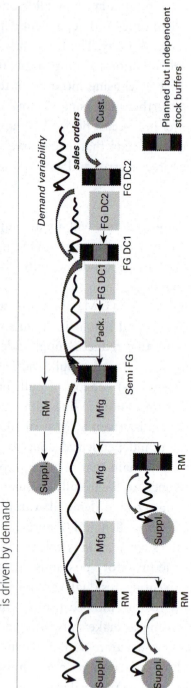

Figure 2.13 Efficient and stable production enabled by Demand-Driven SCM

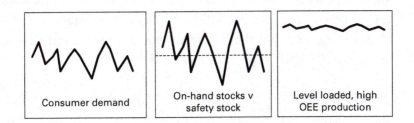

| Consumer demand | On-hand stocks v safety stock | Level loaded, high OEE production |

In a Demand-Driven supply chain forecasting is still important for S&OP, stock target sizing (eg if there is trend or seasonality the targets need to reflect it appropriately) and event management, but high levels of time-phased item-level forecast accuracy are no longer needed and that particular KPI can be dispensed with.

Because of the far lower levels of variability in a Demand-Driven supply chain, relative to that using 'forecast push' MRP, its implementation consistently delivers significant performance improvements due to the elimination of unplanned cost-generating buffers:

- achievement of planned service levels;
- reductions in inventory of 30 per cent to 50 per cent;
- higher-capacity utilization leading to cost reductions of around 20 per cent;
- lead-time reductions of up to 85 per cent;
- without expediting or firefighting and any focus upon high levels of forecast accuracy.

Demand-Driven SCM can now be inexpensively simulated, piloted and implemented across large and complex networks using robust, functionality rich and globally tested SaaS that operates through legacy transaction systems.

Would planned service levels be met with 100 per cent forecast accuracy?

At first one might think that achievement of 100 per cent forecast accuracy would enable companies to make product and ship it to customers straight from the factory without the need for any buffer stock – assuming there was no unreliable supply due to machine breakdowns, quality issues, etc. But even if these supply problems did not occur, due to excellent TPM and TQM for instance, buffer would still be needed and the reason reveals a fundamental flaw in the 'forecast push MRP' replenishment model.

Lead times The logic of 'forecast push MPS/MRP' generates SKU-specific replenishment order recommendations whenever the consumed forecast plus orders exceeds the stock available plus stock on order and is, therefore, consuming the planned safety stock. At the finished-goods level the safety stock is there in case demand exceeds the forecast over the supply lead time, or supply is delayed, and its predicted consumption triggers an exception message. Further up the supply chain the forecast is netted, all processes are expected to meet their individual lead times exactly and no safety stock is planned anywhere.

Lead times, however, are never static. Unless there is infinite capacity, lead times vary with load/capacity utilization and, at higher levels of utilization, they increase in an exponential manner.

The consequence is that, without any obvious cause, such as machine breakdowns or quality problems, lead times will vary and the longer the end-to-end supply chain the greater will be the variation. The reasons are:

1 Each process can only begin when the preceding processes have delivered their materials – any delay is permanently lost capacity that cannot be made up without additional unplanned capacity.

2 Processes are prevented from getting ahead of schedule by their dependence upon material supply from preceding processes. If they do get too far ahead they will starve.

3 The above two mean that delays in a supply chain accumulate but gains cannot.

4 The greater the number of processes in a supply chain the greater the likelihood of delays occurring, the more the delays will accumulate and the greater their impact as they amplify up and down the supply chain – particularly if the delays happen at an early stage in the supply chain.

The consequence is the existence of two of the fundamental rules of Factory Physics (Hopp and Spearman, *Factory Physics*, 1995):

> *In steady state, all plants will release work at an average rate that is strictly less than the average capacity.*

> *In a production line, variability early in a routing increases cycle time more than equivalent variability later in the routing.*

So, without some form of buffer, be it finished goods stock or shipment delay, even 100 per cent accurate forecasts will not deliver planned service levels due to inevitable 'natural cause' supply lead-time variability.

Impact of inaccurate forecasts Average lead times vary directly with the level of supply chain variability and exponentially at high levels of capacity utilization (the variability, utilization, time (VUT), or Kingman equation, in its simplified form, tells us that the average wait in a queue = Variability x 1/(1–Utilization) x average processing Time).

And queues, a major component of lead time, are caused by variation in the rate of arrivals at a workstation and the workstation's processing rate. Together, these sources of variability cause lost capacities and arrival spikes and the development of queues with finite average length. That length is dependent upon the level of variability and capacity utilization, which is why, if planning lead times are extended to compensate for poor OTIF, and more work is thereby released to the factory floor, lead times will actually get further extended because of the consequent increase in capacity utilization.

In a 'forecast push MPS/MRP' environment, a key source of variability is the high level of expediting and schedule changing that tends to occur: MRP exception messages cause planners to reschedule due to demand exceeding forecast and the consequent unplanned consumption of safety stock. Every schedule interruption uses unplanned capacity and, on shared work-centres, impacts the lead times of other products, which ripple out through MRP's dependent demand network.

Minimizing supply chain variability It can be seen that supply chain variability, be it inherent or forecast-induced, causes the development of cost-generating buffers: capacity, queue/lead time and stock. Is there any way it can be minimized?

An obvious approach to tackle significant supply side variability is the implementation of all those tecŸiques that result in reliable supply – TPM, TQM, standard work, 5S etc. It is little wonder that Hopp and Spearman, the authors of *Factory Physics*, describe Lean as: 'fundamentally about minimizing the cost of buffering variability'.[16]

Another key approach is to execute replenishment in response to demand instead of the forecast to avoid the generation of the forecast error-induced variability. Demand-Driven SCM replenishment (in Lean terminology: pull) is not just 'make to order', in an ex-stock environment it involves a make, or ship, to replace mechanism at multiple carefully chosen independent stock positions up and down the supply chain. These decoupling buffers absorb variation and prevent it cascading, as 'bullwhip', up and down the supply chain as well as allowing every work centre to operate independently of each other. In this way, each work centre is protected from inherent lead-time variability and being periodically starved by upstream processes. It also means, of course, that the entire end-to-end supply chain operates in line with demand without any of the rescheduling and expediting that occurs in 'forecast push MRP' because of forecast inaccuracy.

To achieve a more detailed understanding of the 'why and how' of Demand-Driven SCM, see the section 'Demand-Driven SCM: agility thru' stability'.

Summary Forecasts should only be used for supply chain planning (S&OP and abnormal event management). Due to the performance-degrading impact of the variability they generate because of their inaccuracy, they should never be used for driving replenishment through ERP/DRP/MRP/APS.

Demand-Driven SCM replenishment allows the supply chain to autonomously respond to real demand without creating an unplanned cost-generating buffer, and a key step in its implementation is the deliberate positioning of independent and carefully sized stock positions within the supply chain.

And because these stock positions are replenished in line with demand, not inaccurate forecasts, and act to absorb supply side variability, the Demand-Driven Supply Chain operates with significantly less overall buffer than those driven with forecasts through traditional MPS/MRP. Typically they allow planned service levels to be met with 30 per cent to 50 per cent less average inventory and around 20 per cent lower costs due to less unplanned overtime and higher-capacity utilization.

Autonomation

Apart from when exceptional and extreme event management is necessary, a key attribute of the Demand-Driven Supply Chain is that, if set up and managed correctly, materials will flow in line with demand: the supply chain will *autonomously* respond to demand without direct intervention. As demand rises so more will be supplied and, if it falls, so less will be pulled through. If the level of variability is high more variability buffer will obviously be required, depending on the speed with which the supply chain can respond (ie the lead time). If the supply chain is inflexible and lead times are long, clearly more such buffer is necessary.

In a way, the autonomous response of the supply chain is similar to that of the autonomic nervous system in that there is no forethought involved. Whereas the autonomic nervous system bypasses the brain, so the autonomous Demand-Driven Supply Chain does not require a forecast or a planner to tell it what to do in advance – except in the case of abnormal events such as extreme and exceptional demand spikes.

What can sports science teach us about SCM?

An odd question but maybe not so strange? We all want our supply chains to be efficient, which in sports science terms might be translated as 'fit' – and of course the word 'lean' can be applied to both worlds. In the animal kingdom, creatures that are fit and lean tend to be faster and more agile than those that aren't and, in the supply chain world, efficiency and leanness is also associated with speed and agility. The faster that materials are processed into product and shipped out to customers the lower will be their associated costs (eg inventory, waiting, defects and all the other Lean wastes), the more responsive will be the supply chain and the faster will be the cash-generating throughput. All of this might appear a somewhat facile bridge between the worlds of sports science and SCM, but there is another that is less obvious and of far greater relevance.

Complex living creatures have two nervous systems – the sympathetic and the para-sympathetic. The former is that used by the brain to control deliberate actions and is relatively slow because nerve impulses have to travel from the brain to, say, the limb you want to move. The para-sympathetic system manages very fast impulses such as that used when you spontaneously withdraw your hand from a hot surface – the response is autonomic, it does not involve the brain and any thought, it just happens and is very, very fast.[17]

In a related field, Nobel-winning behavioural economist Daniel KaŸeman in his book *Thinking Fast, Thinking Slow* (2011, Penguin) describes how the brain has two thinking processes:

- System 1: fast, automatic, frequent, emotional, stereotypic, subconscious.

- System 2: slow, effortful, infrequent, logical, calculating, conscious.

System 1 often leads us to make incorrect decisions because it effectively reflects 'gut feel'. Experts, however, can use it very accurately and without thinking, when applied to their particular field of expertise, because they have trained it through hours and hours of practice to be reliable. An example is given by KaŸeman of: 'the firefighter who has a sudden urge to escape a burning house just before it collapses, because the firefighter knows the danger intuitively, without knowing how he knows'.[18]

In a similar vein Matthew Syed, in his book *Bounce* (2011, Fourth Estate) makes the same point about how sheer quantity of intensive high-quality practice is necessary for top sports people to achieve world-class performance. Such practice, combined with the right psychological approach, enables them to deliver their brilliant skills and prowess autonomically – naturally, spontaneously and without thinking. Wouldn't it be great if our supply chains could deliver as fast, skilful and agile a performance as George Best, Michael Jordan, Wayne Gretzky and Steffi Graf did when in their prime?

In fact they can but first the means by which most current supply chains respond to their environment needs to be fundamentally changed. Most supply chains are run using the System 2 'big brain' approach in which a master schedule is generated to meet orders and the consumed forecast and supply schedules are calculated using MRP logic to support it. These are then sent to the factory and suppliers for execution. When the schedules prove to be wrong, which they inevitably are because of forecast inaccuracy, exception messages are generated. These prompt planners to expedite and amend the schedules, which leads to unplanned machine changeovers and expensive lost capacity, along with increases in lead times (causing poorer responsiveness and further service issues) and higher stocks. This methodology is also responsible for generating the 'cancerous' side effect called 'bullwhip', which significantly amplifies the impact of these performance-destroying activities.

An alternative, and far more effective, supply chain process would be that which is autonomic in that it responds very quickly and 100 per cent accurately to whatever real demands have been placed upon it – with an absolute minimum of waste (ie customer waiting, excessive stocks and capacity-wasting expediting and schedule changes).

That alternative is Demand-Driven SCM (see the section Demand-Driven SCM: agility thru' stability') replenishment in which execution (ie transport orders, production orders and purchase orders) is triggered only by actual demand. The process involves deliberately positioning independent and decoupled inventories in the supply chain with repetitive stable optimized schedule sequences that simply 'top up' the stock that has been taken from the inventory position immediately downstream.

If the inventory replenishment targets of such a process are correctly managed up and down the supply chain (often called supply chain conditioning, perhaps akin to sports training?) then the entire demand-and-supply network will efficiently and accurately respond autonomously to any customer demand pattern without the need for enormously expensive and ineffective 'big brain' MRP/APS/black box software. And the more frequently production is cycled through the portfolio the more quickly, and in 'real time', will the end-to-end supply chain be responding to demand.

When implemented, this Demand-Driven SCM way of working has been demonstrated to deliver planned service levels with reductions in average inventory of 30 per cent to 50 per cent and costs of around 20 per cent across complex global networks. The rationale for this way of working is based upon what supply chains really are: flows of material for which queuing theory[9] describes how variability eradication (such as that caused by excessively big batches and generated by inaccurate forecasts – analogous to lack of fitness and tecŸique respectively in sport?) is necessary for perfect flow.

None of which is to say that forecasting is no longer important! Forecasting is still necessary to support S&OP for the purposes of financial planning and ensuring sufficient internal and supplier capacity; also for inventory target setting and event management. The important point is that 'big brain' SKU-level time-phased forecasts should never be used to directly drive replenishment execution through any sort of MPS/MRP calculations.

Demand-Driven Collaboration

Demand-Driven SCM's elimination of traditional MRP's use of a dependent demand network driven by (inaccurate) forecasts, and its replacement by multiple independent, but planned and maintained decoupled inventory positions that are replenished in line with demand, means that the process can be applied across company boundaries as much as within a company's own supply chain.

A company that is supplying another and responding to orders generated by that customer's own 'forecast push MPS/MRP' will inevitably be trying to respond to volatile order patterns that are continuously changing as the customer itself tries to align its own supply with demand patterns that are different to those of the forecast. In this situation the supplier will either hold high levels of stock to meet such demand patterns; accede to expedite requests and disrupt their own supply schedules, thereby incurring cost; or simply enforce a rigid order-to-delivery lead-time policy that flips the onus for buffering the variability onto the customer.

In these situations, however the supplier/customer relationship is buffered, the amount of buffer – be it capacity, time or inventory – will be excessive if forecasts are being used to drive execution. In the past, collaborative planning, forecasting and replenishment (CPFR) has been tried to facilitate inter-company replenishment but its reliance upon forecast accuracy for success meant that it wasn't and it just led to antagonism between 'would be' partners because what was planned was never what was needed.

If, however, the downstream partner uses a Demand-Driven replenishment tecȲique (including active collaborative management of extreme and exceptional demand events) instead of 'forecast push MPS/MRP', and places orders upon their suppliers accordingly (or perhaps a vendor managed inventory (VMI) arrangement could be used), then the orders will be far more accurate and stable, which will help the supplier to reduce its own response lead times, stabilize its supply schedules and reduce its costs.

Between mutually dependent suppliers and customers (ie those who account for significant proportions of each other's throughput, and therefore have a common interest in improving efficiency and service) a further step might be taken using 'base stock' replenishment principles, especially if the product being traded is for resale. If the supplier has visibility of its customer's inventory and its consumption, the supplier will be able to actively replenish against an agreed shared stock target and use the customer's inventory as, effectively, its own buffer. (NB this does not imply a consignment stock relationship, which is a matter for commercial negotiation, though the methodology being described will reduce its inventory burden upon the supplier if such an arrangement is in place.) By having visibility of its customer's consumption and using that demand pattern to consume their 'shared' inventory and, thereby, drive its own replenishment activities, the supplier will avoid being subject to 'lumpy' customer order patterns that would otherwise require high levels of variability buffer or the need to integrate large disruptive 'bulk' orders into its schedule.

Demand-Driven Collaboration: key to the fight-back against low-cost competition

During a presentation in January 2015 a senior supply chain director at one of the UK's largest multiples talked about how UK supermarket groups are going to have to work differently with their suppliers in order to successfully compete against the fast-growing grocery discount sector. He described how there needed to be a 'grounded methodology' for establishing real 'end-to-end' collaboration and partnership to drive down 'cost and complexity' but that there were no 'silver bullets'.

In many ways he was echoing the thoughts that Martin Christopher, Emeritus Professor of Marketing and Logistics at Cranfield University, first expressed back in the 1990s, that: 'Supply chains compete, not companies'.[19]

Christopher's words, of course, apply to any industrial sector, not just grocery retailing, but it is perhaps only now, because of the increasing success of the relatively new low-cost retailers, that their truth is being properly recognized by the supermarkets.

Unfortunately in the past, and despite use of 'supportive' processes such as CPFR, truly successful implementations of supply chain collaboration have been few and far between. Apart from the constant issues of trust and capability, one of the reasons has been the difficulty in sharing the essential and accurate inventory and demand data in a timely and robust manner. That barrier has now disappeared with the emergence of SaaS, which allows companies, using different transaction systems, to easily share such information, inexpensively and in a standardized manner, via simple daily flat file upload and download.

The other problem has been the fact that past inter-company collaborative replenishment processes (eg CPFR) have been based on a 'forecast push' process that is simply the wrong model for effective management of supply chain execution. This is unsurprising as nearly all 'make-to-stock' manufacturers currently use 'forecast push MPS/ MRP' to drive their factories. They have been largely unaware of both how very ineffective and costly it is and of the existence of the alternative, and far superior, Demand-Driven SCM approach. Ironically, Demand-Driven SCM, which is really just a cross enterprise(s) version of pull that has evolved out of Lean, was originally inspired by the internal replenishment model used by US supermarkets in the 1950s and that is still in use today!

Demand-Driven SCM replaces the inaccurate forecast as the driver of replenishment with multiple carefully located decoupled inventory positions that are cyclically replenished up to calculated and maintained stock targets – effectively a make-or-ship-to-replace mechanism. The supply chain is therefore able to respond autonomously to all demand patterns except for extreme and exceptional spikes that require anticipatory stock builds via event management.

To get a fuller understanding of Demand-Driven SCM see the section 'Demand-Driven SCM: agility thru' stability'; and for why it reliably delivers planned service levels with up to 50 per cent less average inventory see Chapter 3 (the section 'Why flow?').

Clearly the Demand-Driven SCM approach can be adopted for managing replenishment across company boundaries as long as upstream parties have visibility of downstream inventories, versus target, and there is good collaborative agreement and synchronization of inventory target adjustments. The availability of Demand-Driven SaaS now makes this possible and already many supermarket groups make supplier-specific inventories and point-of-sale (POS) data available to assist the performance of their suppliers. Unfortunately, most suppliers are unable to use such data effectively as they are wedded to the wrong replenishment process!

Collaborative Demand-Driven SCM also needs effective event management so that appropriate actions can be taken in a timely manner (eg advance stock builds), though it is surprising how resilient the Demand-Driven stock buffers are and how capable they are at absorbing 'normal' levels of demand volatility even in, say, a high promotions-based marketplace.

There is a group of supermarket suppliers that actually do use a form of the Demand-Driven SCM approach because their product shelf lives are so short that they have to! Fresh produce suppliers ship product into the retail distribution networks every evening based upon a supermarket multiple's order quantities that replace that day's aggregated POS transactions. The reason their suppliers can respond is that they hold a small amount of finished goods stock (packed the previous day) and every day harvest, wash and pack a quantity up to a daily stock target based on past experience. They may also use a cold storage produce stock-point somewhere between the field and the packing plant as buffer in case of high variability (eg demand spikes and bad weather).

Daily end-to-end response to POS demand may not be appropriate for all ambient manufacturers, or their supermarket customers, but certainly their joint adoption of the Demand-Driven SCM approach to manufacturing supply execution and planning, integrated into the Demand-Driven collaborative approach to distribution, will enable them to make significant progress towards achieving a step change in their service, cost and inventory performances. As such it would be a significant step for both parties on their way towards eliminating a major source of unnecessary cost generation (ie forecast error-induced variability) and allow them to successfully achieve their premium product/service positioning at an appropriately competitive price point.

Demand-Driven SCM may not be the 'silver bullet' but it is almost certainly the next best thing!

A growing number of CPG manufacturers have already begun low-profile implementations of Demand-Driven SCM across their networks – Demand-Driven SCM because it is so very effective; low profile because they know it will give them a considerable competitive advantage.

Figure 2.14   The application of Demand-Driven collaboration – reducing the unplanned buffers and providing two-way visibility

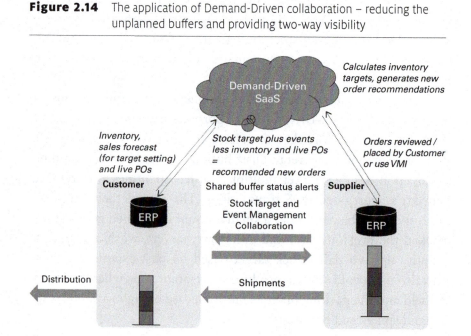

How far away is the first implementation of genuine end-to-end Demand-Driven collaboration between a supplier and a retailer?

Demand-Driven Procurement

As anyone who works in procurement is all too aware, there is continuous pressure to reduce component prices to improve profitability. For many years the 'target costing' and 'Lean' approach has been for supply engineers to guide and train suppliers to adopt Lean tecŸiques that take out 'waste' and then, perhaps, 'share' the benefits.[20] This is clearly a very valid tecŸique that can serve both parties well, but does it always bring the full benefits that had been expected or predicted? When the answer is no, it is perhaps the buying company that needs to make some changes to its own processes in order to unlock the full cost-savings potential of the approach.

The nature of this change is in the way companies drive product replenishment through their supply chain from finished product delivery through to component source. The majority of companies still drive execution using SKU-level time-phased forecasts blown through DRP/MRP calculations. These generate replenishment recommendations aimed at achieving safety stock levels but, because the forecasts are inevitably incorrect, and are always being changed, MRP's exception messages proliferate and both factories and suppliers are frequently asked to amend and change their schedules at short notice. (See Figure 2.15.)

This leads to unplanned machine changeovers and lost capacity, with inevitable knock-on effects further up the supply chain, which

Figure 2.15   The impact upon production of inaccurate forecast-driven MPS/MRP replenishment

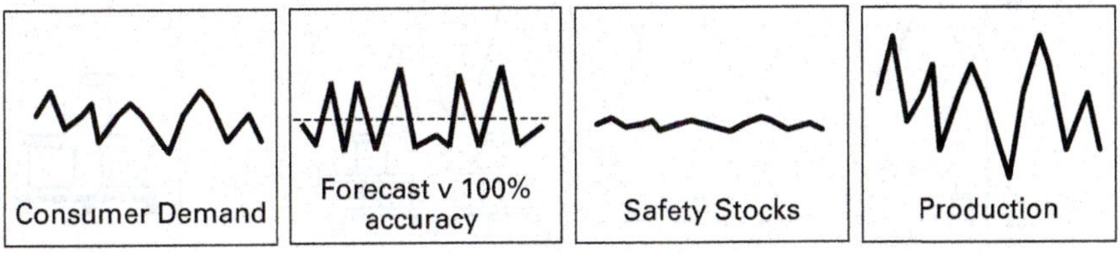

| Consumer Demand | Forecast v 100% accuracy | Safety Stocks | Production |

cause lead times and inventories to grow and require suppliers to have to respond very frequently, and at short notice, to changes in their customers' requirements.

As if these forecast-induced performance issues are not bad enough by themselves, they are a whole lot worse when the end-to-end supply chain is affected by 'bullwhip', which it always is when 'forecast push DRP/MRP' is used. 'Bullwhip' occurs when relatively small changes in downstream demand get amplified by the net forecast, batching and latency[21] as it is propagated up the supply chain, causing factories and suppliers to respond to very much higher levels of SKU demand variability (and its attendant costs) than they otherwise would. (See Figure 2.16.)

So, if your suppliers are working hard to eradicate their own sources of variability then your forecast push DRP/MRP/APS-driven replenishment and ordering process is simply adding another source of that same variability, which is increasing their costs, causing them to have to work with unnecessarily high levels of stock buffer and, as is common, causing them to impose extended response lead times upon their customers' orders. Any unprotected instability can, of course, also disrupt and slow down the supplier's continuous improvement (CI) process as they focus on meeting the latest emergency shipment request instead!

Figure 2.16 Variability being amplified as it is transmitted up the supply chain – bullwhip

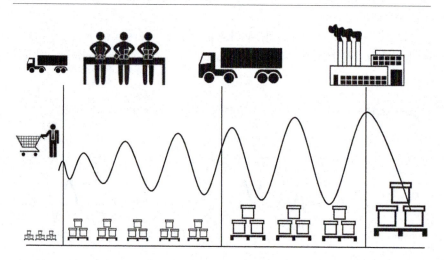

The impact upon product costs of bullwhip volatility has been calculated to reduce margins by up to 30 per cent.[22] This is because all operations (ie those of factories, warehouses and freight as well as those of suppliers) perform most efficiently when under stable conditions – as any operations manager will tell you and as does the well-known Toyota House schematic (Figure 2.17).

If the only way to avoid generating forecast-induced volatility and bullwhip is to stop using the forecast to drive replenishment, is there an alternative? Fortunately there is and it is called 'Demand-Driven SCM' in which, at multiple deliberately positioned and independent stock locations, an appropriate non-forecast-based replenishment tecŸique is selected and, across the full end-to-end supply chain, the tecŸiques, replenishment triggers and buffers are aligned to ensure that they successfully support each other and the rates of consumption at each and every echelon. These tecŸiques do not just apply to a company's internal supply chain of course, they can also be the basis for collaboration with suppliers (see the section Demand-Driven collaboration).

From a stability perspective, these tecŸiques protect operations and suppliers from volatility by preventing it being created by forecast

Figure 2.17 The Toyota House, underpinned by stability

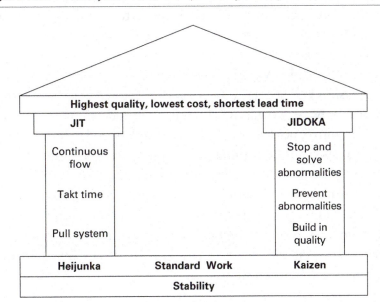

Figure 2.18   Efficient and stable production enabled by Demand-Driven SCM

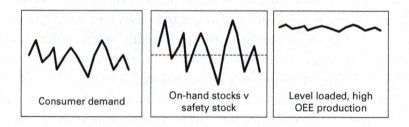

Consumer demand	On-hand stocks v safety stock	Level loaded, high OEE production

error in the first place and ensuring that any remaining is absorbed and minimized. (See Figure 2.18.)

See the section 'Demand-Driven SCM: agility thru' stability' to learn more about the practice of Demand-Driven SCM, including its transformational performance benefits, its recent rapid uptake across industry as well as the role that Demand-Driven S&OP has in providing forecasts of material requirements, including abnormal events, to suppliers so that they can plan their capacities and activities accordingly.

If Demand-Driven SCM is so effective, it is reasonable to ask why is it not practised more widely? In fact 'pull' is increasingly common within the factory walls but rarely across the end-to-end supply chain, let alone through to suppliers. This might explain why many companies often find that all their Lean factory and supplier engineering efforts have not translated into the significant performance benefits they expected.

By now the reader will know why.

The reasons for the relative scarcity of end-to-end Demand-Driven SCM can only be speculative but might include the fact that it is counter-intuitive, neither widely or fully understood, and difficult to implement successfully without appropriate software support.

Clearly procurement and supply management have an interest in how their company's supply chain is managed as it has a significant impact upon their performance and ability to contribute to the bottom line, let alone its impact upon the material shortages and service issues that they have to manage. In some companies their CEO might also be interested.

Fortunately, the outlook for Demand-Driven SCM is very positive with the impact of a Lean education upon the new generation of supply chain leaders, the training and publicity being provided by the Demand Driven Institute and the emergence of functionality rich and globally tested enterprise-wide Demand-Driven SaaS systems that can be inexpensively and easily piloted before a low-risk step-by-step roll out.

How would successful implementation of Demand-Driven SCM affect procurement and supply management activities? The good news is that it will remove a lot of tedious and non-value-added work such as continuously cutting and recutting of supply plans, expediting and then having to explain why late deliveries are holding up operations. You should be able to share your now relatively stable requirements with suppliers and allow them to reliably schedule their operations accordingly... and, perhaps, even manage their own VMI replenishment schedules if a Demand-Driven SCM collaborative shared-visibility portal and ways of working have been established. This will all allow you to spend more time on value-add activities such as source selection/evaluation, price/cost analysis, supplier engineering, CI initiatives, etc. Perhaps, most importantly, having significantly stabilized demand patterns upon your suppliers, they should be able to operate with shorter lead times and far more efficiently... and some of the cost saving should accrue to their customers!

Notes

1 Exception messages are generated whenever the safety stock is in danger of being used so forecast error tends to be 'bounced' up the supply chain from it and through the dependent demand network. Many companies protect their operations with time fences that are effectively a lead-time extension, which represent more stock buffer (and exacerbate the situation by increasing load), but will still eventually suffer service issues unless some schedules are amended

2 And traditional MRP uses fixed lead times within its upstream BOM, which means that variability-caused delays and lead-time extensions tend to ripple out across the network and become cumulative unless additional capacities can be found to catch back

3   Hopp and Spearman describe Lean as 'fundamentally about minimizing the cost of buffering variability', in (2004) To pull or not to pull: what is the question?, *Manufacturing & Service Operations Management*, 6 (2), pp 133–48. It does so by improving supply reliability (eg TPM, TQM, poke-yoke, standard work, etc) and flexibility – the latter, such as postponement, quick changeovers, multipurpose work centres, multiskilling, etc, reduce the amount of aggregate buffer (time, capacity, inventory) required or created by a particular level of variability

4   Forecasts are used in Demand-Driven SCM for inventory buffer sizing and S&OP; in both cases high levels of item level, time-phased accuracy are unnecessary because, in the case of buffer sizing, we use an average of the forecast over three or four months and service is achieved mainly through autonomous supply chain response to demand, and for S&OP we only need good aggregate forecast accuracy, which is very easy to achieve. Adequate forecast accuracy for these purposes can be achieved using automated simple historical extrapolations (ie naive tecŸiques) leaving demand planners to focus their attention, by exception, upon anticipatory event management and working with supply planners to ensure that appropriate advance stock builds are planned in

5   Productivity increases of up to one-third have been recorded as a consequence of regular and predictable schedules being introduced into operations through 'economies of repetition'

6   An optimal sequence will not always be followed, in that certain items may be skipped if they are off cycle – what should never happen though is that a sequence is reversed; if the buffers are sized correctly and there is an effective event management process this will never happen

7   It is important that level schedules are not used to unnecessarily drive up batch sizes as these reduce flexibility and generate variability reflected in higher stock levels, service issues (due to non-availability of capacity when it might be needed) and higher inventory costs – storage, damage, deterioration etc

8   See the section Demand-Driven Collaboration later in this chapter

9   Flow variability at constraints generates queues according to the Kingman/VUT equation: Q = Variability x 1/(1 – Utilization) x Time. It quantifies how they increase directly in line with V (and T) and exponentially with U, especially at high levels of U. Thus queue/lead

times can only be reduced through use of expensive spare capacity or minimization of variability. See Hopp and Spearman (1995) *Factory Physics*, and any text on queueing theory. Also see 'Can SCM be deductive' and 'Why flow?' (Chapter 3).

10 Personal communication

11 See [Online] https://www.linkedin.com/pulse/fastlane-from-roi-rip-how-effectively-kill-success?trk=hb_ntf_MEGAPHONE_ARTICLE_POST (last accessed 4 October 2016)

12 See the section 'Supply chain optimization – what does it really mean?' (Chapter 3).

13 The Kingman equation, see Hopp and Spearman (1995) *Factory Physics*

14 Hopp and Spearman, To pull or not to pull, pp 133–48

15 The only demand events that cannot be absorbed by the inventory targets are those that are extreme and exceptional – these become the focus of active event management

16 Another key Lean tecŸique is SMED to enable batch size reduction. Smaller batches reduce levels of variability because they can more quickly be processed by a work centre than can an excessively big batch, thereby allowing a greater mix of products to be processed and causing less upstream delay. Think of how much quicker a short train will flash through a road crossing as compared to that of a long train travelling at the same speed

17 The ideas and concepts described here are not original, they were first described by Taiichi OŸo (1983) *Toyota Production System: Beyond large scale production'*, Toyota Production System Productivity Inc., p 45:

A business organization is like the human body. It contains autonomic nerves that work without regard to human wishes and motor nerves that react to human command to control muscles. The human body has an amazing structure and operations; the fine balance and precision with which body parts are accommodated in the overall design are even more marvellous.

In the human body the autonomic nerve... performs... functions that respond automatically to changes in the body. These functions are performed unconsciously without any directive from the brain.

At Toyota we began to think about how to install an autonomic nervous system in our own rapidly growing business organization. In our production plant, an autonomic nerve means making judgements autonomously at the lowest possible level; for example, when to stop production, what sequence to follow in making parts, or when overtime is necessary to produce the required amount.

These discussions can be made by factory workers themselves, without having to consult the production control or engineering departments that correspond to the brain in the human body. The plant should be a place where such judgements can be made by workers autonomously.

... a business should have reflexes that can respond instantly and smoothly to small changes in the plan without having to go to the brain.

The larger a business, the better reflexes it needs. If a small change in a plan must be accompanied by a brain command to make it work, the business will be unable to avoid burns or injuries and will lose great opportunities.

Building a fine-tuning mechanism into the business so that change will not be felt as change is like implementing a reflex nerve inside the body.

Toyota's just-in-time supply process is a way to deliver exactly what is needed when it is needed. This method does not require extra inventory.

18 D KaŸeman (2011) *Thinking Fast, Thinking Slow*, Penguin, London, p 237

19 See [Online] www.martin-christopher.info (last accessed 4 October 2016)

20 Cox (2001) Managing with power: strategies for improving value appropriation from supply relationships, *Journal of Supply Chain Management*, **37** (2), pp 42–7

21 Latency bullwhip occurs between trading partners when the customer experiences a short lived demand increase about which their supplier learns when receiving a much larger order than usual. They interpret it as a permanent increase in demand and raise production and capacity in anticipation of it persisting – only for the whole process to later go into reverse leaving the supply chain full of excess (queues of) stock and capacity. Latency is also the form of variability that causes the phantom traffic jams that appear out of nowhere in fast-moving motorway traffic

22 Metters (1997) Quantifying the bullwhip effect in supply chains, *Journal of Operations Management*, **15** (2) pp 89–100

Why Demand-Driven SCM? 03

Chapter 2 described what a Demand-Driven supply chain is, and Chapter 4 will describe, in some detail, how they are set up and operated. The subject of this chapter is about *why* Demand-Driven supply chains are so effective.

Agility, flexibility, stability and the other 'i-t-y-s'

Frequently used words to describe desired supply chain behaviour include agility, flexibility, stability, reliability and, in more recent years, sustainability. Some of these might appear to overlap (eg agility and flexibility) while others can be perceived as being in conflict (eg agility and stability). In reality they all have particular and specific meanings and contribute to a higher ideal called:

Flow – in a supply chain, perfect flow occurs when the end-to-end supply lead time (from raw material through to end customer) is composed wholly of 'value-add' activity (ie no cessation of movement in the form of static inventory whether planned, such as in a finished good warehouse, or as WIP and RMs, awaiting processing) as materials are converted into products and delivered to customers. This definition is sometimes formalized as:

Process Cycle Efficiency: Value Add time/Lead time = 100 per cent
= Perfect Flow

Most supply chains achieve less than 5 per cent efficiency when this measure is applied to individual units of material, due to the impact of queuing/waiting and batching, which are, respectively, a symptom and cause of the *variability* that destroys flow.

Variability

Variability refers to the arrival patterns of materials at constraints such as work centres (including warehouses) and the rate of processing by (or demand patterns at) those work centres. So, for instance, when large quantities (relative to capacity or demand) arrive at a work centre (eg due to excessively large batch sizes or, simply, due to uneven arrivals) so the backlog queue immediately grows. And when a work centre slows down or stops, capacity is irretrievably lost. It is the interaction of these two forms of variability that causes queues, not lack of capacity per se, and the average queue length is directly related to the level of variability. The queue length also depends upon the level of capacity utilization and they are longer, as we would intuitively expect, when capacity utilization is higher. The relationship is demonstrated below and, as you will notice, the average queue times (and, therefore, the inventory levels) grow in a highly non-linear fashion with the level of capacity utilization (Figure 3.1).

Figure 3.1   Demonstration of how increasing levels of supply chain variability and capacity utilization increase lead times and inventory

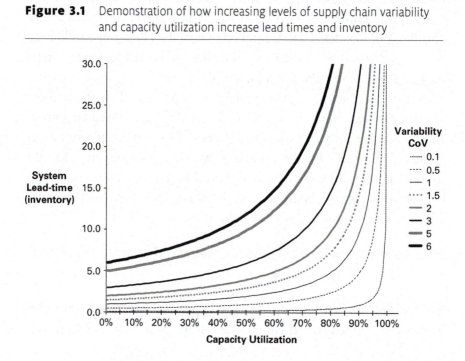

The relationship between average queue time (or average inventory) is quantified by the Kingman (or VUT) equation, which is a foundation of simple queuing theory:[1]

> average **Q**ueue time = **V**ariability x 1/(1 – **U**tilization) x average processing **T**ime

So, by reducing our levels of supply chain variability we can achieve higher capacity utilization with lower levels of inventory and shorter lead times – and assuming we are replenishing what our customers are buying, we will be achieving our planned service levels too. That is why we want our supply chains to flow!

Reliability

Now that we know about the destructive properties of variability, we can begin to understand why reliability is so important. Reliability describes the ability of supply chain 'value-add' activities to deliver their agreed and planned level of capacity when called upon. This capacity can be measured in terms of throughput over planned up-time. If the work centre is unable to process product at the planned level of throughput then supply will obviously be delayed (thereby potentially starving downstream work centres and wasting their capacity too) and it will cause an upstream queue with an unplanned addition to lead time. And without the existence of spare capacity to enable catch-up, this delay will be permanent (and a service threat) or, if caught up with at the expense of other supply schedules, will cause further delays across the supply chain through MRP's network of dependent demand relationships. Factors that reduce reliability are obvious: machine breakdowns, labour shortages and quality rejections – all which can, of course, be minimized/eliminated through Lean practices such as TPM, TQM, poke-yoke, standard work, etc.

Flexibility

As we have learnt, supply chain variability creates buffers (queue time, inventory, unplanned use of capacity) but the supply chain's flexibility reduces the size of the required aggregate buffer for any given level of variability.[2] An analogy is how water, which is very flexible, quickly flows down a hill and around obstructions, whereas glaciers, with very little flexibility, can do neither. In supply chains flexibility comes from a number of design features. One that is very important is the deliberate positioning of independent inventory buffers between multiple value-add activities to decouple them and, thereby, prevent the entire supply chain being impacted by local delays. Flexibility is also aided by holding 'generic' upstream inventories in support of a postponement response to demand, use of multipurpose assets and multiskilled people who can quickly respond to a changing mix/level of demand with fast changeovers. Another example is use of annualized hours contracts to support seasonal demand patterns. Small batches, enabled through SMED, are also a contributor to flexibility by allowing fast and short lead-time response to changing demand patterns. Fast response is, of course, synonymous with short lead times to which network design and sourcing decisions contribute (eg local versus offshore – which is one of the reasons why the fashion retailer Zara has been so successful using local sourcing in combination with postponement).

Stability

Contrary to common belief, stability is not about operations having visibility of future firm schedules many weeks in advance that can be planned for with a high degree of certainty. Very often companies try to achieve this form of rigidity through time fences but fail, thereby generating flow variability and its buffers, as they reschedule/expedite to prevent back-order threats caused by the fact that their MPS is being driven by very inaccurate forecasts. Some pertinent questions and points in this context are:

1 Should safety stocks really be designed to absorb the average forecast error of >40 per cent that is typical of most SKUs (those of medium to low volume, medium to high variability) in a portfolio achieving world-class 80 per cent forecast mix accuracy?

2 Forecast error is always far greater than the variability of demand around an average and MRP logic actually encourages planners

to reschedule, and plan not to use those safety stocks by generating exception messages whenever their use is predicted by those (inaccurate) forecasts.

3 Despite planned and firm time fences of anything between one and 12+ weeks, are MPSs really firm or are they always disrupted to meet real demand anyway? And why is all the work put into developing them always overwritten a week or month later anyway?

4 Why do operations need to know what they think they are going to make (but probably won't) next week/month anyway? Of far greater importance is that they have the necessary capacity, they make in a predictable and efficient sequence, the materials for processing are available in the quantities required when they are needed, and they are not forced to disrupt their rhythm by switching schedules at short notice!

In contrast to its commonly understood meaning, operational stability is not a fixed schedule for up to 12 weeks into the future (which always gets changed anyway), it is the various supply chain value-add activities working to their *own* efficient and predictable *sequence* with minimal unplanned stoppages, changes and interruptions. The exact timing and quantity of each item that will be made is maybe unknown (it will depend upon how much, if any, has been sold or consumed, and the quantities, if any, will always be above the planned minimum and rounded to the nearest multiple), but operations just need to focus upon making what is required – knowing that the necessary materials are available, they have sufficient capacity, there will be no schedule interruptions, what they are making will meet demand and, unless aggregate demand declines very rapidly, they will be kept busy!

Operations obviously need to be capacity-sized correctly but this is a function of aggregate forecasting and planning, high accuracy of which is quite easy to achieve – it has nothing to do with needing firm schedules.

The benefits of stability are, of course, that costs can be minimized through working to a sequence that maximizes change-over efficiencies and can be relied upon so that people, materials, machines, etc can be prepared as necessary so that there is no loss of throughput.[3]

So, if use of forecasts to directly drive replenishment execution should be avoided (at all costs!) and safety stocks and their exception messages dispensed with entirely, how should stable replenishment be driven? The answer is via:

Agility – which is the ability of a supply chain to autonomously respond to demand (as does water respond to gravity when flowing in a river), and its variations, with planned buffers that are minimized, albeit of the right size, and in the form that best serves both the company and its customers - and is 'designed in'.

The essence of 'agility' is in the use of the terms:

- '*Autonomously respond to demand*': responding to changing demands immediately and without prior thought and preparation.

- '*Planned buffers that are of the right size and in the right form*': buffers are always associated with variability unless the supply chain is so flexible that it is able to meet demand exactly while operating at 100 per cent utilization without customers either being kept waiting or supplied ex-stock. The aggregate of these buffers (time, capacity and stock) should be minimized in terms of their cost generation and be in a form that 'delights' the customer.

- '*Designed in*': it is in how the supply chain is planned, operates and is improved upon that delivers high service with ever decreasing levels of buffer: continuous improvement to achieve flow and thereby minimizing lead times, inventory and the necessity to use spare capacity.

Clearly such an *agile supply chain*, with its minimal cost-generating buffers, is also going to have a high degree of *sustainability*. It will help the company(s), of which it is a part, to be extremely competitive and, therefore, be able to sustain its own existence. And by eliminating unnecessary 'waste' it will also be sustainable from an environmental perspective by minimizing use of unnecessary carbon-generating energy and materials.

Supply chain agility is clearly achieved through flexibility, reliability and stability, all of which in their own way contribute to minimizing variability – and this includes Lean, which Hopp and Spearman define as: 'fundamentally about minimizing the cost of buffering variability'.[4]

Figure 3.2 The Toyota House, underpinned by stability

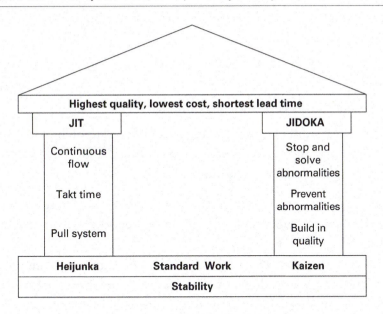

It is also worth noting that the famous Toyota House graphic, see Figure 3.2, is built on stability. The Toyota House also provides a clue as to how agile, flexible, reliable, stable and sustainable supply chains should operate. The appropriate term is 'just in time', which is delivered through a pull system. But, unlike most Lean implementations that are focused on just the factory floor, the full power of pull is harnessed when it is implemented right across the enterprise(s). In this form it is now more commonly known as Demand-Driven SCM.

Demand-Driven SCM can be implemented across even the most global/complex supply chain networks (including between companies) using simple, but aligned, reorder point/reorder cycle mechanisms at multiple independent inventory positions that ensure material is processed in line with demand and with adequate buffer to absorb local variability and prevent it being propagated/amplified up and down the supply chain.

Typical benefits achieved by companies that replace their 'forecast push MRP/DRP/APS' with Demand-Driven SCM, due to elimination of forecast error-induced variability and the dampening of residual process variability, are:

1 achievement of consistently high planned service levels, with

2 reductions in average inventory of between 30 per cent to 50 per cent, and

3 increases in OEE, enabling cost reductions of around 20 per cent, with

4 planning lead-time reductions of up to 85 per cent, and

5 with no expediting or firefighting and no focus upon high levels of forecast accuracy except for very exceptional and extreme events that require planned stock builds

– and it can be operated successfully no matter the character of the demand patterns (volatile or stable, with trend or seasonal) or the length of the lead times.

The reason is that Demand-Driven SCM treats supply chains as what they really are: flows of materials that are prone to develop queues in the presence of variability. Instead of using expensive capacity to keep materials moving, Demand-Driven SCM eliminates forecast error-induced variability, positions multiple and independent inventory buffers to absorb process variability and uses multiple 'loose pull' mechanisms to ensure that resource is only used to buy/make/ship what is needed, when it is needed and in a manner that allows planned service levels to be met with right-sized (and reduced!) inventories and minimal waste of capacity.

Why flow?

The term 'flow' has been associated with excellence in supply chain/operations management for many years. It is one of the five key components of Lean (along with value, value chain, pull and continuous improvement) as described in *Lean Thinking* by JP Womack and DT Jones (1996). Lean is also a core concept in the Theory of Constraints (ToC) and even the pioneers of MRP (such as Orlicky, Plossl and Mather) emphasized its importance.

'Flow', of course, is synonymous with how water behaves in a river and the analogy is often extended when we talk about upstream and downstream in a supply chain. But what exactly is supply chain flow and why is it so important?

It helps to think about some of the characteristics of how water actually flows. The key features are that water, when flowing in a river, is continuously moving and is doing so because it is entirely flexible and responds autonomously to gravity. Perfect flow in a supply chain is exactly the same – it occurs when materials continuously flow through the various value-add activities to customers, and does so through autonomously responding to the rate of demand.

The importance of supply chain flow is that it means materials are continuously having value added without incurring any unnecessary costs due to becoming stationary stock (be it 'in process' or as finished goods in a warehouse). In consequence, *perfect flow* can be said to occur when the lead time of the finished goods is composed entirely of value-add activity, as demonstrated by the well-known *process cycle efficiency* (PCE) ratio at 100 per cent:

PCE = Customer Value-Add Time/Total Cycle Time %

The other main element of supply chain flow (ie autonomous response to the rate of demand) now becomes clear – if product is made too slowly there will be service issues; if it is made unnecessarily fast, cost will be incurred while holding stock. In the real world, of course, certain products have to be made faster than they sell because they are manufactured on multiproduct machines as part of a predetermined cycle. But if batch sizes become excessive it means that capacity is being used when it is not needed, lead times are excessive, responsiveness is lost and unplanned service-saving schedule interruptions become inevitable.

Another perspective on supply chain flow is that offered by simple queuing theory. Queuing theory is particularly applicable to supply chains because most are composed of a series of stationary queues of materials waiting to be processed by machines/people or waiting in warehouses to be sold – and queuing theory shows us how to minimize those queues of inventory to achieve efficient flow.

At the heart of queuing theory are two equations:

> *Little's Law: System Lead time = System Inventory/System Throughput*

– which simply tells us what we intuitively already know: that the greater the average amount of stock in a supply system, the longer the average time it takes for any item to pass through it. A simple implication of Little's Law is that items should be processed in as small a size of batch as is feasible[5] in order to minimize waiting time and the accumulation of stationary stock. Also, of course, value-add processes should never be delayed, break down or produce unsellable product (fundamental attributes of any good Lean process) because this would reduce throughput and increase lead time (as well as wasting capacity).

The other equation is:

> *Kingman equation: average **Q** time = **V**ariability x 1/(1 – **U**tilization) x average processing **T**ime... or Q = VUT*[1]

– which can be graphically represented as follows:

Figure 3.3   Demonstrating how increasing levels of supply chain variability and capacity utilization increase lead times and inventory

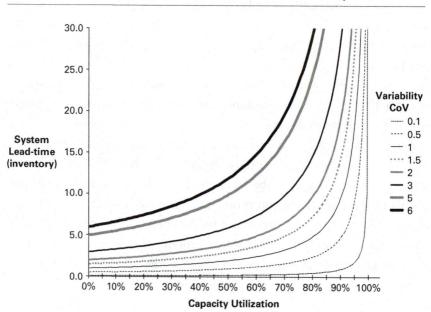

This shows that total system inventory, or lead time, grows as capacity utilization increases and does so exponentially at high levels of utilization. The implication, of course, is that if your supply chain is getting congested with inventory, one obvious (expensive) option is to increase capacity.

The other key relationship shown is that between the level of variability and system inventory/lead time: each curve from right to left represents a greater level of variability, so the other option for reducing lead time/inventory is to reduce variability.

In a supply chain, variability refers to the materials' rate of arrivals at work centres (eg high variability is caused by irregularity in arrivals of inventory and is exacerbated by batches that are excessively large relative to demand) and the rate at which the materials are processed (eg if the machine keeps breaking down, suffers long changeovers or there are large volumes of rejected material the variability is high).

By now you will probably have recognized that the various activities that come under the Lean umbrella (eg elimination of the seven wastes, or muda, and its two main forms: mura – uneveness, and muri – overburden; also tecŸiques such as TPM, TQM, SMED, standard work, etc) are actually all about reducing variability – in agreement with Hopp and Spearman's assertion that 'Lean is fundamentally about minimizing the costs of buffering variability'[4] – and the buffers are those of capacity, inventory and queue time, all of which generate supply chain cost. Whether they are planned or not, these buffers are always created in the presence of variability and it is excessive variability that creates excessive buffer. The first to be noticed tends to be growth in queue *time*, when supply delays occur (ie lost capacity) or demand has unexpectedly increased significantly, which causes customers to get shorted (remember MRP assumes known and fixed supply lead times), then buffer *stocks* are often deliberately increased (and maybe also planning lead-time parameters, which release more work to the factory floor that actually further increases lead times and inventories) and eventually unplanned *capacity* is used to catch up on service levels (bear in mind that the amount of capacity that had been required before this particular service issue is always in excess of that actually required, due to all the unplanned service-saving changeovers caused by the forecast errors).

Use of capacity is an expensive alternative to the creation of supply chain agility. In this context *agility is the entire supply chain's ability to respond to changing demand patterns with minimal levels of cost-generating buffer*; it requires two key capabilities:

- *Flexibility*: this reduces the amount of buffering required in a production/supply chain system for a given level of variability. Examples of flexibility include the use of planned but independent inventory positions within the supply chain, which prevent local delays impacting the network; the holding of 'generic' upstream inventories (or 'bright stock' as it is known in the United States) in support of a postponement response to demand; use of standard-ized multipurpose capacity such as assets and multiskilled people; small batches/fast changeovers that support quick response to changing demand patterns; and local sourcing that increases responsiveness with short lead times. In addition, annualized-hours contracts support flexible response to aggregate levels of demand variability such as seasonality.

- *Autonomation*: this is the ability of the entire supply chain to operate with a high degree of *stability* (ie the various supply chain value-add activities working to their own efficient and predictable sequence with minimal unplanned changes and inter-ruptions) while responding to changing demands without any preplanning (ie without forecast-driven master production sched-ules, use of time fences and schedule expediting): the way water does not have to think about how it *flows* in a river. This is in contrast to the way many companies, perhaps using pull/kanban within their factory walls, still drive their supply chains using forecast-driven schedules. This 'forecast push MPS/MRP' process inevitably causes significant levels of variability because supply is driven by the inac-curate forecasts,[6] not demand, so the schedules have to be amended to avoid service misses and it is this that generates the unplanned, cost-generating buffers – time, capacity and inventory.

Summary

Supply chain flow minimizes costs and maximizes cash-generating throughput by reducing lead times towards that of the value-add time and can be achieved through:

- *Lean*: maximizing *reliability* through, for instance TPM, TQM, poke-yoke, 5S and standard work, and improving supply *flexibility* through, as appropriate, quick changeovers, right-sized batch sizes, design for manufacture, local sourcing and postponement.

- *Autonomation*: designing the supply chain replenishment process to enable it to autonomously respond to demand.

In companies using 'forecast push MPS/MRP', the first priority should always be to replace it with a process that enables the supply chain to autonomously respond to demand, as it is the easiest and quickest 'kaizen' to achieve with the maximum benefit (achieve planned service levels with 30 per cent to 50 per cent less average inventory and 20 per cent cost reduction through higher capacity utilization). Such *Demand-Driven supply chains* also allow the full benefits of Lean to drop directly through to the bottom line instead of being swamped by forecast error-induced variability. To learn more about the benefits and operation of Demand-Driven SCM, see the section 'Demand-Driven SCM: agility thru' stability' in Chapter 2.

Why pull?

In the previous section, 'Why flow?', it was described how flow, in a supply chain context, delivers transformational performance in terms of service, inventory and cost. The section describes how *perfect flow*, or absence of variability, means that an item's lead time is composed of 100 per cent value-add time with no materials sitting around as stock (either in process or in a finished goods warehouse) and no requirement for spare capacity.

Of course perfect flow is an ideal that cannot be achieved, but much can be done to make progress towards it. Many activities that fall into the Lean tool set are aimed at improving flexibility and reducing what W Edwards Deming called 'common cause variability' (eg TPM, TQM, standard work, SMED). But there are far more significant sources of variability in most supply chains that are totally unnecessary and generated by management policies – that Deming called 'special cause variability'. The most significant such example is the variability created by driving supply chain replenishment with forecasts through MPS/MRP.

World-class forecast accuracy across a portfolio is around 80 per cent (ie 20 per cent wrong!) and this can only be achieved because the relatively few, large-volume/low-variability SKUs attain around 95 per cent accuracy, which strongly skews the overall measure away from the 60 per cent achieved by the rest of the portfolio (ie those with lower volumes and higher variability). (See Figure 3.4.)

Figure 3.4   Typical range of forecast mix accuracies across a product range

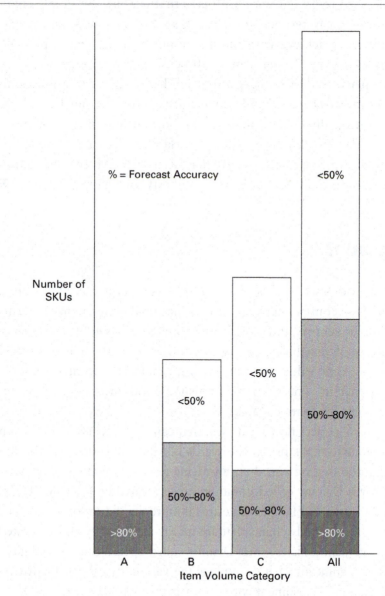

This forecast error leads to the wrong quantities of the wrong products being made and sent to the wrong places, which inevitably causes service issues and schedule amendments/factory frustration triggered by MRP exception messages. In this way the forecast error leads directly to the commonly seen 'unholy trinity' of unbalanced and excessive inventory levels, excessive lead times (and time fences that inevitably get broken) and low levels of OEE due to all the unplanned service-saving schedule changes. (See Figure 3.5.)

So the first step on the journey to *flow* is to attack the most significant source of variability that is also the quickest to eliminate. For this reason, replacing the inaccurate forecast as the driver of end-to-end replenishment execution should be the first activity to be undertaken by companies wishing to significantly improve supply chain and operations performance.

The alternative to forecast-driven replenishment execution is Demand-Driven SCM (which is essentially enterprise(s)-wide pull and can be defined as:

Figure 3.5   The inevitable picture of unbalanced and excessive on-hand inventories as a consequence of inaccurate forecast-driven MPS/MRP replenishment execution

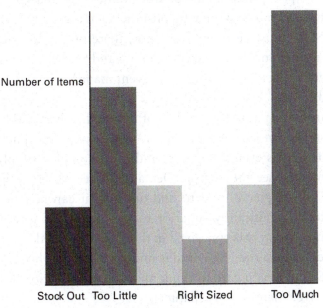

A segmented multi-echelon supply chain reorder process featuring multiple deliberately positioned and planned, but independent, inventory locations that are each replenished, in an efficient and stable sequence, to a calculated stock target in line with real demand – not the forecast.[6]

In essence, the process allows materials and products to be pulled through the supply chain in line with demand, using multiple reorder point or reorder cycle mechanisms. The key to its success[7] is correctly positioning, sizing and maintaining the multiple inventory buffer targets with respect to the average level of demand, and its variability, over the local replenishment lead time and allowing each replenishment activity to follow its own stable and efficient sequence in line with demand – which also allows those lead times to be reliable. Within the range of historical average demand variability, this process will successfully deliver planned service levels with right-sized inventories without any schedule interruptions, right through the supply chain, so capacity utilization can be very high too. By exception, of course, extreme and exceptional demand events do occur so it is a key focus of demand-and-supply planners to work with sales people and customers to get early visibility of them and build in an appropriate advanced stock build. Demand-Driven SCM is, therefore, a 'pull' system with 'push' when it is required. Demand-Driven SCM most certainly does not, therefore, ignore forecasts, they are needed for the capacity-planning and S&OP process, inventory target sizing and, of course, the event management. (See Figures 3.6a and 3.6b.)

To learn more about the practice of Demand-Driven and how new SaaS systems can support its robust, sustainable and quick implementation across even the largest and most complex supply chain/ERP networks, see the section 'Demand-Driven SCM: agility thru' stability' in Chapter 2. And to find out how it can be conclusively proved to be significantly superior to the ubiquitous forecast push MRP process (that was conceived in the 1950s, codified in the 1960s, commercialized in the 1970s and is under the bonnet (hood) of every ERP/APS system you care to think about, see the section 'Can SCM be deductive?' (later in this chapter).

Figure 3.6a Demand-Driven SCM – strategically positioned inventory buffers prevent variability transmission and replenishment is driven by demand

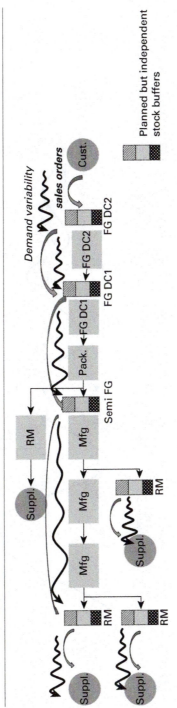

Figure 3.6b Forecast push MPS/MRP – replenishment is driven by an inaccurate and volatile forecast and variability is amplified as it is blown up the dependent demand network

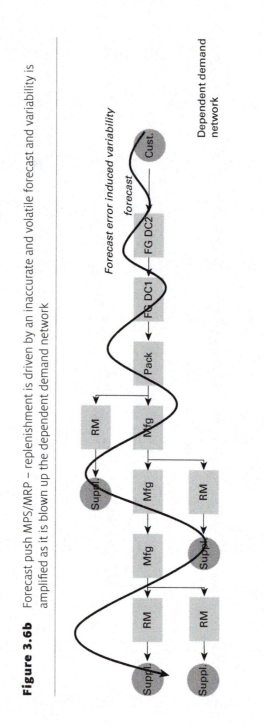

Should planners ignore MRP's exception messages?

The bane of many a planner's working life is responding to MRP's avalanche of exception messages – or trying to work out which are important and should be responded to, and ignoring the rest and hoping that the right decisions have been made.

But should exception messages be responded to at all? Is there a case for ignoring not just some but all of them?

There is, but before it is described let's remind ourselves of what exception messages are telling us. They are triggered when:

(On hand inventory + on order quantity at due date) – (backorders plus sales orders plus unconsumed forecast at due date)
= < or > zero or safety stock

Their recommendation is to push back or pull forward the timing of supply orders so that the future on-hand inventory balance is zero or, for finished products, is at the safety stock level. Unsurprisingly, given that the time-phased accuracy of all forecasts is always wrong (and world-class portfolio accuracy of 80 per cent hides the fact that the majority – lower volume/higher variability – will be < 60 per cent accurate), exception messages, calculated in this manner, are legion (and in MTO supply chains they are just as much an issue whenever the schedule is calculated to miss the due date, which is most of the time due to natural process variability).

One of the problems is that MRP/APS software packages don't help planners to ascertain which are the most important exception messages amongst all of those generated by, let's face it, what everyone knows is an inaccurate forecast.

Inevitably, planners tend to focus on those threatening a service issue and often drop their plans into XLS and use some form of 'rule of thumb' (eg day's cover) to help them judge which are the most urgent and should be pulled forward. And there is always an understandable tendency to focus on the service risks and 'pull forward', rather than the excessive inventories and 'push back'. This is why average on-hand inventories, in 'forecast push MRP' supply chains, are rarely equivalent to safety stock + 50 per cent of average supply quantity. Instead, the average tends to be safety stock + around 70 per cent of the average quantity, because of the propensity to avoid use of the safety stock.

And anyway, these average inventories are always higher than need be, because the 'safety' element is based on the aforementioned high levels of forecast error (which is always significantly higher than real demand variability) and all that pulling forward of supply orders interrupts the lead times of other products. After a while, in order to help supply OTIF performance, the planning lead times get increased, which means that even more safety stock is required (and more work is released to the factory floor, which itself tends to increase lead times yet further). The other impact of pulling forward supply orders and interrupting the supply of other products is, of course, use of unplanned and expensive capacity, both immediately and later, to enable supply of the other delayed products to catch up.

So, what would happen if all exception messages were ignored?

One benefit would be that supply orders would no longer be rescheduled, thereby helping to stabilize lead times and preventing use of unplanned capacity. In addition, of course, the safety stocks would definitely get used and, if they were not sized correctly, service misses would occur – as it would if there was persistent negative bias in the forecast.

If planners spent more time on setting the correct safety stock levels, eliminating forecast bias and actively managing events, and less time expediting and responding to exception messages, the outcome would be less use of expensive unplanned capacity and achievement of planned service levels, though average inventory levels would have to be very high.

In fact, some companies protect their factories from service-saving disruptions to their schedules by simply level-scheduling supply of all products in line with the long-term forecast. This approach can certainly work well where demand volumes are high and stable, but otherwise, if volumes are lower and inevitably more variable, the average inventories have to be extremely high to avoid service issues.

In both cases, the reason for the consequently high levels of inventory that result (and that have replaced the expensive capacity buffer) is, of course, the variability of demand and the use of inaccurate forecasts to drive replenishment.

> *Would such companies prefer a replenishment process that is equally efficient in terms of capacity utilization to that of level schedule but which also delivers minimal service issues, shorter lead times and significantly less inventories – and requires very little focus upon forecast accuracy?*

Such a process does exist and is being quietly adopted by some of the world's most admired companies using new SaaS systems – quietly because it gives them a distinct competitive advantage.

> *Not only does Demand-Driven planning and execution process deliver significantly improved service, inventory and OEE KPIs, it also empowers the factory to have greater control and responsibility for its own, now more stable and efficient, schedules.*

If you would like to know more, go to the section on 'Demand-Driven SCM: agility thru' stability' in Chapter 2.

Can SCM be deductive?

It is well known that in science nothing can actually be proven. The means by which science makes progress is through the process of falsifiability and, unless a theory is falsifiable (ie can be shown to be false by observation or experiment), it is not regarded as scientific. As a result, 'knowledge' claimed through induction cannot be regarded as scientific. For instance, the fact that the sun has always risen in the morning is not a logical basis upon which to claim it will rise every morning.[8] Or, as Karl Popper put it in *The Logic of Scientific Discovery* (1934):

> No matter how many instances of white swans we may have observed, this does not justify the conclusion that all swans are white.

On the other hand, mathematics progresses through a process of deductive reasoning in which absolute proof can be achieved through use of 'already known to be true' statements, or premises, that mean, if the rules of deductive logic are followed, the conclusion is also necessarily true. A simple example is that if 1 + 1 = 2 then we can also say that 2 – 1 = 1.[9]

Why is this difference between induction and deduction important to the 'science' that is SCM?

It is important because it can be deductively *proved* that the currently most common form of supply chain replenishment process is significantly inferior to the Demand-Driven SCM process that is, with the availability of appropriate SaaS systems, now beginning to be adopted in place of that 'forecast push ERP/DRP/MRP/APS'.

In line with scientific principles we cannot, of course, claim that Demand-Driven SCM is more effective than 'forecast push' just because its typical performance improvements are:

- achievement of consistently high planned service levels, with

- reductions in average inventory of between 30 per cent to 50 per cent, and

- reduction in unplanned overtime, or increase in capacity utilization, enabling cost reductions of around 20 per cent, with

- planning lead time reductions of up to 85 per cent.

But we can legitimately claim that Demand-Driven SCM is superior if we are prepared to accept that supply chains are effectively a flow of materials through various value-add processes on their way to consumers.

If we accept that supply chains are about flow then we also have to accept that flow in the presence of flow variability at 'value-add' constraints (eg machines, warehouses, etc) causes queues, as described by the simplified, mathematical Kingman formula (also known as the VUT equation)[1]:

$$\text{Average waiting time in Queue}$$
$$= \text{Variability} \times 1/(1 - \text{capacity Utilization}) \times \text{average processing Time}$$

Flow variability relates to the rate of arrivals at constraints and the constraints' rates of processing. The average queue time grows proportionately in line with the variability (and average processing time) and, as capacity utilization increases, the queue time increases exponentially, as demonstrated in Figure 3.7.

Figure 3.7 How increasing levels of supply chain variability and capacity utilization increase lead times and inventory

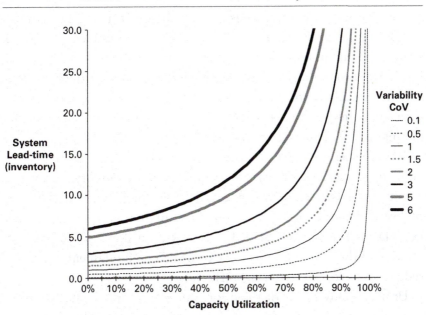

In a supply chain environment queues develop, despite the existence of adequate average capacity (if there was a real capacity deficit the queue would grow indefinitely), because of arrival spikes temporarily above capacity (eg uneven arrivals and excessively big batches) and periodic capacity losses due to non-arrivals and processing-rate dips (eg quality rejections, run rate issues, unplanned schedule interruptions and changeovers).

What VUT tells us simply is that, for a given level of throughput and assuming no change in average processing time, *supply chain queues of inventory (be it components, WIP or FGs) can only be reduced if flow variability is reduced or capacity is increased.* And when one considers that, in most companies, the process cycle efficiency (value-add time/lead time per cent) is rarely above 5 per cent it becomes clear that supply chains are plagued with significant levels of variability.

Clearly, if it can be demonstrated that use of Demand-Driven SCM results in less variability than 'forecast push ERP/MRP/DRP/APS', then we can be certain that Demand-Driven is the superior process because it thereby creates less of the cost-generating buffers – queue time, capacity, inventory. And if it is found that 'forecast push MRP' actually generates variability we could also say that it is actually perverse and harmful to use it.

Of course many companies achieve high service levels despite supply chain variability because they work with significant levels of spare capacity, tolerate long lead times and hold high levels of FG buffer inventory. But in all such companies there is continuous pressure to reduce inventory levels, reduce lead times and reduce costs (eg through achieving higher levels of capacity utilization) while maintaining or increasing service levels.

With the aid of 'deductive reasoning' we now know that we can do all of these together by reducing supply chain variability, and many companies have been busy trying to do so for many years in the form of Lean/CI initiatives. When you think of the various Lean tools (SMED/smaller batches, TQM, TPM, standard work, poke-yoke, DFM, etc) they can all be recognized as being: 'fundamentally about reducing the cost of buffering variability'.[4]

Unfortunately much of the effort put into Lean to date has been something of a waste. Although kaizen events achieve local efficiencies their benefits rarely drop through to the bottom line because they are swamped by the cost-generating buffers (time, capacity and inventory) created by forecast error-induced variability which is propagated and amplified through the supply chain by MRP's use of dependent demand.

Forecast error-induced variability, propagation and amplification

It is well known that all forecasts are incorrect and 80 per cent portfolio accuracy (ie 20 per cent wrong) is considered 'world class'. Due to the 20:80 rule, such performance means that most medium- and low-volume SKUs (usually the majority) actually achieve accuracies that are significantly worse, not least because with lower volumes the variability is higher and so is the level of forecast inaccuracy. Manufacturing or purchasing schedules based upon inaccurate SKU forecasts lead to the production of unbalanced stocks with potential service issues, and expediting inevitably follows as planners respond to exception messages.

Service-saving production schedule changes cause expensive, unplanned machine changeovers, schedule congestion and increased lead times with knock-on effects upon other schedules up and down the factory routings. In consequence, average lead times increase and become volatile (contrary to the DRP/MRP assumption of fixed lead times, therefore causing a further service risk) and stock becomes both excessive and unbalanced with service issues often continuing to occur. The further up the supply chain, and away from end-customer demand one goes, the variability is propagated by MRP's dependent demand relationships (the assumption that every supply chain activity has a known and fixed lead time with no buffer) and is amplified by batching and latency.[10]

To enable supply chains to fully benefit from Lean, and to eliminate the performance-eroding impact of forecast error-induced variability, we now know that we should not be using 'forecast push MRP/DRP/APS'.

How does the Demand-Driven process compare?

A definition of Demand-Driven is:

A segmented multi-echelon supply chain reorder process featuring multiple deliberately positioned, planned and maintained but independent/decoupled, inventory locations that each are replenished, in an efficient and stable sequence, to a calculated stock target in line with real demand – not the forecast (which is used for S&OP, event management and inventory target sizing).

To learn more about the 'why and how' of Demand-Driven SCM go to the section 'Demand-Driven SCM: agility thru' stability' in Chapter 2.

*The reason that we can now **know** that Demand-Driven SCM is superior to 'forecast push DRP/MRP/APS' is that it eliminates the forecast error-induced variability, and through its multiple (independent shock-absorbing) planned buffers, minimizes any that is residual, thereby also minimizing the cost-generating supply chain buffers of stock, time and capacity.*

As Demand-Driven SCM can be demonstrated and deductively proven to be genuinely superior to 'forecast push MPS/MRP' in all supply chain configurations,[11] it is reasonable to ask why it is so rarely seen. The answer can be attributed to the low data-processing capability of the early supply chain IT systems. These early MRP systems were designed to simply support just in time (JIT) purchase of materials to support a known MPS. They then evolved into manufacturing resource planning (MRPII) but were too unsophisticated to support simultaneous end-to-end replenishment of multiple independent echelons. And that can still be said of today's ERPs and APS. But the recent emergence of functionality rich and robust Demand-Driven SaaS systems (that operate through legacy transaction systems) now support the Demand-Driven process both across a single company's various echelons and the extended supply chain (see the section 'Demand-Driven collaboration' in Chapter 2). An added benefit of SaaS is that it can be used to quickly and inexpensively simulate and pilot Demand-Driven before a revenue-expensed wider implementation.

A fast-growing number of companies are now quietly piloting and implementing Demand-Driven – quietly because they know it will give them a competitive advantage!

Supply chain optimization – what does it really mean?

Optimization is a term frequently used in the context of SCM, particularly with reference to inventory, but it seems impossible to find a definition of what it is actually supposed to be.

Looking at a commonly used dictionary, we find the definition of 'optimize' is: 'make the best or most effective use of (a situation or resource)' – which, in supply chain management, would mean something along the lines of: 'making most effective use of resource capacity, and/or inventory, in terms of service and cost'. Given this definition, it might be thought that there is some form of trade-off between cost, capacity, inventory and service.

For pragmatic purposes, let's assume the cost element excludes raw materials and that we are only concerned with product cost related to labour and overhead. With this in mind we know that product cost is inversely related to throughput; also the quicker our stock turn the greater will be our cash flow and the lower will be our asset base and, if we are working with a third-party logistics (3PL) that charges us for warehouse pallet space usage, the lower will be our distribution costs too. So we want high-capacity utilization and low inventories, which means we need to size our capacity correctly and make product that will sell quickly.

But isn't there a trade-off between inventory levels and service?

Of course there is, we all know that there is a relationship between service level and the amount of inventory buffer we need in order to achieve it. And we also know that the amount of buffer required is related to our replenishment lead time – usually expressed through the square root of that lead time. And to complicate things further, the bigger are our supply batches the longer will be our lead times but the greater could be our factory throughput due to less 'changeover' downtime.

Is there a tecŸology that can help us to achieve real supply chain optimization across this web of relationships? Not one that I know of!

So, what can we do about optimization?

Let's go back to that dictionary definition... it's about making the most effective use of our resources, yet there seems to be all these complicated trade-offs.

Why do we have these trade-offs? Is there an underlying hidden variable that we could eliminate, or at least reduce, that would allow us to achieve our planned service levels with higher-capacity utilization, with lower inventories and shorter lead times?

If so, shouldn't that be the area we should be focusing our 'continuous improvement' efforts upon instead of throwing money at expensive so-called 'optimization' tecŸologies?

The answer is 'yes' and the hidden variable is 'flow variability'.

In a supply chain context variability refers to the arrivals of materials at constraints such as work centres (and includes warehouses where arrival patterns do not exactly match demand patterns) and the rate of processing by those work centres. So, for instance, when material arrives at a busy work centre for processing it has to wait – maybe join a queue. And when a large batch arrives, relative to capacity (or demand) at a work centre (or in the warehouse), the backlog queue immediately grows significantly. Alternatively, when a work centre slows down or stops, capacity is irretrievably lost and the queuing time is extended.

It is the interaction of these two forms of variability that causes queues and, for a given level of capacity utilization, the queue time grows directly in line with the variability. These queues have a finite average length for a given level of capacity utilization (if there was insufficient capacity the queue would grow without limit) and they are longer, as we would intuitively expect, when capacity utilization is higher. The relationship is demonstrated by Figure 3.7, above and, as you will notice, the average queue times (and, therefore, the inventory levels) grow in a non-linear fashion and exponentially at the highest levels of utilization.[1]

So, by reducing our levels of supply chain variability we can achieve higher-capacity utilization with lower levels of inventory and shorter lead times – and assuming we are making product that our customers want to buy we will be achieving our planned service levels too.

So how can we achieve this service-satisfying flow of materials and products with lower levels of supply chain variability?

Most manufacturing companies have, in fact, been working on this for some time and calling it Lean. If you think about all those factory Lean tools such as TPM, TQM, SMED/smaller batches, poke-yoke, 5S, etc they are all about reducing process variability.[4]

Unfortunately most such companies have failed to achieve the full benefits of Lean because they are still driving their end-to-end replenishment execution with incorrect forecasts of demand through ERP/MRP/APS systems – hence they buy, make and move the wrong quantities of the wrong stuff at the wrong time so inevitably suffer service threats, which they try to avoid by amending and disrupting their schedules, using up unplanned capacity and increasing lead times (MRP assumes they are fixed!). They also, sometimes, buffer their factories with excessively long-planning lead times/time fences (eg planning lead times are typically just 5 per cent value add, the rest is queue time buffer), which means they have to hold more work in progress and need to hold yet more finished goods inventory and still, usually, service issues persist!

'Forecast push' supply chains are plagued by high levels of forecast error-induced variability and these accompanying cost-generating buffers – queue time, inventory and use of unplanned capacity. So the first step on the road to true supply chain optimization (read trade-off elimination or, put more simply, performance improvement) is to eliminate this forecast error-induced variability. This is not a call for more accurate forecasts because short-term, time-phased item-level mix forecast accuracy at 80 per cent is world class and, with today's increasing demand volatilities (eg promotions, SKU proliferation, longer lead times), it is not going to improve (and bear in mind that such a level of accuracy hides the fact that most of the SKUs in the portfolio – those of medium/low volumes and medium/high volatilities – will be achieving accuracies no greater than 60 per cent, or >40 per cent wrong!).

The alternative to today's ubiquitous 'forecast push MPS/MRP' replenishment process is the Demand-Driven SCM process that typically delivers, through it suffering significantly less variability:

- planned service levels;
- up to 50 per cent less average inventory;
- planning lead-time reductions of up to 85 per cent, and requiring
- around 20 per cent less capacity;[12]
- without expediting or firefighting and no focus upon high levels of forecast accuracy.

And it can be applied in all supply chains (ie across inbound supply, manufacturing, distribution, retail and the extended supply chain/network) be they MTS, ATO or MTO (in fact wherever stock is held), whether demand is stable, seasonal or volatile and lead times short or long.

Can so-called 'optimization' get near these levels of performance improvement?

To learn about the 'what, how and why' of Demand-Driven SCM go to the section 'Demand-Driven SCM: agility thru' stability'.

High variability? Go Lean, adopt pull!

Conventional wisdom has it that Lean is all about waste and cost reduction (and only viable when demand is relatively stable) whereas agility is focused upon responding to volatile demand patterns – but this is wrong.

Lean is actually all about minimizing supply chain variability and maximizing the efficiency with which the supply chain and operations respond to demand no matter how volatile it might be.

There are two main sources of variability in all supply chains: on the supply side and the demand side. Many of the basic Lean tools are aimed at reducing the former such as TPM, TQM, poke-yoke, standard work, etc, which increase supply reliability. Quick changeovers also reduce supply-side variability by enabling batch-size reduction that smooths the flow of arrivals at work centres and, likewise, enables smooth flow of upstream components.

But the greatest source of variability in most supply chains is not supply side and it is not market demand either. It is self-inflicted and is generated through use of forecasts blown through MPS/MRP to drive replenishment execution.

As we all know, forecasts are inaccurate and the more variable is demand the more inaccurate they will be. Companies achieving world-class forecast mix accuracy of 80 per cent do so because they have a small number of high-volume/low-variability items at 95 per cent+ but will find that 80 per cent of their SKUs are at less than 60 per cent. These dreadfully inaccurate forecasts lead to exception messages and service threats that cause planners to change the supply schedules that cause unplanned use of changeover capacity and longer lead times on the interrupted items. And because MRP assumes fixed lead times these too suffer service threats and so the vicious circle continues, leading to planning lead-time increases to protect supply OTIF and more 'safety stock' – both of which put yet more pressure upon an increasingly destabilized factory floor.

The Lean solution to this forecast error-induced variability is, of course, pull. Unfortunately, pull has, until recently, been mostly confined to the factory floor through use of kanbans. And, because of this, Lean itself has largely failed to deliver most of its potential benefit as improvements in factory floor reliability and flexibility have been offset by companies now efficiently making the wrong mix of products and having to live with excessive/unbalanced inventories and capacity-hungry service-chasing schedule interruptions – and still suffering service issues! In fact, most companies do not recognize how bad their performance is. After all, their competitors are no better as they all use forecast push MPS/MRP too and benchmarking tells them they are in the right 'ball park'. But if they were to benchmark themselves against one of the small, but growing number of companies that have adopted enterprise-wide pull, or Demand-Driven SCM, they would find that their supply chain and operations performance (in terms of service, inventory turn and capacity utilization) is woeful – and perhaps a threat to their future prosperity.

So how does Demand-Driven SCM, or enterprise-wide pull, enable companies to respond to volatile demand?

It is important to realize that Demand-Driven supply chains are decoupled – inventories are deliberately positioned in the supply chain and each is replenished independently of the other and in a sequence that is both efficient and stable for the upstream value-add activity. The replenishment tecŸique is simple reorder point or reorder cycle and the 'order up to' stock targets are set according to average demand and local variability, with rounding to recognize minimum order quantity (MOQ) policies. And as long as the stock targets are set reasonably accurately the end-to-end supply chain is able to respond autonomously to demand using a series of independent 'make/ship to replace' mechanisms – and do so without factory floor schedule instability. These deliberately located inventory positions deliver the added benefit of preventing residual supply-side variability from being propagated up and down the supply chain, which is another reason why such supply chains suffer far less aggregate variability than do their 'forecast push MPS/MRP' equivalents and, therefore, far less unplanned buffer – be it use of unplanned capacity, inventory and lead time.

Counter-intuitively, the more variable is a supply chain the greater will be the benefit from adopting Lean. Obviously supply-side variability should be reduced by using the appropriate Lean tecŸiques, while the more variable is demand the more inaccurate would be the forecasts – so the greater the benefit from eliminating this source of variability.

Of course pull, or Demand-Driven SCM, cannot cope with variability that is exceptional and extreme. But, on one hand, now that consistent variability is fully buffered, the supply planning, demand planning, commercial teams and, perhaps, customers, can focus upon anticipating such events and building the required stock in advance. On the other hand, if your demand history is full of promotional spikes and very variable, you can build such variability into your buffers and just focus upon the major TV campaigns and any seasonality... and your average inventories will still be significantly below that which you are currently experiencing. The graphs in Figures 3.8a and 3.8b show the difference between 'easy to buffer' consistent but high variability, and an exceptional/extreme event.

Figure 3.8a   Consistently high-demand volatility that will not disrupt a Demand-Driven supply chain

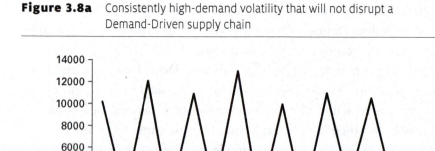

Figure 3.8b   The same demand pattern but with an abnormal demand spike that should be anticipated and built for – event management

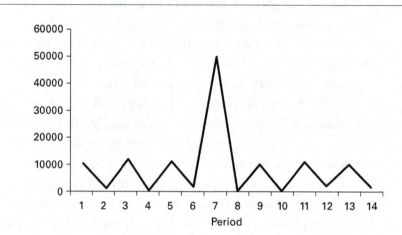

Much of the Lean tool set is part of day-to-day business these days and maybe you are looking for your next high-impact continuous improvement initiative? If you are working in a business with 'forecast push MPS/MRP' replenishment you will probably have realized that it is your company's greatest source of variability and, as such, should be tackled as a priority.

How do you start?

Have a read of the section 'Demand-Driven SCM: agility thru' stability' in Chapter 2. You will learn that Demand-Driven SCM is catching on fast and that its implementation does not require a high-risk/big-bang approach. It can be introduced at very low cost and step by step through your supply chain so that the sceptics can see it delivering the promised results and hear your commercial, operations and finance colleagues joining you, and your planners, in advocating its full-scale roll out – what are you waiting for?

The impact of SCM upon quality

The commercial president of a medical device company took the opportunity, at a quarterly business update meeting, to take his operations people to task for their apparent lack of a good manufacturing practice culture. A machine operator had stood by, seemingly without noticing, as his machine screamed like a banshee as metal-on-metal friction contaminated the supposedly sterile product.

'Why was this?' demanded the clearly incredulous president.

'Are operators not aware that they are making products for sick and vulnerable people?'

'Isn't there a TQM culture that instils quality into every aspect of the manufacturing process – including empowering operators to turn off machines when there is obviously a problem?'

These were all good questions – and factory floor staff then went through an appropriate training programme to ensure it didn't happen again.

But was the issue really just 'lack of quality awareness'? Or were there other factors at work?

In 'water cooler' discussions it soon became clear that there were probably other factors involved. Customer service had been a serious problem for some time. In the past 18 months virtually everything that could go wrong had: an attempt to change the distribution network had had to be reversed – and, into the bargain, the planning system interfaces had broken; a new low-cost packaging supplier had been found to have too little capacity so unplanned material lead-time increases had destroyed service levels and two weeks of production had been lost due to snow cracking the factory roof. As a result, the period and quarter-end sales pushes had become even more exaggerated than usual, forecast accuracy (never good) had fallen off the edge of a cliff and the factory was doing its best to maintain sensible output levels while responding to planners as they chopped and changed the schedules in an attempt to head off the next back orders – when they weren't 'calculating' their daily period end back-order prediction!

Maybe the cause of a 'lack of quality culture' rested with senior management? Maybe pressure upon the factory to maintain output, while being jerked about by planners due to the company's addiction to forecast-driven execution, was at least partly to blame through its negative impact upon stress levels, concentration and morale. When this was suggested the commercial president, to give him credit, agreed that such 'ways of working' were probably a significant contributory factor.

Okay, so the scenario described is not typical but the forecast-driven replenishment process certainly is and so are its symptoms: service issues, excessive and unbalanced inventories, high costs, stress, pressure, quality issues and no possible improvement.

Why is this?

Putting aside insanity as one possible cause of why most supply chains can make little performance improvement,[13] it is well known that all forecasts are incorrect and 80 per cent portfolio accuracy (ie 20 per cent wrong) is considered 'world class'. Due to the 20:80 rule, such performance means that most medium- and low-volume SKUs (usually the majority) actually achieve accuracies that are significantly worse, not least because with lower volumes, variability is higher and so is the level of forecast inaccuracy.

As noted above, manufacturing or purchasing schedules based upon inaccurate SKU forecasts lead to the production of unbalanced stocks with potential service issues, and expediting inevitably follows as planners respond to exception messages.

Service-saving production schedule changes cause expensive, unplanned machine changeovers, schedule congestion and increased lead times, with knock-on effects upon other schedules up and down the factory routings (they also disrupt factory floor stability and generate quality risks). In consequence, average lead times increase and become volatile (contrary to the DRP/MRP assumption of fixed lead times, therefore causing a further service risk) and stock becomes both excessive and unbalanced with service issues often continuing to occur. The further up the supply chain, and away from end-customer demand one goes, the variability is propagated by MRP's dependent demand relationships (the assumption that every supply chain activity has a known and fixed lead time with no buffer) and is amplified by batching and latency.[10]

Taiichi OŸo, the father of the Toyota Production System, likened the ideal factory to one being run by tortoises rather than hares – steady and predictable manufacturing being far more conducive to steady, predictable and high-volume, high-quality production than that allowed by rushed stop-and-start schedules.

Figure 3.9   'The slow but consistent tortoise causes less waste than the speedy hare that races ahead and then stops occasionally to doze. The Toyota Production System can be realized only when all the workers become tortoises' (Taiichi Ohno (1988) 'The Toyota Production System')

The Tortoise and the Hare

What is...   What could be...

But how can such a 'stable' approach to production ever be 'agile' enough to meet the volatility of today's demand patterns?

The answer is simple – though counter-intuitive. To appreciate how, the definitions need to be clarified in terms that are accurate (but often misunderstood) in a supply chain context:

Stability – is the various supply chain value-add activities working to their own efficient and predictable sequence with minimal unplanned changes and interruptions.

The benefits of this form of stability are that factory operators can focus on working to a sequence that maximizes changeover efficiencies and can be relied upon so that, for instance, people, materials and machines can be prepared in advance as necessary. Operators can also concentrate upon making product efficiently and to high quality levels while developing better ways of working through continuous improvement. To achieve such stability there obviously needs to be a minimum of interruptions, such as urgent and sudden changes to the schedule to prevent service threats.

On the other hand:

Agility – is the ability of a supply chain to be autonomously responsive to real demand, and its variations, with buffers that are of the right size and in the form that best serves both the company and its customers – and is 'designed in'.

The essence of 'agility' is in the use of the terms:

- *'Autonomously flexible'*: responding to changing demands immediately and without prior thought and preparation.

- *'Buffers that are of the right size and in the right form'*: buffers are always associated with variability unless the supply chain is so flexible that it is able to meet demand exactly while operating at 100 per cent utilization without customers either being kept waiting or supplied ex-stock. The aggregate of these buffers (time, capacity and stock) should be minimized in terms of their cost generation and be in the form that 'delights' the customer.

- *'Designed in'*: it is the design of how the supply chain is planned, operated and improved upon that delivers high service with ever-decreasing levels of cost and inventory (ie continuous improvement).

Agility can be achieved with stability by designing a supply chain process that simply involves positioning, sizing and maintaining inventory locations at strategic points in the supply chain, and replenishing them independently, in line with demand (or consumption), in an efficient, stable and predictable sequence. Overlaid with *exceptional* event management and planned advanced 'push' stock builds, this Demand-Driven SCM process will deliver the following performance improvements:

- achievement of consistently high planned service levels;
- reductions in average inventory of between 30 per cent to 50 per cent;
- reduction in unplanned overtime and increase in capacity utilization enabling cost reductions of around 20 per cent;[12]
- lead-time reductions of up to 85 per cent;
- without expediting or firefighting and any focus upon achieving high levels of forecast accuracy.

> *The reason that Demand-Driven SCM is so effective is that it enables the end-to-end supply chain to flow autonomously in line with demand by eliminating forecast error-induced variability – thereby also eliminating expediting and firefighting and their consequent generation of excessive inventory, volatile long lead times, use of unplanned capacity and risks to quality through broken concentration, urgency and poor morale.*

Demand-Driven SCM is a major change in the way most companies manage their supply chain, but tecŸical implementation is relatively simple. Robust, functionality rich and globally tested SaaS that supports the critical processes of positioning, sizing and maintaining the independent inventory positions is now available; they also support the 'work to' list generation and operate through legacy ERP transaction systems. In addition, via system-supported forecast-driven simulations through the relevant replenishment rules, the planner can understand future inventory and capacity requirements, which of course form the basis of S&OP decision making.

The SaaS model also facilitates quick simulations of your supply chain's historical performance versus that which Demand-Driven supply would have delivered, as well as low-cost, fast pilots prior to a revenue-expensed implementation and roll out.

A rapidly growing number of CPG and life science companies are quietly piloting and implementing Demand-Driven SCM – quietly because they know that 'agility with stability' will give them a significant competitive advantage, and not only in terms of product quality!

Assuming you are not insane, can you afford not to join them?

Has Lean been a waste?

For around 30 years manufacturing companies have been applying Lean and, latterly, Six Sigma tecŸiques as a means to improve their efficiencies. They have undoubtedly had some positive impact but I would argue that the vast majority of companies have failed to benefit to anything like the extent that they should because they have not addressed a key root cause of their unnecessarily high supply chain cost base – variability (despite, ironically, the explicit focus of Six Sigma being the management of that very phenomenon!). Variability minimization is the greatest source of sustainable cost reduction in any manufacturing supply chain and both Lean and Six Sigma will certainly help – but their contribution, in most companies, is being completely undermined by their choice of a supply chain replenishment process that actually generates significant variability.

Flow

One of the key components of Lean is flow. One-piece flow is often stated to be the ideal, but have you ever wondered what it is about flow that makes it such a powerful supply chain concept?

Perfect flow is achieved when materials continuously move through value-add processes to the customer and occurs when a supply chain's end-to-end process cycle efficiency (PCE) (ie value-add time/total cycle time) is 100 per cent. When one considers that most companies rarely exceed 5 per cent it is obvious that perfect flow is somewhat difficult to achieve!

What are products doing when they are not moving and not having value added? The answer, of course, is standing still as stock – and incurring storage costs and reducing cash flow while they're at it. The relationship between lead time, an important measure of responsiveness, and stock is direct (as described by Little's Law: System Lead Time = System Inventory/System Throughput) so, at a stroke, we can improve responsiveness, reduce inventory and improve our cash flow by raising our PCE through the reduction of that element of lead time that is not value add – or the time that materials are stationary.

Of course, some materials are deliberately held as stock, such as finished goods, to ensure that downstream service levels are adequately maintained. And other *unplanned* stock positions can be found throughout the supply chain. All these stock positions exist, despite average supply rates being aligned with that of capacity and demand, because variability prevents the timing of finished product arrivals exactly matching that of demand. The challenge is to keep materials and products moving in line with demand and most companies, inadvertently, try to do so by having lots of spare capacity. Unfortunately, of course, spare capacity impacts the cost base – so is there another way of keeping product moving continuously through value-add processes without adding to costs or, ideally, allowing them to be reduced?

Hopp and Spearman's *Factory Physics*[1] provides the answer in the form of the VUT equation, a simple version of which is:

$$\text{average wait in Queue} = \text{Variability} \times 1/(1 - \text{Utilization}) \\ \times \text{average processing Time}$$

Here we see that reduction in flow variability is the key to minimizing queues and keeping stock moving without having to maintain and use expensive spare capacity.

What causes variability?

If a process capacity constraint is 100 per cent we know that a queue will be created that will grow without limit. But, even if we have enough average capacity at a constraint, be it a supermarket checkout counter or a factory work centre, we will still get a queue and it is caused by variability in both the rate of arrivals and in the processing time. These two sources of variability cause demand spikes in excess of capacity as well as lost capacities and the consequent development of a queue with finite average length – and the queue will usually be visible unless there are very high levels of spare capacity.

Interestingly, if whatever is moving through the constraint has infinite flexibility (eg river water running through and around rapids is a good example, though even water is not infinitely flexible so rapids do cause an indiscernible upstream backlog), no queue will develop. For this reason, in a supply chain context and on shared work centres, smaller batches flow better than big batches because they cause less variability.

Quick changeovers and batch-size production are a core tool of Lean – and now we know why. And all the other Lean tools can also be seen as tecŸiques that reduce not only waste, but also flow variability and, thereby, help to keep product moving, eg TPM, TQM, standard work, poke-yoke, etc.

It is now clear that Lean and Six Sigma are both focused on variability reduction, because they help minimize its inevitable creation of cost-generating buffers – queue time, stock and use of unplanned capacity. Earlier it was said that these tecŸiques were being undermined by most companies' choice of replenishment process and the reason is that forecast-driven execution actually creates very high levels of supply chain variability.

Forecast error-induced variability

It is well known that all forecasts are incorrect and 80 per cent portfolio accuracy (ie 20 per cent wrong) is considered 'world class'. Due to the 20:80 rule, such performance means that most medium- and low-volume SKUs (usually the majority) actually achieve accuracies that are significantly worse, not least because, with lower volumes, variability tends to be higher and so is the level of forecast inaccuracy.

To reiterate, manufacturing or purchasing schedules based upon inaccurate SKU forecasts lead to the production of unbalanced stocks with potential service issues, and expediting inevitably follows as planners respond to exception messages.

Service-saving production schedule changes cause expensive unplanned machine changeovers, schedule congestion and increased lead times with knock-on effects upon other schedules up and down the factory routings. In consequence, average lead times increase and become volatile (contrary to the DRP/MRP assumption of fixed lead times, therefore causing a further service risk) and stock becomes both excessive and unbalanced with service issues often continuing to occur. The further up the supply chain, and away from end-customer demand one goes, these problems amplify due to latency (ie bullwhip caused by batching, response delays and misinterpreted demand signals).

A typical reaction to this set of problems is for management to increase ERP/MRP system parameters such as planned lead times and time fences. Unfortunately these just make matters worse by leading to more work being released to the factory floor, which puts more pressure upon capacity and further increases both lead times and stock while reducing responsiveness. In this way, companies using 'forecast push MPS/MRP' end up with the characteristic buffer combination of unsatisfactory service, excessive but unbalanced aggregate stocks and lots of unplanned overtime and poor OEEs. Frequently seen expensive 'solutions' to these problems are technologies for increasing forecast accuracy and 'optimization' tools for inventory and scheduling. Neither can offer significant supply chain performance improvement, however, because they are both based upon the wrong replenishment process.

So, if companies should not be using the forecast to directly drive replenishment, what should they be using? The answer is quite simple, they should use *demand* instead. Using demand to drive replenishment is often thought to mean 'make to order' (MTO), and while MTO is indeed 'Demand-Driven', so too can be 'make to stock' replenishment through the Demand-Driven SCM process. To learn more about the rationale and practice of Demand-Driven SCM go to the section 'Demand-Driven SCM: agility thru' stability' in Chapter 2.

The new planning

The implementation of Demand-Driven SCM has a significant impact upon the planner's role. Instead of constantly expediting and recutting inaccurate forecast-driven replenishment schedules (and generating variability!) the planner can concentrate properly upon value-add activities such as supply chain conditioning.

'Conditioning' enables the supply chain to flow and autonomously respond to demand. It is undertaken at each stock level position through demand profile analysis, replenishment tecŸique selection and calculation of rate and stock targets. These activities are performed regularly (eg tecŸique selection annually and parameters monthly) but changes are very much by exception – only around 5 per cent of targets usually need changing at any one time.

Planners will continue to be involved with new product launches, phase-outs and, on extreme and exceptional occasions, event management and, as the Demand-Driven principles can be applied to manage replenishment across company boundaries, planners will also have time to work a lot more collaboratively with key suppliers and customers.

In addition, of course, forecast-based S&OP continues to be an essential supply chain support process. As it is forward looking it incorporates the rate and stock-target setting process as part of aligning material and capacity availability with the demand plan. In fact, use of Demand-Driven SCM improves the value of S&OP by eliminating 'firefighting' and use of unplanned capacity, thereby allowing the process to focus more accurately upon the future and to be less short term and review-orientated in nature.

The benefits and implementation of Demand-Driven SCM

The concepts behind Demand-Driven SCM are not new, they have been around since 1961 (and before at Toyota) when Kingman formulated the VUT equation, a proof of Little's Law was first identified and Forrester and Burbidge initially wrote about 'bullwhip'. In recent years Cranfield University's Martin Christopher has also written extensively about them with the late Professor Dennis Towill from the Cardiff Lean Enterprise Research Centre (see the reading list at the end of the book).

The reasons for the current relative scarcity of the Demand-Driven SCM approach in companies are that it is counter-intuitive and difficult to implement successfully across modern enterprises without appropriate and robust software support.

Its outlook, however, is very positive as its rationale becomes more widely known and the performance deficits of 'forecast push MPS/MRP' become ever more exposed by increasing demand volatility and growing lead times (think of emerging markets/promotions/tenders and asset consolidation/offshoring/globally integrated supply chains, respectively). And, with the emergence of functionality rich, scalable and globally tested single-instance SaaS systems, especially designed to support Demand-Driven SCM (as well as forecast-based S&OP), it is now possible to quickly and inexpensively simulate, pilot and implement these tecŸiques both within and across company boundaries (and the boundaries may be real or within the same organization). The major challenge for companies that wish to go down the Demand-Driven SCM route are actually those of 'change management' because the ways of working are so different to that of 'forecast push MPS/MRP'.

But with the step-change performance benefits that the Demand-Driven SCM approach delivers, such as reductions in average inventory of 30 per cent to 50 per cent and around 20 per cent cost reductions, while meeting planned service levels, it is not surprising that some major companies in the CPG and life science sectors are proving extremely successful early adopters. Such companies, of course, also then start to fully benefit from all the effort that they had hitherto put into variability reduction using other Lean and Six Sigma tecŸiques.

Demand-Driven escalator management successfully applied at Holborn tube station

No, this is not about those escalators that only start moving when you step on them, or the way the Underground/Tube/Subway operators change the mix from two going up/one going down to vice versa, depending on the weight and direction of traffic at rush hours – although both are indeed a form of Demand-Driven escalator management.

This is about a subtle but ingenious way to accelerate people up the extremely long exit escalators at Holborn tube station in central London, where there is a tendency for the crowds to be queuing up the platform at rush hours.

As you probably know, the English are fantastic at queuing – be it for buses, taxis or trains – usually very polite, few sharp elbows and, on escalators, very disciplined at standing on the right to let those in a hurry pass by on the left.

So what they have done at Holborn is quite a culture shock: standing on the right *and left* is now obligatory! The reason is that the tube operator reasoned that, by encouraging people to enter the escalator in pairs (rather like the animals entering Noah's Ark), the effective capacity of the escalator would be increased and the platform queues cleared more quickly. What this would mean is that individuals in a hurry would not be able to get through on these escalators but the *average* wait time for all those in the queue (or the *average* speed with which all people exit the platform) would be increased. In effect, the underused capacity on the left-hand side of the escalator would no longer be sacrificed for the benefit of those in a hurry.

And initial trials demonstrated the truth of the hypothesis: the queues cleared 30 per cent more quickly. So, now at Holborn tube station, be very un-English: stand on the right *and left* sides of the escalator and perhaps be prepared to have a chat with your neighbour for a few minutes – on any subject, of course, other than the British weather!

What has this to do with Demand-Driven SCM?

Well, what are static inventories in a supply chain if they are not queues of materials waiting to be moved: either bought by customers or processed by machines or people? And, just as the operators of Holborn tube station were able to reduce the queues (or inventories) by improving capacity utilization and throughput by fully filling the left-hand side of the escalator with passengers, instead of it being partially used by those in a hurry, so supply chain managers can make far better use of their scarce supply capacity. They can do so by eliminating its use by expedited and 'hot list' items that disrupt otherwise efficient schedules and use up unplanned capacity through, for instance, expediting supply orders and causing unplanned machine changeovers.

If you would like to know more about how the principles of successful queue management can be used to significantly accelerate your supply chain's throughput, and substantially increase both your service levels and inventory turns (without having to invest in more capacity!) take a look at 'Demand-Driven SCM: agility thru' stability' in Chapter 2.

SCM – a comedy of errors?

Is it a little strange to even suggest that there might be a link between William Shakespeare and SCM?

Possibly, but given that 2016 was the 400th anniversary of Shakespeare's death and the link is about what makes us laugh, something the Bard was very good at, it might be worth a try...

The link is in the importance of timing. Good comedy is all about good timing – a great joke can fall flat if told poorly, whereas an average joke told well can bring the house down.

Shakespeare knew this; in *Hamlet* he advises that 'Brevity is the soul of wit' (Act II, Scene II) and the stage directions for his comedies are very particular: not only on how the words are spoken but also when – down to the split second.

The same is true of SCM: much of what goes wrong is down to poor timing. A typical supply chain is one in which there are excessive levels of inventory but it still suffers from frequent services misses – and that is due to the timing of replenishment.

What happens is that the planners set up perfectly sensible (perhaps even, so called, 'optimized') schedules based upon forecasts, actual demand, available capacity, stock on hand, stock on order and planned safety stocks. Then, when the forecasts prove to be incorrect and service issues loom, they reprioritize the affected SKUs, disrupt the schedules and use up unplanned capacity right through the routings with unplanned machine changeovers. In addition, of course, the lead times of the interrupted SKUs are extended and these later become service threats too. And, over time, the lead times of all the SKUs get extended far beyond that really necessary, safety stocks get increased and still the exception messages proliferate as forecast versus safety stock calculations continue to generate yet more exception messages and service threats.

What has all of this to do with timing?

The answer lies in the poor timing of the planners' replenishment decisions. Planners know full well the most efficient sequence that should be scheduled through their work centres and also know the economic minimum quantities and sensible increments... so the timing of replenishments, given the forecast, seem easy to determine for the MPS. Unfortunately, due to the inaccurate forecasts, exception messages appear and sooner or later the planner feels obliged to intervene, so the replenishment timing and sequence get changed and become sub-optimal – and, for those involved on the factory floor, this is anything but funny as they have to perform unplanned and complicated machine changeovers that negatively impact their OEE.

What planners and factory management really want is to set up schedules that follow a repeatable, predictable and efficient sequence that results in planned service levels being achieved with right-sized inventories.

That might seem like something of a surreal joke but it is not – in fact that is exactly what they can, and should, be doing. The really rather sick joke is that most don't and it is because their company has spent millions on SCM software systems that force them to plan schedules that they have no chance of achieving. These are 'forecast push ERP/MRP/DRP/APS' systems that do nothing more than translate inaccurate forecasts into inaccurate MPSs that inevitably have to be changed, with significant performance-eroding consequences.

The alternative is Demand-Driven SCM that uses enterprise(s) wide multi-echelon decoupled reorder point/cycle but only uses forecasts for S&OP, event management and inventory buffer-target setting. The way it works is that, as inventories are consumed by downstream activities or customer demand, upstream work centres 'make, or ship, to replace', and as long as the inventory targets have been set correctly, including enough buffer for demand and supply variability (which, with modern-day Demand-Driven SCM software is very quick and easy to calculate and set up), customer demand will be met and aggregate average on-hand SKU inventories capped at variability buffer plus half the reorder quantities – no longer will inventories swing between too much and too little, and planned service levels will always be achieved.

What has this to do with good timing?

It is that when supply chain execution is Demand-Driven the timing of replenishment is always correct and schedules can be efficiently sequenced and relied upon without any need to change them. In effect, the end-to-end supply chain operates in a highly stable, but autonomous, manner while delivering a very high, and highly agile, level of service performance with right-sized inventories[14] and elimination of forecast error-induced wasted capacity – and that is definitely not a joke!

If you would like to know more about how to seriously improve the performance of your supply chain and operations, have a look at the section 'Demand-Driven SCM: agility thru' stability' in Chapter 2.

And if you are hesitant, remember something else that Shakespeare advised: 'Our doubts are traitors, and make us lose the good we oft might win, by fearing to attempt' (*Measure for Measure*, Act I, Scene IV).

Notes

1 See Hopp and Spearman (1995) *Factory Physics*. The full Kingman or VUT equation, valid for a single-server queue, is:

$$\text{Average waiting time in Queue} = \left(\frac{Ca^2 + Cp^2}{2} \right) \frac{1}{(1-U)} T$$

– where T is the mean processing time, U is the rate of utilization (ie mean processing rate/mean arrival rate), Ca is coefficient of variation for arrivals and Cp is the coefficient of variation for processing times

2   See Wallace J Hopp (2007), *Supply Chain Science*, McGraw Hill, New York

3   Also, productivity increases of up to one-third have been recorded as a consequence of regular and predictable schedules being introduced into operations through 'economies of repetition'

4   WJ Hopp and ML Spearman, 'To pull or not to pull: what is the question?', *Manufacturing & Service Operations Management*, 6 (2), pp 133–48

5   This is why quick changeovers are so useful: they allow smaller batches without loss of capacity

6   World-class 80 per cent accuracy hides the fact that most SKUs in a portfolio – the medium- to low-volume/high-variability items – will be achieving less than 60 per cent

7   Typical supply chain/operations performance improvement from implementation of Demand-Driven are:

- achievement of planned service levels;
- average inventory reductions of up to 50 per cent;
- higher potential capacity utilization enabling capex avoidance and around 20 per cent overhead cost reduction per unit;
- lead-time reductions of up to 85 per cent.

Remember that forecast push supply chains always have significant, and excessive, multiple inventory positions that are **not** planned, they are there as a consequence of the variability that is injected by the inaccurate forecasts and propagated/amplified by batching and MRP's network of dependent demand relationships.

8   This example goes back to the 18th-century Scottish philosopher David Hume, of whom Karl Popper said: 'I approached the problem of induction through Hume. Hume, I felt, was perfectly right in pointing out that induction cannot be logically justified' (Popper (1963) *Conjectures and Refutations*, Routledge and Kegan Paul, London, p 55)

9   This statement is subject to the caveat that even after the over 300 pages it reputedly took Russell and Whitehead to prove that 1+1=2 in their opus *Principia Mathematica* (1913), Kurt Godel then showed with his 'incompleteness theorems' (1931) that even within mathematics there is an inherent limit to what can be known

10 Latency is when significant changes in the rate of downstream demand fails to be matched further upstream leading to shortages of materials, in the case of accelerations, and the late and unexpected need for catch-up activities, which are often then exaggerated leading to the well-known bullwhip phenomenon

11 Given that all physical supply chains involve a flow of materials, all such supply chains can be managed with Demand-Driven principles using active selection and management of the three buffers – time, capacity and inventory

12 Due to the reduction in service-saving expedites and unplanned schedule changes that use up capacity, OEEs are improved and expensive overtime reduced. In addition, the consequent stability that is brought to the factory floor results in greater levels of productivity from less stressed and more highly motivated staff who become more efficient by no longer being constantly interrupted

13 Einstein reputedly said: 'Insanity is doing the same thing over and over again and expecting different results'

14 Average inventories will stabilize at variability buffer plus 50 per cent of replenishment quantity across the portfolio, which is considerably less than achieved by forecast push MRP because of overforecasting and the tendency of planners to pull forward schedules far more than they delay them. In addition, lead times can be reduced due to the reduction in schedule interruptions and this also allows planned variability buffer to be reduced too

How to operate a Demand-Driven Supply Chain

04

There are five key stages to the operation of Demand-Driven SCM. The first three are all strategic – buffer types, buffer sizing and buffer maintenance – and are effectively an integral part of the S&OP process that, as will be seen, Demand-Driven SCM totally transforms and reinvigorates. The remaining two stages are simply the day-to-day execution and the monitoring of the flow process – with intervention only if absolutely necessary.

In addition to these five key stages are three no less important aspects of successful Demand-Driven SCM. The first of these is its beneficial organizational implications that are a natural consequence of the process. Another concerns the business performance metrics that, if not amended to reflect the new and real business priorities, can undermine the entire transition to Demand-Driven SCM and, thereby, its delivery of transformational business performance. Finally, there is the all-important change management process that, because Demand-Driven SCM is so fundamentally different to the way most companies run their supply chains, should be actively managed during its implementation.

Strategic

Buffer types

Supply chains are simply flows of materials through multiple conversion processes on their way to consumers but, like all flows, if they are not perfectly flexible, they are prone to turn into queues when they meet any form of 'constraint'. In supply chains these constraints are work centres and warehouses where processing rates, or rates of demand, and supply rates do not exactly match. Variability in these patterns of demand (or processing) and supply result in unplanned buffer, of which there are only three types:

- *Capacity*: if material arrives late at an available work centre then capacity can be lost. Similarly, if a work centre slows down, or stops, that capacity is also lost, as it is if machine changeover times are long. Lost throughput as a result of lost capacity can, of course, only be recovered with the addition of more capacity.

- *Time*: if material arrives at a work centre that is already busy it has to wait – this is queue time. Intuitively we know that the greater its level of capacity utilization the more likely it is that when material arrives at a work centre the more likely it is that it will have to join a queue – and the longer that queue will be. That is indeed the case; the average waiting time in a queue is related directly to the level of variability and increases exponentially at higher levels of capacity utilization.

- *Inventory*: material queues behave like queue time – they are related directly to the level of variability and increase exponentially at higher levels of capacity utilization. Material queues in front of work centres are, of course, simply a form of inventory, often called 'work in progress'. Sometimes the quantities of factory WIP are so large that they 'justify' their own warehouses (be it raw materials or semi-finished goods). Most companies would say that their finished products are not in a queue but, in fact, they are: they are in a queue waiting to be sold.

If a company knew exactly what customers were going to buy and when, they could, theoretically, plan their supply to synchronize exactly with demand so that customers were neither left waiting nor having to be supplied from stock. As this is impossible, companies either plan to meet customer demand from a finished stock buffer (ie 'make to stock', MTS) or require their customers to wait until they can supply what they order.

If customers are prepared to wait then, broadly, there are three forms of this time-buffered approach:

- *Engineer to order* (ETO): in which the supplier makes exactly what the customer wants using a customized design. The customer has to wait for the design to be finished, the materials to be supplied and for the product to be fabricated.

- *Make to order* (MTO): in which, from a finite range of design options, the customer is supplied with their specified product after waiting for its components to be purchased and then processed by the supplier.

- *Assemble to order* (ATO): as with MTO, customers choose from a finite range of designs but only have to wait for the supplier to make or assemble the product from materials and sub-assemblies that are held in stock.

The speed with which a company can respond to an order obviously depends upon its response strategy, conversion lead times and level of spare capacity. It should choose how to respond to orders using explicit calculations of risk, cost and opportunity:

- *Opportunity*: by holding stock the company can provide customers with a quick delivery response, which may be an order-winning strategy – or simply a competitive imperative.

- *Risk*: the holding of stock by a company implies that the company is confident that it can and will be sold before it becomes obsolete and the cash-flow implications are manageable.

- *Cost*: capacity utilization can be very high under MTS as there is no need to await customer orders, and supply schedules can be stable and efficient because the stock buffer decouples order patterns from supply; although it has to be remembered that holding stock does incur a cost in that it takes up space and ties up cash.

Because inventory is the buffer that can be most easily quantified and sold directly (unlike time and capacity), it is used as the main planning buffer in Demand-Driven SCM. However, in certain circumstances, demand or supply is so unpredictable that different buffers have to be used instead. For instance, the demand pattern for ships is fairly unpredictable and no two ships are the same so they tend to be sold on an ETO basis, which means that a time buffer is being used. The building of a ship takes quite a long time so the ship builder's challenge is to have a replacement order in place when each ship is completed in order to avoid having unused capacity or layoffs. Clearly the customer's order-to-delivery lead time is determined, in this case, by the design time, 'build time' and, maybe, a 'queue time', in contrast to customers of 'make to stock' (MTS) products that simply have to wait for ex-stock delivery.

A pure MTO response involves the manufacturer buying in the materials and performing the fabrication upon receipt of the order. In some circumstances, a long lead time MTO customer proposition can be improved upon if, say, the finished product can be assembled from 'generic' ex-stock items and components that can be fabricated, or customized, to order. Such an ATO service allows a quicker response than pure MTO but is a far less inventory-hungry strategy than that permitted by an ex-stock service.

Many car manufacturers have moved towards this form of ATO from both the MTS and MTO ends of the buffer spectrum. These companies have effectively adopted a 'mass customization' proposition. Instead of selling discounted standard models ex-stock and expecting customers to wait weeks for more expensive non-standard configurations, they have designed their cars, manufacturing processes and supply logistics in such a way that customers can order one of literally millions of different car specifications, which are then configured and built within a standard and relatively short response time – and without any price penalty except that to cover cost of optional and "luxury" materials. When you consider the number of components that go into making a car, the level of capital investment in a car plant and their need to maintain very high levels of throughput/capacity utilization, this is an exceptional feat. It is achieved by the manufacturer, using the details of individual customer order specifications, to plan both component deliveries and their supply to the production line in a predetermined sequence that allows each customized car to be assembled in turn and on time. This allows them to provide their customers with a relatively quick ATO response time for an immense range of options (so much so that the same exact model may never be made more than once) and avoids the need to forgo the profit from heavily discounted 'standard' models.

An ATO response can also, of course, be a very sensible way for manufacturers to respond to exceptional and extremely large orders for standard products that, for a MTS company, might otherwise cause a stock out. In this case the assembly would be from raw materials and components for which the company deliberately plans to hold an additional stock quantity to enable them to meet such orders relatively quickly. Of course, this type of response would require the company also to be able to quickly turn on additional capacity. Thus, the ability to provide this form of stock/time buffered response is dependent upon the availability of spare capacity – and without it the time-buffer element will be considerably longer.

To summarize, companies should design their supply chain response to orders using a mix of the three available buffers – capacity, time and inventory. The mix of buffers selected will be influenced by a company's marketing strategy, the competitiveness of the market, the predictability of demand, and the cost of holding inventory and response capacity. In general, competitiveness is aided by fast response, high capacity utilization and low levels of inventory. Although there may be trade-offs between the three buffers, it is essential that companies try to minimize their aggregate cost and, as has been demonstrated earlier with the VUT formula, this can best be achieved by minimizing supply chain variability.

Inventory buffer positioning

Any manufacturer that wishes to provide customers with a supply response that is no longer than its own fabrication supply lead time must, by definition, plan to hold inventory of some raw materials. Thus all ATO and, of course, MTS companies must plan to hold at least one inventory buffer. This is often known as the decoupling point because it is positioned at the point in the supply chain where response to customer orders is separated from upstream forecast-driven response. The decoupling point is still of relevance to Demand-Driven Supply Chains but there are two subtle, but very significant, additional features:

- *Forecast-driven versus Demand-Driven*: for execution purposes, Demand-Driven Supply Chains use item-level forecasts not to develop a time-phased MPS designed to meet it, but to size decoupling inventory positions that will be replenished by upstream value-add activities according to the rate of *actual* demand.

- *Multiple decoupling points*: unlike the traditional *single* decoupling-point model of a supply chain, Demand-Driven Supply Chains often use multiple decoupling inventory points – be they finished goods actually at the customer (as in a collaborative supply chain), the company's own finished goods and raw materials and, perhaps, even, sub-assemblies in the factory. The reason for using multiple decoupling points is that they absorb natural process variability (and prevent it being transmitted through the supply chain) and allow each buffered value-add activity (or group of activities) to be scheduled and replenished independently of others up and down the supply chain.

This decoupling has the enormous benefit of significantly simplifying the development of efficient and stable schedules that meet demand and allow operators to efficiently focus upon their own 'value-add' activities with minimal interruption due to sources of variability such as material delays or expedite messages. As a consequence, OEEs are higher and lead times are shorter as materials flow in line with demand.

The decision as to where to position planned independent inventories in the Demand-Driven Supply Chain is often very simple. In distribution companies, for instance, it is in the customer-facing warehouse(s) and in many fast-moving MTS companies it is as finished products in the FGs warehouse (and/or, ideally, at the customer's location), at raw materials and, perhaps, somewhere in the factory before the packing process. An example of the latter might include bulk pharmaceutical tablets that are packed into multiple finished packs and where imme-diate packing and distribution is not as critical as it is with, say, some food products because of short shelf life considerations.

But even the assumption that raw materials should be stocked can sometimes be overturned if the business decides to plan downstream replenishment execution a week, or maybe two, out. In this way the materials can be bought in (line-side) to support the schedule. Such a tactic will significantly reduce the need for goods-in warehouse space, though because the effective replenishment lead time has been increased, will result in an increase in finished goods stocks.

In companies with a deep and complex bill of materials the position-ing of stock can be a more complex process. A key factor that impacts whether and where stock might be held is the level of commonality of component parts/sub-assemblies across the company's finished prod-uct portfolio: the greater the commonality the stronger the case for them being planned stock items. This applies whether the company is MTS or ATO, and MTO companies may decide to bring in a level of component and sub-assembly standardization so that response lead times can be economically reduced.

A reasonable level of part standardization is important for posi-tioning Demand-Driven SCM decoupling points, simply because of the cash impact. Independent inventory positions are there for many reasons such as supporting/beating customer response expectations and cushioning supply/demand variability, but it is clearly impor-tant that the net cash implication is beneficial (ie that the inventory cash implications of an upstream inventory position are more than compensated for by a reduction in downstream inventory positions). Careful consideration and analysis is needed to ensure that proposed upstream inventory positions genuinely improve responsiveness and reduce enough inventory positions downstream to justify themselves.

Replenishment technique selection

Wherever it is decided that an independent stock location is to be positioned, the next step is to decide its default replenishment tech-nique. This does not mean that the chosen process will be followed slavishly – sometimes events, hopefully planned, will be an overrider and, of course, the selected tecÿique should be revisited periodically and changed if required.

One factor that is not a determinant of the chosen replenishment tecÿique is that being used at other stock positions – even those directly upstream or downstream. The reason is that one of the key characteristics of Demand-Driven SCM is that the multiple independent inventory locations decouple the supply network activities to prevent variability being propagated and amplified through its batching policies. This decoupling means that each stock position can be replenished using its own optimal process and, as long as the inventory targets are set correctly, each echelon will be able to follow its own independent cycle without reference to other supply chain activities.

What are the factors that influence the choice of replenishment tecÿique? There are simply two: demand volume and demand variability.

It is a statistical fact (known as the central limit theorem or the 'law of large numbers') that a random sequence of numbers from a high-magnitude range will be less variable than that from a lower such range. In this sense we are not referring to the absolute variability (which will obviously be higher when taken from a high-magnitude range) but the relative variability. The absolute variability is best measured using standard deviation; to calculate relative variability we simply divide it by the average. Sometimes this is known as 'normalized variation' or the 'coefficient of variation', and is the type of variability referred to throughout this book whenever it is described as high, medium or low.

Just as a series of random numbers from a high-magnitude range tend to exhibit low variability, so the same occurs with demand volumes. Demand for high-volume products is always less variable than of low-volume items and, for this reason, forecast accuracy on such items is usually better too. Following the pareto, or 20:80, rule however, although a company's relatively small number of high-volume products may account for most of their volume, it is the large tail of products (that account for a small aggregate volume share) that suffer the highest levels of demand variability. For these items, time-phased forecast accuracy will also be very low, which is why it is these items, in a 'forecast push MPS/MRP' environment, that cause the vast majority of the expediting, firefighting, cost and unplanned buffers.

Another implication of the 'central limit theorem' is that forecasts of an annual volume will be more accurate than monthly volumes and considerably more accurate than weekly or daily volumes. Many 'forecast push MPS/MRP' companies have moved to weekly forecast buckets in an attempt to improve their alignment between supply and demand but, as you will now be able to appreciate, the consequence for forecast accuracy is such that this is a fruitless tactic.

The relationship between demand volume and variability is shown in Figure 4.1 and it demonstrates the typical pattern seen at most Demand-Driven decoupling points. As you can see, there are a small number of high-volume/low-variability items, many of medium volume and medium variability and some with very high variability because of extremely low volumes.

Figure 4.1   Demand volume and variability analysis for replenishment technique selection

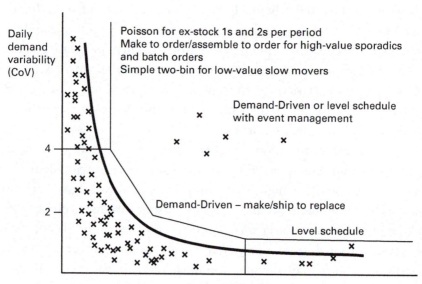

High variability/low volume

Clearly the case for *not* using forecast push MPS/MRP *gets stronger the more variable is demand because the more inaccurate will be the forecast*. As has been discussed earlier, sometimes demand is so variable that it is best to use MTO or ATO. These strategies work well when customers are prepared to wait and there are very high levels of customization (eg for a very highly specified yacht) or the order is exceptionally large of an otherwise standard ex-stock item.

How do we manage demand for consistently low-volume items that are also low value? Given that they are low value it is often the case that they can be replenished using a simple two-bin system with a relatively infrequent cycle. Clearly the amount of stock held relative to demand is very high, but if the cost of goods is very low too then this may not be an issue.

For items that sell only in 1s or 2s per period, and space or value prevent a simple two-bin system, then what is called a poisson variability buffer can be used. In statistical terms, a poisson distribution measures the likelihood, based on past experience, of an event occurring in the next time period (such as an order for a single unit or, in another context, a bus arriving at a bus stop). Based on the level of probability of an order occurring over the replenishment lead time it therefore becomes possible to calculate the reorder point to provide a desired level of service.

Low variability/high volume

Replenishment of items with high demand volumes and, due to the central limit theorem, low variability can work reasonably well with 'forecast push MPS/MRP', but a far more effective methodology exists. High-volume items also tend, seasonality aside, to show little in the way of significant trend, in other words their volumes are flat or only trending quite gradually. So instead of using 'forecast push MPS/MRP', and being on the receiving end of unnecessary forecast error due to the addition of 'marketing intelligence' into the forecast, why not a 'level schedule'? In other words, work out the average level of demand per period (and because we are dealing with averages of high numbers, we will be quite accurate), make it every period and plan to hold an appropriate variability buffer for those periods when actual demand is higher than average. And, periodically, check inventory and demand levels to decide whether the batch size/frequency should be amended. Clearly such a process offers enormous benefits in terms of simplicity of planning and shop floor predictability.

In Lean terminology this level schedule (or rate-based) process is known as mixed-model scheduling or heijunka and, quite rightly, the process emphasizes the need for batch sizes to not be excessive relative to average demand. This is because, obviously, excessively big batches drive up average inventory levels but, also, because big infrequent batches cause demand upon upstream supply to be very variable and, consequently, buffer hungry and difficult to stabilize. In addition, and quite counter-intuitively, it is nearly always the case that when a company reduces its excessive batch sizes its frequency of non-productive changeovers also diminishes – more may be planned but far less of the unplanned variety occur. This is because, with infrequent supply, excessively large batches and excessively long lead times, unplanned service saving interruptions to the schedule become very much more common.

Another counter-intuitive aspect of the level schedule process is that, the greater the supply lead time, the stronger the case for using it. As has been discussed, high-volume item estimates are always more accurate than that for low-volume items (eg percentage error estimates for an unknown large volume tend to be more accurate than that for smaller volumes) and the longer the lead time, of course, the larger will be the level of lead-time demand. For replenishment purposes, the longer the lead time the larger the lead-time volume, so the more accurate will be the level schedule orders versus the average. This means that a correctly calculated level schedule will be very accurate and require proportionately less variability buffer. In consequence, replenishment from long lead time offshore sources lends itself particularly well to level schedule. But again, care needs to be taken not to oversize the batches. Although big batches can reduce the need for variability buffer (less deliveries meaning less stock-out risk exposures), they are also a source of demand variability for the supplier and are a supply continuity risk for the buying company (eg customs delays through to shipwrecks!).

Medium variability/medium volumes

These items are those that should be replenished using a reorder point (ROP) or reorder cycle (ROC) mechanism. Effectively this means that stock is replenished as it is consumed, with a frequency determined by the planned order interval or batch size – for which earlier comments about excessive size also apply.

It might be thought that these items could be replenished using a level schedule. Their higher demand variability, however, means that the variability buffer would have to be very high across a relatively large number of items. And there is no reason why items on ROP/ ROC should suffer significantly less productive efficiency than those on level schedule. The fact that supply schedules can be sequenced efficiently and are never interrupted means that the equivalent benefits of supply stability can accrue to these items as well.

The way these two processes operate is as follows:

- *Reorder point*: as soon as the stock on hand plus on order falls below the reorder point (ie variability inventory plus average demand over the supply lead time) another supply order is placed following order quantity policies. By adding an offset to the lead time (and therefore increasing the reorder point) multiple mixed orders for a certain supplier or work centre can be periodically collated and sent together.

- *Reorder cycle*: some companies prefer to work with specific order cycles for different products. Typically, the higher-volume items are ordered more often than those of lower volumes. Depending on the day of the week, or week in the month, and which products fall into that particular cycle, item orders are placed for a quantity that takes the stock on hand plus on order back up to a target level. That target level is calculated by adding the variability buffer to the average demand over the supply lead time and over the planned order interval.

  When ROC is used in a manufacturing environment, the scheduling sequence can be 'hard coded' into the orders that are sent to the factory floor or that can be left to the factory floor operators. Either way, the best sequence of supply can be selected and followed without fear of interruption if the variability buffers have been sized correctly, spike orders are managed effectively and, of course, there are no significant supply-side issues.

ROC is tecŸically less efficient than ROP because it builds in additional and artificial lead time (ie the cycle period) that needs to be covered by the variability buffer. In most situations where ROC is used there is an enforced or desired ordering cycle due to, say, shipping schedules or planned production cycles.

Effective ROC requires the minimum order quantity (MOQ) to be consistently below average demand over the order interval otherwise, when the cycle comes around and it is ordered, the target inventory may be exceeded. Alternatively, if it were skipped there could be a strong risk of a stock out.

ROP is most useful when there is no requirement for a disciplined order cycle and, clearly, ROP minimum order quantities must be sized to reflect available capacity (eg too small and changeover time might be excessive). If, as was suggested earlier, an offset to the lead time is added to enable collation of ROP orders, ROP's inventory efficiency advantage over ROC is lost.

A theoretical benefit of ROP is that it is less likely to result in a service issue if the parameters are not properly maintained. For instance, if demand increases ROP will keep up by requesting more frequent replenishment, albeit using more capacity, while ROC could suffer a stock out.

High variability/medium to high volume

Some medium- to high-demand-volume products occasionally do experience exceptional and extreme demand spikes. The impact of these should not be allowed to prevent adoption of a level schedule or ROP/ROC if it is otherwise sensible. Unexpected significant demand spikes that require immediate fulfilment would disrupt any replenishment process but such events are very rarely unexpected – someone somewhere in the business, or at the customer, almost always has knowledge of them a long way in advance. If Demand-Driven SCM is replacing 'forecast push MPS/MRP' all the firefighting that was being caused by item-level forecast error will be eliminated from the business. This means that those working in supply planning, demand planning and commercial can begin to focus upon active event planning and demand management so that such 'spike orders' are anticipated, and built for, in a planned and an efficient manner.

Buffer sizing

The purpose of the multiple deliberately positioned inventory buffers in a Demand-Driven supply chain is threefold:

1 Activate the initiation and quantity of supply-side value-add activity when stock levels get to a 'trigger' point (ROP) or when an order cycle comes around (ROC).

2 Supply materials on demand to customers or downstream value-add processing activities.

3 Absorb and prevent the propagation of variability (eg supply delays/demand surges) up and down the supply chain.

The sizing of the buffers is therefore an important element of Demand-Driven SCM to ensure that, across the end-to-end supply chain, all the value-add activities occur in an aligned manner, without disruption, so that materials flow and capacity utilization is maximized.

Although there might appear to be a considerable amount of complexity in the buffer-sizing activity (eg there are three options for simply choosing how to calculate an average – see below) in reality it is not something that should pose any great challenge. Good Demand-Driven SCM software support systems will do all the calculating and generate user-friendly exception reports that indicate which parameters need changing. It is also worthwhile bearing in mind that, unlike the need for highly accurate time-phased forecasts in 'forecast push MPS/MRP', Demand-Driven inventory buffer sizing only has to be roughly right. As long as the buffers are set approximately at the correct level (which is very easy to achieve because we are only estimating demand averages over multiple periods, not exact quantities per period, *and* we are building in a quantity for error) the supply chain will respond *autonomously* to actual demand (eg as you sell more you make/ship more, as you sell less you make/ship less).

There are three components of the planned inventory buffers (Figure 4.2): lead time, variability and order quantity. It is important to note that it is not the intention, usually, to hold this entire buffer quantity as 'on-hand' inventory. The majority of the lead time inventory should, as much as possible, be 'on-order'.

Figure 4.2   Inventory buffer target and its components

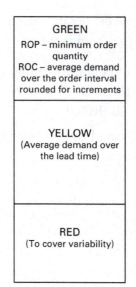

Lead time

In a perfect world where ex-stock supply could be in single units, then every time a single unit of material was consumed another would immediately arrive to replace it. In order for this to happen there would need to be a continuously full pipeline of single units that moves at the same speed as demand. In this ideal state the lead time would be the value-add time from the previous inventory position and it would be full of single units streaming along behind each other in line with demand. In the real world, however, the lead time we use is the 'planned lead time', and the lead-time volume is the average of demand over it.

Notice we are not referring here to an average lead time. In real life it is extremely difficult to measure actual lead times correctly, and calculating an average is fraught with difficulty. As we have seen, actual lead times continuously change in line with variability and capacity utilization, or load, and if we used an average we would set ourselves up to fail 50 per cent of the time. It might be suggested that we could hold a supply variability buffer (see below) but this assumes that lead-time error follows a normal distribution – which it never does, it is always skewed by the propensity of deliveries to be on time or late. We therefore set a best-estimate lead time that covers, say, 90 per cent of actually achieved lead times, and focus on eliminating the causes of the outliers.

If deliveries for a particular material from a particular supplier start to become persistently late we need to ascertain whether it is due, say, to a series of unfortunate incidents or because supply is becoming capacity constrained – which, as we have learnt, always causes queues to expand, especially in the presence of high variability. In either case we need to avoid simply increasing the planning lead time because, in the case of the former it is unnecessary (instead, understand the events and take action to prevent a recurrence) and, in the case of constrained capacity, we will only make the situation worse by further increasing demand upon the supplier or resource. If lead times are growing because of growth in capacity utilization, additional capacity is most likely required! In this situation, if lead times are increased, be aware that further increases may be necessary, especially if the lead time is from a supplier who has other customers, because your action is likely to be replicated by them and a vicious circle initiated: constrained capacity –> delayed deliveries –> increased planning lead times –> further constrained capacity.

Given a sensible planning lead-time parameter, how do we calculate the average demand element? There are a number of options, which makes it sound rather complex, though, in reality, it is not. Those to choose amongst are generally quite obvious and rarely need revisiting – and will be the same for most products, even in a reasonably heterogeneous portfolio:

- *Forecast or history*: not withstanding the tecÿical point that an average calculated from history is just as much a (naive) forecast as an average taken from a forecast (and given lack of trend they should be identical), which should be used? In general, as we are planning for the future, we should use the forecast, especially if the demand pattern contains trend or seasonality. But if experience shows that the forecasts always have a serious amount of bias in them then an average taken from history – or a blend – might be more effective.

- *Roll period*: whether we are using a forecast or history, over how long a period should we calculate the average? The longer the period selected, the less responsive it will be to changes in demand, and if they are meaningful it could mean that the buffers are sometimes wrongly sized. On the other hand, of course, too short a roll period could be just as inaccurate as it reflects meaningless short-term variability. In general, companies tend to use three or four months unless trend and seasonality are such that something shorter is more appropriate.

- *Offset*: an average can also be selected for a roll period from any time bucket in the past or the future (eg a three-month period from last year, earlier this year, starting in two months' time, etc). Again the selection criteria are dictated by the relevance of the period being chosen to that being planned for, so trend and seasonality are, again, relevant factors. It is common to use a forecast offset equivalent to the supply lead time and, if there is one, the order interval combined.

Variability

With no variability in demand it would be possible for a supply order to be placed when stock on hand plus already on order equates to the lead time 'average' (ie the reorder point), and for the next delivery to arrive exactly when the last unit of on hand is being consumed. The fact that we are dealing with averages, of course, means that sometimes it would arrive before or after those last units are consumed. We obviously do not want the latter to occur because it implies a service miss, so we hold a quantity of variability buffer that we know sometimes will and, of course, sometimes will not be used. In a perfectly 'normal' world (statistically speaking) the frequency and degree of usage and non-usage at every supply delivery will balance out so, over a period of time, both the actual and planned average level of stock in the warehouse will include all of it.

As was described in the above section on lead times, we do not want to try calculating a statistical level of inventory buffer for supply variability, which leaves us just having to manage that of demand. The calculation is designed to quantify the amount of additional inventory we should plan to hold on hand to deliver a specified level of service given the calculated level of variability of demand around the average over the replenishment lead time (and in the case of ROC this would include the cycle interval too – see below).

The best predictor of future variability is that which has occurred in the past, so we use historical demand variability. In order to do this there is a well-known approximation as follows (though there are more sophisticated calculations that factor in the frequency of replenishment and consequent exposure to a stock-out risk):

Variability Buffer = z factor for service level x standard deviation of demand x square root of lead time

(And be careful to ensure that your demand and lead time units of measure are the same – eg days or weeks – and don't use periods below one unit – ie fractions – for the lead time.)

The higher is the variability and/or the level of service we desire, the more variability buffer that we will need. Also, the longer the lead time the more buffer we need, which makes sense because the longer the lead time the greater the average, so the greater will be the absolute level of variability. But, as we learnt earlier, the bigger the numbers we are dealing with, the lower the level of relative variability, which is why the lead-time effect only increases in line with its square root.

In fact, this square-root-driven estimate of variability over the lead time becomes increasingly generous as lead times become longer and with very long lead times, such as those associated with offshore sourcing, they can be very excessive. When companies use a real calculation of lead-time demand variability for their buffer calculations, they find that long lead time items deliver some of their most significant inventory reduction opportunities. The real calculation of variability over the lead-time parameter (that we would multiply by the z factor to get the variability buffer) involves calculating the standard deviation of 'demand over the lead time' actuals for a series of relevant historical lead-time periods. Conceptually quite simple to understand, and good Demand-Driven SCM software will do it for you.

The variability calculation for use in a level schedule is exactly the same as that for ROC as it uses the order interval added to the supply lead time to calculate the lead-time parameter.

Order quantity

Using ROP, if the order quantity is one then, clearly, every time a single unit is sold another is ordered, so the pipeline is filled with a sequence of single units, and the variability buffer ensures that there is always enough on hand to cover variability over the lead time. In the real world we tend to have minimum order quantities but the principles are exactly the same.

The key feature of ROP is that the order quantity is always the same and it is ordered whenever stock on hand plus on order drops to the ROP (variability buffer plus average demand over the supply lead time) – the trigger point. This can mean, if daily throughput is high relative to the order quantity, that multiple orders have to be placed every day. If, in these circumstances, it is desired that only one order should be placed per day then we have effectively moved to a reorder cycle mechanism in which the order quantity becomes variable while the daily cycle stays fixed.

ROC eliminates the need for a reorder trigger point. Instead, whenever the cycle comes around an order is placed (ie the minimum plus any incremental rounding) that takes the level of stock on hand, plus on order, up to a reorder target. That target is composed of variability buffer, plus the average demand over the supply lead time plus the average demand over the reorder cycle. The last of these is why, if ROC is to be used, the average demand over the reorder interval should be consistently above the minimum order quantity – clearly if it is not then either the new order will result in the target stock being regularly exceeded or, if the order is skipped and placed on the next cycle, there will be a gap in the future sequence of deliveries that poses a service risk.

In general, ROC is applicable whenever a fixed order cycle is desired and the order quantity is variable (usually subject to a minimum and, sometimes, increments) and, because the order interval in ROC should not be interrupted the order cycle is effectively an addition to the lead time for calculating the variability buffer, as described in the variability buffer section.

The sizing of minimum order quantities/increments and order intervals is deliberately not being addressed here. When multiple products have to flow through single processing machines there is an inevitable loss of capacity whenever there is a changeover, so some degree of batching is inevitable. The calculation of optimal batch sizes, in this situation, involves consideration of the number of items being made on the same machine, average demand volumes, speed of processing, changeover times and available capacity. Other overriding considerations include the fact some processing machines have to be full when operated (eg liquid containers), sometimes there are batch-size rules (eg as in pharmaceutical bulk manufacture) and sometimes there are transport and purchasing economies to consider. These are all considerations that feed into the Demand-Driven SCM order-sizing process and different situations will use local decision-making policies.

In general, the smaller the MOQs/increments and the higher the frequency of replenishment the lower will be batching as a source of flow variability and the quicker will be the supply chain response to demand. But, of course, achieving this responsiveness at enormous expense (eg using high levels of expensive non-productive capacity for frequent changeovers) means that we are just using capacity to keep the materials moving. Instead, we should constantly be improving our supply chain flexibility, which is its ability to respond to demand with minimal aggregate buffer from whatever source. In the case of manufacturing batch sizes, of course, this would mean working on speeding up changeovers to enable their reduction and, unsurprisingly, SMED has become a key component of Lean for this very reason.

Inventory too high and wondering why?

SCM tends to be about two key objectives: achieving good service and reducing aggregate inventory levels. Much of a supply chain manager's working life is about preventing the former from becoming a high-profile issue and trying to work out why any progress on the latter causes risk to it.

We all know that attacking inventory levels through the safety stock is a naive approach (unless you are replacing an arbitrary 'x weeks of forecast' policy with a more sophisticated calculation using a target service calculation) and the alternative (ie increasing replenishment frequency/reducing order quantity) can be time-consuming to achieve if there are price breaks to consider or capacity restrictions – though this route is definitely worth pursuing and persisting with.

But assuming sensible safety stock calculations and stable average order quantities, aggregate inventories still usually tend to exceed what they should be. Theoretically, average on-hand inventory for any individual finished product should be equivalent to the planned safety stock plus half the average order quantity. But if you do the analysis across a portfolio, the actuals always come out at the aggregate of those safety stocks plus quite a bit more than that 50 per cent.

Of course, some of the excess can be due to the surplus inventory still hanging around due to overly optimistic new product-launch forecasts but, even with this accounted for, the surplus is usually significant.

Further analysis will show that the 'guilty' items are not the few that account for the majority of sales volume (ie the top 20 per cent by volume items[1]) but mainly those that account for the balance – the remaining 80 per cent of the SKUs that account for 20 per cent of the volume. You will find that most of these have an average inventory level of planned safety stock plus 70 per cent+ of their average order quantity.

The reason is that the small number of really fast-moving items experience relatively low demand variability, and high-frequency stable volumes are supplied with little interference from planners – with the result that a large proportion of their safety stocks are frequently being used. The opposite is true, however, of the 80 per cent of higher-variability/lower-volume items that are supplied less frequently. These items tend to have excessively high planned safety stocks that never get used so the average inventory actuals are always far higher than both calculated or needed.

The reason is that they suffer very poor levels of forecast accuracy so planners tend to schedule and reschedule them a lot (ie responding to exception messages) to avoid use of the safety stocks as a means to protect service. In consequence the safety stocks do not get used and the early stock arrivals result in the effective safety stock being in excess of that planned. Unfortunately, planners have a propensity to pull forward schedules when demand appears to exceed forecast, but rarely to push them back, so even where there is overforecasting the same result occurs. These high-variability items also tend to have very generous planning lead times reflecting all the variability-induced queue time, and to guarantee their on-time arrival, which leads them to arrive early as well as inflating their calculated size through the safety stock's square root rule.

You can easily check this for yourself: simply calculate every item's daily or weekly demand (or sales or ship) average and standard deviation, and then divide the latter by the former to get the coefficient of variation – CoV.[2] Then calculate the forecast accuracy being achieved by each item (ie aggregate absolute error/aggregate forecast as a percentage), their actual average stock and their theoretical average stock (ie safety stock + 50 per cent average order quantity). You will find that those items with higher levels of CoV suffer the poorest levels of forecast accuracy and proportionately higher inventories versus their theoretical levels. And if you look at their service-level record you will find that this tends to be poor too!

So the root cause of excess inventory, and ironically most service failures, is not forecast inaccuracy per se (as it is often suggested) but demand variability. The more variable is demand the more inaccurate the forecasts will inevitably be and, if those forecasts are being used to drive replenishment through DRP/MRP/APS, the greater the misalignments between supply and demand.[3] And this leads to planners overcompensating with their planning parameters and intervening with their well-meaning, but inventory/lead-time-increasing and capacity-hungry schedule interventions.

Can companies significantly downsize (and right size) their inventories and still achieve planned service levels – while also ceasing to waste capacity with unplanned service-saving schedule amendments and all the associated firefighting?

The answer is 'yes' and it starts with *not* using forecast push MRP/APS and involves adopting Demand-Driven SCM instead. When implemented, Demand-Driven SCM consistently delivers:

- planned service levels;
- right-sized average inventories at up to 50 per cent of their previous level;

- significantly lower demand for capacity due to reduction in unplanned changeovers (that allows for more frequent planned changeovers and small-order quantities);
- planning lead-time reductions of up to 85 per cent, without:
  - any firefighting or expediting, and without
  - any focus on trying to achieve high levels of item-level forecast accuracy.

To find out more about the 'why and how' of Demand-Driven SCM see the section 'Demand-Driven SCM: agility thru' stability' in Chapter 2.

Buffer maintenance

Sizing the inventory buffers is obviously not a one-off activity. Over time, demand levels change as demand grows or declines and there might need to be active management of seasonality. And within the growth and decline categories, of course, there are the product life-cycle launch and phase-out stages to manage as well as possible item substitutions.

If the buffers were left untouched then, in the case of ROP, any sales growth or decline would inevitably result in growing or declining demand for capacity, and with ROC demand increases can eventually cause stock outs when the rate of supply fails to match that of demand. Only an increase or decrease in buffer target size can help realignment. And in the case of demand variability, clearly that element of buffer should also be maintained to ensure planned service levels continue to be met when levels of variability are changing.

A case can be made for highly frequent buffer adjustments on the grounds that the changes will be smooth, but counter to this is the inevitable increase in planning effort. Most companies find that a monthly buffer-sizing review process is adequate and this is also convenient as it aligns nicely with most companies' S&OP process. As such, buffer adjustments, and their aggregate consequences for capacity and inventory levels can be reviewed and approved by senior management as part of that process.

The buffer maintenance process is something that is undertaken by supply or demand planners. In effect, this aspect of Demand-Driven SCM replaces the focus upon high levels of time-phased forecast accuracy, MPS development and the expediting process that takes up so much time in 'forecast push MPS/MRP' supply chains. Unlike these activities, however, effective management of the buffer levels is not fruitless effort as it enables the supply chain to flow autonomously and efficiently. It is, however, a data-intensive process and unless the data is robust and managed correctly it can be done poorly and consequently generate supply chain performance issues. For this reason it is strongly recommended that good Demand-Driven SCM software is used to facilitate the process instead of, say, high-risk spreadsheet systems that can easily contain errors, can be broken, have limited functionality and are often high risk as they are supported by only one person.

The sort of basic functionality that buffer-sizing and maintenance software should consist of are:

- *Variability*: calculate the buffer quantity required to achieve a planned service level based on historical demand variability over the replenishment lead time using an appropriately selected period from history.

- *Average demand over the lead time*: calculate the average demand quantity over the lead time (and the order interval for ROC) from a similarly appropriately selected period in history or the forecast (or both).

- *Evaluate the new buffer and compare with the old*: to indicate to planners any significant percentage changes so that investigation can take place before confirmation, as appropriate.

- *Spike recognition*: a significant demand spike, whether planned or not, is usually excluded from both of the variability and average demand calculations because they are not part of the day-to-day demand for which the buffers are designed to accommodate. If the forecast contains significant demand spike it should raise an alert for further investigation and appropriate action.

Different demand profiles require different approaches to buffer sizing and maintenance as follows:

- *Trend*: whether negative or positive, it is important that the buffers are adjusted every month in line with the trend as it occurs. In this situation the buffers should be sized using the forecast, with appropriate adjustments for any known bias. If the replenishment lead time is significant, and with it the trend, it might be necessary to select the forecast with an offset equivalent to that lead time.

- *Seasonality*: this requires a slightly different approach to that of simple trend if the capacity available during the peak period is insufficient to meet it. Where this is the case, the buffers need to be artificially raised in advance of the peak, and continuously raised as necessary, until the desired level of preseason volume has been built. If the peak is very short-lived then 100 per cent of the seasonal peak will have to be built and the accuracy of the forecast will determine the extent to which the final service/inventory performance pans out. This is also the case if the supply lead time is very long compared to the length of the selling season. In both of these situations the business should treat the advance stock build decision like it would any other cost-benefit decision in which there is an element of risk. Unless you are extremely lucky you will end the season either with unmet demand or unwanted stock that might, if it has a short shelf live, need to be written off. For this reason it is sensible for the advance build-quantity decision to be the subject of a cross-functional assessment so that a fully informed, and recorded, consensus can be reached.

If, however, the supply lead time is relatively short and some peak season capacity is available then a good risk management approach is to make in advance, say, 70 per cent of the forecast requirements and to top up as required during the season so that, when it is over, all demand has been met and no unwanted stock is left over.

- *Upstream buffer targets*: upstream from finished products, the stock targets are composed of the same three buffers:

  - *Variability*: should be calculated based upon actual consumption by the relevant downstream value-add activities. This means that, if downstream consumption is very uneven, the upstream variability will be quite high (such as if there is a high degree of irregular batching). If, however, downstream activity follows a stable pattern then, despite any batching, the variability of consumption over the lead time can be relatively low. Similarly, the greater the range of finished products that the component or sub-assembly is a part of, the more stable is its likely demand due to its volume being that much larger and subject to the benefits of the central limit theorem. And, for this reason, it is often the case that multipurpose raw materials and sub-assemblies can be replenished using a level schedule despite the downstream SKUs being ROP/ROC or, if a postponement strategy is in place, ATO.

- *Average demand over the lead time*: should be calculated through the BOM based upon demand for the relevant finished products with an allowance for consistent wastage.

- *Order quantity*: the same as for finished products: the MOQ for ROP or average demand over the order interval for ROC.

If there is a one-to-one relationship between the demand for a finished product and one of its components then it is important that their inventory targets should be kept aligned and changed at the same time when trend and seasonality is present. If the component has a long lead time, however, it might have to be changed in advance to ensure the right level of inventory is available when required. When a component is used in many different products, however, its sensitivity to demand changes is diluted and the software should perform the somewhat onerous calculations and let you know when changes have to be made based upon the appropriate aggregate demand trends.

By now it should be clear that there is a need for alignment between upstream and downstream inventory targets, and within a single company using a single Demand-Driven SCM software instance this is obviously quite easy to achieve – especially if the company has introduced a centralized and end-to-end inventory target management process. If, however, a collaborative Demand-Driven replenishment process has been entered into it is important that the trading parties actively synchronize their inventory target changes, in line with downstream demand, to keep them aligned.

- *Product launch*: the challenge with new product launches is that you do not have any demand history upon which to base the variability buffer. Actually, this doesn't matter a great deal because the real challenge is in guessing how much is going to be sold how quickly and, therefore, how much product should be built prelaunch. Unlike the case with seasonality, however, the forecast cannot be informed by demand levels from previous years, though you may be able to refer to experience with other similar new products. In consequence, and as was described for seasonality, a cross-functional consensus decision-making process should be employed to estimate the prelaunch stock build so that the service and inventory risks are assessed thoroughly. Ideally the prelaunch stock cover should be as short as possible, commensurate with available capacity, so that replenishment can be aligned as closely as possible with actual demand. In general, the sales of new products should be the subject of close review during the introduction and growth phases of their product life cycles so that the inventory targets can be manually kept aligned with demand until a suitably stable demand history and forecast can be used as the basis of a more steady state Demand-Driven SCM replenishment process. A huge benefit of Demand-Driven SCM is that, with the absence of continuous expediting, planners have adequate time to carefully and effectively manage such new product launches.

- *Product phase-out*: Demand-Driven phase-outs simply require the elimination of the stock target so that product continues to be sold until all residual inventory has been consumed. Some control over the timing of inventory exhaustion can be achieved through use of the forecast and management of the stock target, though its accuracy depends on the level of forecast accuracy. This might be done in conjunction with analysis of upstream component inventory target management to minimize pipeline inventory write-off. Sales can always, of course, be halted exactly on a date, and earlier than stock exhaustion, just by using a block on sales-order entry.

- *Substitutions*: very often, within a product's own life cycle, there is a need to change its components. If a component is being replaced by a new component then the former's inventory target can simply be transferred to that of the latter, subject to order quantity policies. On the other hand, if it is a case of changing a component to another that already has a buffer target then, in addition to any change in order quantity policy, the replaced item's element of the average demand over the lead time needs to be transferred and an increment made to its variability buffer to reflect the larger volumes.

With both finished product and component substitution phase-in/phase-outs, the timing of these changes can be managed using a hard stop (ie setting a date when the substitution will occur) and a soft stop (ie allowing the change to be made when full consumption of inventory is complete).

Why all the focus upon sales and operations planning?

Since the acronym first appeared in the early 1980s, sales and operations planning (S&OP) has cost companies millions of dollars in consulting effort to get it up and running, and more in management time to actually operate the process. Over the years S&OP has been reincarnated a number of times and is now sometimes known as Integrated Business Planning (IBP). Whether it is S&OP, IBP or core commercial cycle (CCC), which is another term I came across recently, the process is justified by 'evidence' that its implementation improves corporate performance by somehow aligning/synchronizing/unifying the activities of the commercial, supply and innovation functions. And to this, nowadays, can be added, with the advent of new optimization IT capabilities, the potential for companies to use S&OP to evaluate the financial 'best' use of resources under conditions of constrained capacity using 'what if' scenario exploration across a global network.

According to many SCM analysts, however, the vast majority of companies, on an S&OP maturity scale of one to five, fail to develop beyond the stage-two version.

Why is this? A key reason is that companies have been focusing on S&OP far too early on their road to supply chain excellence. S&OP obviously cannot be of value to companies that are totally incapable of delivering a plan. And most companies, due to the inadequacy of their SCM processes, find that all the effort they put into planning proves so divorced from the reality of what actually happens that S&OP becomes discredited and little more than a mid-level management review process instead of the C-suite strategic forum it is designed to be.

This is not to suggest that S&OP is of no potential value. Its value can be immense but first companies need to implement SCM processes that can be planned, *and* delivered, with some degree of accuracy. Unfortunately, most companies use replenishment processes that are so ineffective that they are, in effect, out of control and no amount of S&OP/IBP/CCC is going to be of any benefit.

How forecasts degrade supply chain performance   These companies are using forecasts for both planning *and* replenishment and, while the former is obvious, the latter is plain wrong and leads to totally inadequate supply chain performance that is always different to that which had been planned – in terms of service, inventory and capacity utilization.

As forecasts have been driving supply chains for many years in most companies, and their use for this purpose appears fairly intuitive, the above paragraph might be considered something of an exaggeration. Its truth, however, is borne out by evidence and very robust scientific principles.

It is well known that all forecasts are wrong and 80 per cent portfolio mix accuracy (ie 20 per cent wrong) is considered 'world class'. Due to the 20:80 rule, such performance means that most medium- and low-volume SKUs (usually the majority) actually achieve accuracies that are somewhat worse, not least because with lower volumes, variability tends to be higher and so too is the level of forecast inaccuracy. Manufacturing or purchasing schedules based upon inaccurate SKU forecasts lead to the production of unbalanced stocks with potential service issues, and expediting inevitably follows as planners respond to exception messages.

Service-saving production schedule expedites are a major source of flow variability and cause costly unplanned machine changeovers, schedule congestion and increased lead times with knock-on effects upon other schedules up and down the factory routings. In consequence, average lead times increase and become volatile (contrary to the DRP/MRP assumption of fixed lead times, therefore causing a further service risk) and stock becomes both excessive and unbalanced with service issues often continuing to occur. The further one goes up the supply chain, and away from end-customer demand, these problems are amplified by MRP's dependent demand network, batching and latency (ie response delays and misinterpreted demand signals).

A typical reaction to this set of problems is for SCM to increase ERP system parameters such as lead time and time fences. Unfortunately these just make matters worse by leading to more work being released to the factory floor, which puts more pressure on capacity and, thereby, increasing both lead time and stock while reducing responsiveness. In this way, companies end up with the classic combination of unplanned and unsatisfactory service, excessive stocks and higher than planned use of overtime.

Another common response, of course, is even greater expenditure upon forecasting software (eg demand sensing) followed by inventory and schedule 'optimization' tecҰology. Both routes are actually misguided because they are attempting to improve a replenishment model that is entirely inappropriate for what is, in effect, a non-linear system.

Simple queuing theory, Lean and flow The relevant underpinning of SCM and operations is queuing theory, which recognizes that any process involving at least one conversion stage, be it a supermarket checkout counter, a factory production line, a distribution channel or supplier, has finite throughput capacity (ie is a constraint) and always suffers from queues. If demand exceeds capacity the queue will grow indefinitely. Even if demand is below 100 per cent capacity, however, there is still a queue. This is because variability in the rate of arrivals at a work station and/or its processing time will cause both lost capacities and demand spikes and the development of a queue with finite average length. (NB If there is plenty of spare capacity, however, no queue will actually be observable for most of the time.)

The average waiting time in one of these queues, for a given level of capacity utilization, is directly proportional to the flow variability. On the other hand, the relationship between the queue length and the level of capacity utilization is exponential, and very noticeably so when variability or utilization is high. Both relationships are demonstrated as follows.

The relationship between queues, variability and capacity utilization can also be modelled using the Kingmand or VUT equation, a simplified version of which is:

Figure 4.3   Demonstrating how increasing levels of supply chain variability and capacity utilization increase lead times and inventory

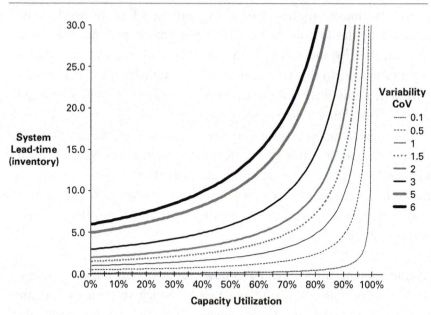

$$\text{Average wait in queue} = \text{Variability} \times 1/(1 - \text{Utilization}) \times \text{processing Time}$$

We know that queue time is a major component of lead time and through Little's Law we also know that lead time is directly related to inventory level:

$$\text{System Lead Time} = \text{System Inventory}/\text{System Throughput}$$

Little's Law and the VUT equation are at the heart of Hopp and Spearman's 'Factory Physics' and are used to explain the underlying rationale for why the tools of Lean are so effective.

Conceptually we can understand that if supply was unconstrained and totally flexible we could meet any demand (ie volume and mix) and achieve perfect continuous *flow* without holding any static stock, either in process or as finished goods. In the real world, any inability by the supply conversion process to respond instantaneously to demand changes implies the existence of a constraint (eg a processing machine) that inevitably suffers flow variability, which causes the creation of cost-generating buffer. The default buffer response to variability is an immediate increase in lead time due to queuing, ameliorated by use of spare capacity (if any); management may respond with an increase in capacity (eg overtime) and finished goods inventory upsizing often follows to prevent service issues.

Lean activities such as TPM, TQM, SMED, 5S, standard work, DFM, etc, eradicate not only wasted effort and cost, they also reduce flow variability, including that caused by excessively big batches (thereby supporting flexibility), which means less cost-generating buffer is created or needed. And this is particularly valuable when working at high levels of capacity utilization. In consequence, the Lean supply chain uses less unplanned capacity and can operate at higher levels of capacity utilization (ie lower costs), with shorter queue/lead times (ie greater responsiveness) and lower levels of stock. Reducing flow variability is actually synonymous with minimizing cost and inventory while increasing responsive flexibility, and is why Hopp and Spearman describe Lean as: 'fundamentally about minimizing the cost of buffering variability'.[4]

Lean's full potential has rarely been fully exploited, however, because most companies, through their inaccurate forecast-driven replenishment execution processes, are (as has been described) still unwittingly introducing huge amounts of reschedule and expediting variability (ie forecast error-induced) into their supply chains and operations.

Demand-Driven SCM and flow In addition to the 'shop floor' Lean that increases flexibility and minimizes factory variability, operations and supply chain leaders can significantly reduce the performance-destroying and plan-confounding impact of the supply chain variability that they generate themselves through their use of inaccurate forecasts to drive replenishment execution.

The Demand-Driven SCM approach uses replenishment processes that are autonomously responsive to real demand, and its variations, with minimized cost-generating buffers that are of the right size and in the form that best serves both the company and its customers.

Companies that adopt these tecŸiques sustainably achieve their desired service levels with inventory reductions of between 30 per cent to 50 per cent, planning lead-time reductions of up to 85 per cent and cost savings of around 20 per cent through better use of capacity and higher OEEs. These companies no longer, of course, have any further concern for high levels of item-level weekly, or monthly, forecast accuracy.

The definition of Demand-Driven SCM is:

> A segmented supply chain execution process featuring multiple deliberately planned and positioned, but independent/decoupled, inventory locations that are each replenished, in an efficient and stable sequence, to a calculated and maintained stock target, in line with real demand – not the forecast (which is used for S&OP, event management and buffer sizing).

To learn more about the practice of Demand-Driven SCM, go to the section 'Demand-Driven SCM: agility thru' stability'.

The new planning and S&OP   The implementation of Demand-Driven SCM has a significant impact upon the planner's role. Instead of constantly expediting and recutting inaccurate forecast-driven replenishment schedules, the planner can concentrate properly on value-add activities such as supply chain conditioning.

'Conditioning' enables the supply chain to autonomously respond to demand; it is undertaken at each planned stock position through demand profile analysis and replenishment tecŸique selection (effectively level schedule or ROP/ROC) and calculation of rate and stock targets. These activities are performed regularly (eg tecŸique selection annually and stock targets/rates monthly) but changes are very much by exception – only around 5 per cent of targets may need changing at any one time (and these tend to be those experiencing strong trend or for which stock builds are necessary such as for planned supply interruptions and seasonality).

Planners will continue, of course, to be involved with new product launch, phase-out and event management for extreme and exceptional orders and promotions, though if demand history is littered with promotional activity the planned stock targets will cope with them without further intervention. And as the Demand-Driven SCM principles can be applied to manage replenishment across company boundaries, planners will also have time to work a lot more collaboratively with key suppliers and customers.

In addition, of course, forecast-based S&OP can now add real value as a senior management planning process. The elimination of forecast error-induced variability means that actual aggregated supply chain activity and performance (eg service levels, inventory levels and capacity requirements) will closely match that which had been planned – and 'firefighting' will be a thing of the past. As a result, S&OP will earn credibility in the eyes of senior management and can become a valued, reliable and accurate forum able to support real evidenced-based tactical and strategic decision making.

Tune your supply chain (and forget the MPS!)

Before reading this short section it is worth reading either 'Demand-Driven SCM: agility thru' stability' or 'Forget the forecast accuracy KPI' (Chapter 2).

You probably know that, when using 'forecast push MPS/MRP', the MPS is a statement of what a factory can and will build over the ensuing planning periods. It is generated by planners using a forecast of what is expected to sell, knowledge of what is already on order and in stock – and is designed to be achievable with current capacity. The MPS is then further cascaded through the BOM to generate replenishment requirements (ie MRP) for sub-assemblies and materials that will support its achievement. Most MPSs have a frozen period in which no changes are permitted without senior management approval, as changes to factory floor commitments are very disruptive and costly.

A longer-term version of the MPS is also used by planners to identify capacity constraints so that they can be either removed before they constrain supply or to signal the need for an active order-rationing process to be put in place. Thus, the same forecast-driven MPS is being used for both planning and execution purposes.

A key feature of Demand-Driven SCM, however, is the *separation* of the planning and execution processes, as follows:

- *Planning: strategic* – positioning and review of the independent inventory buffers up and down the supply chain and selection/ review of the most appropriate replenishment tecYique at an item/ echelon level. Also, of course, evaluation of capacity requirements over the medium and long term through use of 'what if' forecasts and simulations through the BOMs and routings.

- *Planning: buffer sizing* – sizing of the planned but independent inventory buffers at each echelon using an estimate of *average* demand (ie a naive forecast) plus the correct quantity for variability and rounded for order quantity policies.

- *Planning: buffer maintenance* – the process of ensuring that the inventory buffers continue to align with demand patterns as they change over time.

- *Execution: replenishment* – the actual replenishment process, through work-to list generation, in the appropriate time buckets (eg daily, weekly, two-weekly etc with/without offsets) in line with demand using ROP or ROC or a level schedule and including, by exception, advance stock builds for events such as significant promotions, seasonality, holiday shutdowns, etc.

- *Execution: monitoring* – checking that the materials and products are flowing as planned within the supply chain via on-hand inventory alerts and, by exception, expediting if there have been delays or unexpected demands that threaten service levels.

As you will have noticed, the Demand-Driven SCM approach does use forecasts for both the planning and execution activities – but in neither case is high-level accuracy needed at the item/period level. For capacity planning, easily achievable long-term aggregated-level forecast accuracy is sufficient, and for buffer sizing a reasonably accurate item-level average over numerous periods is sufficient along with a quantification of the variability about that average. The reason that accurate short-term forecasts are no longer required for driving execution is that, firstly, they are always wrong[5] and secondly, the Demand-Driven SCM process allows the supply chain to *autonomously* respond to actual demand by replacing the stock that is consumed in an efficient sequence and cycle. This process, and the planned buffers, are designed to service variability in the demand pattern – the only demands that such a process cannot accommodate are extreme events that require anticipation, which become a key focus, by exception, of demand and supply planning.

It is clear that the Demand-Driven SCM approach does make use of a medium- to long-term MPS for the purposes of capacity planning, as well as financials (including cash flow/inventory levels), by blowing the item-level forecasts through the selected replenishment tecŸiques/targets, BOMs and routings and evaluating/acting upon the outputs (ie S&OP). In effect, an equivalent of item-level forecast-driven planned orders are being created and used at an aggregate level but they play no role whatsoever in the execution world.

Instead of an MPS for execution, the Demand-Driven SCM effectively uses a statement of the demand volume/mix that can be met over a given time period as determined by available capacity and the way the buffer parameters have been set up. This is sometimes known as supply chain *conditioning* or *tuning* and is effectively a statement of *potential capability* – to be realized depending upon the actual volume/mix of demand that occurs. Of course, depending upon the frequency with which shop floor activities are scheduled, 'work to' lists will still be generated, which are a statement of what should be built – but these are not forecast-driven schedules, these are statements of what *should* be made and *will* sell.

Demand-Driven S&OP

If you have read 'Demand-Driven SCM: agility thru' stability' in Chapter 2, you will understand that 'forecast push MPS/MRP' supply chains suffer significant levels of forecast error-induced variability and unplanned buffers (queuing lead time, excess and unbalanced inventory and unplanned changeover/catch-up capacity).

In consequence a forecast-driven S&OP process is always inaccurate because it fails to account for the unpredictable (ie in terms of magnitude, timing and form – inventory, capacity, lead time) unplanned buffers and tends to be overrun by the serious performance issues that this inaccuracy causes (ie particularly the service and inventory levels).

Perhaps this is why, in so many companies, S&OP fails to become top management's strategic and unifying forum – it is simply unreliable and swamped by fruitless discussions about forecast accuracy, schedule adherence and how to recover from today's service and inventory performance crisis.

By contrast Demand-Driven supply chains eliminate forecast error-induced variability and minimize residual process variation through the deliberate positioning of multiple planned, but independent, inventory locations. As a result they behave in a much more linear and stable fashion than forecast push MPS/MRP supply chains, as illustrated by the typical performance improvements:

- achievement of consistently high planned service levels;
- reductions in average inventory of between 30 per cent to 50 per cent;
- increases in OEE enabling cost reductions of around 20 per cent;
- planning lead-time reductions of up to 85 per cent;
- stable, predictable replenishment orders upon suppliers that allow shorter supply lead times and greater upstream efficiency that can convert, subject to negotiation, into significant procurement cost savings;
- without the continuous and time-consuming expediting and fire-fighting typically seen in most supply chains and operations.

This supply chain predictability means that S&OP in Demand-Driven supply chains is very accurate and the process can deliver genuine value by supporting both tactical and strategic decision making.

So what does Demand-Driven S&OP look like?

One important feature is that, unless S&OP is being used to manage delivery of the annual budget numbers (in which case it should not really be called S&OP as S&OP should use a rolling 24-month planning period), a top-level executive meeting does not actually need to be held every month. Although there does need to be a monthly planning process it is not always the case, unless the environment is particularly volatile or the business is sufficiently large and complex, that a formal meeting is required so frequently. The reason for this suggestion becomes clear when one considers the key activities that compose a Demand-Driven S&OP process.

The key S&OP activities are:

- Aggregate capacity planning: focusing on potential bottlenecks such as machines, skilled labour, warehouse space, etc – and making the relevant decisions to avoid them developing into a flow constraint.

- Financial planning: covering both revenue and profitability as well as cash-flow forecasting.

- Inventory planning: providing an estimate of future on-hand inventory levels, usually as a cash value and maybe in terms of their storage space requirements.

Each of the above are typical of any S&OP process and involve blowing the sales forecast through the replenishment rules, inventory parameters, bill of distribution (BOD), BOM and routings using the relevant replenishment processes and the right-sized inventory parameters.

A key attribute of Demand-Driven SCM is that maintenance of flow is achieved through the reviewing and resizing of the planned multiple independent inventory buffers and it is this activity that composes most of the pre-S&OP activity. Resizing of inventory buffers obviously impacts inventory levels and cash flow as well as warehouse space and capacity (eg higher demand levels without an increase in inventory targets will absorb more changeover capacity), so it is the purpose of pre-S&OP to plan these changes and alert senior management to any that may have a significant corporate impact.

Other key S&OP activities are:

- Event management: companies that are subject to significant levels of seasonality and/or have a high-rate of new product launch will want to consider how to plan for these forms of event and, in particular, the forecast and management of inventory risk. Some companies might also want to consider how to respond to significant spike orders, particularly if they are from new markets or customers and represent an inventory risk.

- Strategic issues: with the elimination of forecast error-induced variability and its unplanned buffers, the Demand-Driven S&OP process becomes a reliable data source for supporting strategic decision making. When it comes to deciding, say, how best to allocate finite resources when demand is growing faster than supply, S&OP data and 'what if' simulations become the obvious tool set for evaluating the options. And the same can be said of how companies choose to make investment decisions or, in recessionary times, how to retrench.

This latter form of strategic analysis is the real 'value add' of a Demand-Driven S&OP process – if it warrants a monthly meeting so be it, but in some companies it might more naturally follow a quarterly and annual review. One thing is for certain – companies that become Demand-Driven no longer need a monthly crisis review meeting to discuss the most recent service/inventory metrics and decide how best to try to recover!

Execution and event management

There are arguably just two key replenishment execution decisions – when and how much to buy/make/ship. Under 'forecast push MRP' both are always answered wrongly because they are driven by an inaccurate forecast and assume that all the other materials needed to allow execution to begin will be available too. We have seen how these grossly incorrect assumptions are corrected by Demand-Driven SCM through its use of demand as the driver of replenishment and multiple independent, but planned, inventory positions that cushion process variability and ensure that dependent materials are always available when required.

Level schedule

The timing and quantity of replenishment in a very stable demand environment can be made extremely simple indeed through use of level schedule in which the quantity and timing of replenishment is fixed, in advance, in line with the appropriately stable demand forecast. It will only be changed when demand and supply become seriously misaligned, and early alert systems using on-hand inventory versus planned should indicate this early enough to avoid stock outs or excessive inventory levels.

When demand is slightly less stable and ROP/ROC is in use then either the timing of replenishment is variable and the order quantity is fixed (ROP), or the timing is fixed and the quantity is variable (ROC). The detail of both is as follows.

Reorder point

When stock on hand plus stock on order (less today's orders and unfulfilled past orders and selected future events) falls to the combined level of variability buffer plus average demand over the lead time: order the fixed order quantity.

Reorder cycle

When the planned order cycle comes around order the difference between the 'order-up-to' target and current stock on hand plus stock on order (less today's orders and unfulfilled past orders and selected future events), rounded according to the minimum/multiple order quantity policy.

Event management

Both ROP and ROC can accommodate most demand spikes that fall within the threshold that the planned variability buffer is designed to accommodate. As the variability is measured using standard deviation it might, at first, be thought that this means any level of variability that has occurred in the past can be fully buffered in the future. This is not the case, however, as historical *exceptional* and *extreme* events, if contributing to the measured level of standard deviation, will not be fully covered by the resulting variability buffer. In fact, such events should be planned for in advance (see below) and eliminated from the demand history for the purposes of inventory target sizing. The only demand variability that the stock targets will successfully cover is that which is *consistent*, no matter how variable. So, if an item's demand history is full of promotional demand spikes the planner can be confident that future such demand patterns will be covered by the variability buffer without the need for detailed promotion planning and manipulation of the forecast.

Exceptional and extreme events are a different matter. Without preplanning, such events, if processed as orders and shipped, will cause a stock out/backorders (either immediately, or in the near future) and the need for expediting and/or customer order rationing until supply

Figure 4.4a   Consistently high demand volatility that will not disrupt a Demand-Driven supply chain

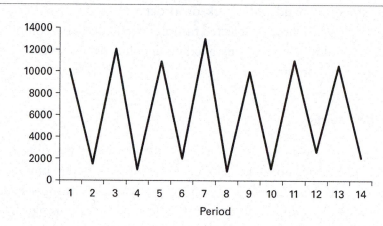

Period

Figure 4.4b   The same demand pattern but with an abnormal demand spike that should be anticipated and built for – event management

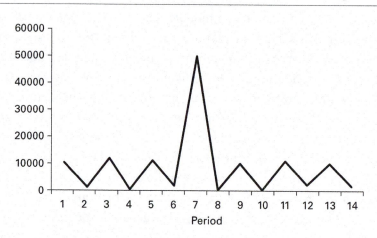

Period

has fully caught up. This eventuality can be prevented if planners are able to see such spike orders far enough in advance to allow the necessary stock to be built in time to meet the order.

This brings us to the true meaning of the frequently used terms demand planning and demand/order management. These should be more than just forecasting (which in Demand-Driven SCM can effectively be automated as time-phased item-level forecast accuracy has ceased to be important) and order processing. They should be more about getting visibility of extreme and exceptional demand events early enough, so that supply planning can accommodate them in their supply schedules if it is decided that they should be met. And in large global multinationals this can only be achieved through the implementation of a disciplined, empowered and policy-driven order management and communication process involving commercial, order management and the supply planning teams (and maybe even customers themselves).

The sort of demand management policies that should be considered include:

- The definition of an extreme and exceptional order. It will be different for every item and will be related to its size versus aggregate demand for that item and whether it is a regular order from that customer or a one-off. Automated order processing blocks should be considered to prevent inappropriate response to such orders.

- How early supply planning should be made aware of such orders to enable efficient response (and this may vary depending on the size of the order).

- Risk management – should the order be responded to anyway? Is it real or speculative and who placed it?

- If the order is urgent and within supply lead time, how should supply respond? (For example: incur cost through disrupting the schedules to meet the shipment date, smooth supply and ship in multiple deliveries or ship immediately and ration the remaining stock accordingly?)

In some companies this process operates entirely separately from forecasting; in others the forecast is considered a good vehicle for alerting supply to the presence of demand spikes but it means that the Demand-Driven SCM software should be able to recognize such spikes so that they can prompt the right questions and discussion regarding how such orders should be managed.

Order prioritization

As any planner knows, it is not good practice to release supply orders for which there is a shortage of materials or insufficient capacity.

Demand-Driven SCM software will alert planners to both and retain the orders on the planning board until they can be executed. The software should also prioritize the orders according to their urgency so that, for instance, the planner can hold back those that are less important if there is a capacity constraint, or allocate finite materials to those most urgently required. The prioritization is usually based upon a calculation of current stock on hand plus on order, expressed as a percentage of the combined variability and lead-time buffer with the urgency related to the level of buffer penetration. There might also be a form of colour coding, representing the degree of buffer penetration, to provide a visual alert. The urgency of any supply order that is being held will clearly change daily as inventory is consumed.

Shelf-life management

Products with shelf-life limits can pose difficulties for any replenishment process as the 'on hand' inventory quantity is usually based upon 'live stock', not whether it will be 'sellable' on the day it is consumed. Companies can therefore find themselves having to expedite a replenishment through manufacturing because it is suddenly found that yesterday's generous on-hand stock levels have almost disappeared overnight because they have either expired or customer shelf-life requirement thresholds have been breached. With the aid of modern-day Demand-Driven SCM software, it is now perfectly possible for stock on-hand quantities and their shelf lives (with an offset, as necessary, to meet customer requirements) to be evaluated against demand and the planner alerted as to the value of possible write off and the need to replenish inventory 'early' if some of it is likely to expire before it can be used.

It is to be hoped that in companies with these challenges the root cause of the problem is overly optimistic product launches and not consistently excessive batch sizes!

Ordering groups

It is not uncommon, in a manufacturing environment, for certain products to have to be co-produced. There are numerous examples such as the packing of liquids or creams, and the like, in which a base material is made in a certain batch size that is used to fill many finished products. In this situation there is often a desire to use up the entire batch to minimize the frequency of having to clean down the filling equipment or, perhaps, the material cannot be stored because of shelf-life considerations, or the need to use the holding tank for another purpose. Whatever the scenario, it is often the case that only some of the finished product items actually need to be replenished at that point in time and they will not account for the entire batch. Ordering groups are a facility that is designed to show the planner the entire portfolio of items that use the base material. They can then execute the order for those items that need replenishing and allocate the surplus across all the other items according to need (ie their stock position versus the stock target) and fully use up the material.

Container filling

Similar to ordering groups is the useful 'container filling' functionality. Transport economics often require movements of products between warehouses – or between factories and warehouses – to be in full loads, be they trunking vehicles or shipping containers. Such shipments are often planned on a regular cycle with a finite cube or weight per shipment. Good Demand-Driven SCM software will allow the planner or shipping agent, based upon each item's shipping parameters, to fill the container with the items that must be moved – plus, to fill it completely, those with the higher levels of stock target penetration or, if the container is of insufficient size, to decide whether some items can be delayed to the next cycle or should be shipped as a special. Irrespective of this container-filling functionality, one of the immense benefits of Demand-Driven SCM, in a pure distribution environment, is that – because the process results in right-sized and balanced inventories at every distribution point – the need for highly expensive emergency shipments (either from a hub or via cross-shipments) is virtually eliminated.

Monitor (but don't touch!)

Events aside, be they demand spikes or supply disruptions, correctly sized buffers combined with disciplined execution (ie orders placed on time and in the correct quantities that are supplied within lead time) will deliver planned service levels and right-sized inventories without any further intervention from planners. But, of course, things can go wrong: unexpected spike orders might be mistakenly processed and there may be significant hold-ups in supply, be it due to material delays, quality issues, machine breakdowns, etc. For this reason, Demand-Driven SCM software alerts planners to such 'flow disruptions' in the form of 'on-hand buffer' alerts. These are similar to the execution alerts discussed above, in that they use colour coding and a percentage penetration calculation, but these alerts focus purely upon the level of on-hand stock versus the variability buffer.

It is, of course, to be expected that variability buffer will be consumed in a Demand-Driven SCM environment – unlike in 'forecast push MRP' in which exception messages encourage planners to prevent its usage. But the flow alerts indicate to planners the depth of variability buffer penetration and are often set to yellow when it falls to below 100 per cent of variability buffer, and red when below 50 per cent. Planners might then wish to check whether supply is imminent, which it should be and usually is. Of course, if it is not then perhaps some fast-track expediting might be considered and/or the implementation of order management rationing.

Sometimes the supply delivery might be scheduled to arrive on time yet there is still a serious on-hand inventory alert due to the processing of an unplanned spike order. What this demonstrates is that no longer should suppliers be judged *solely* on the basis of 'on-time in full'. Instead the focus should be upon buffer maintenance and the disciplines required to ensure that they are sized correctly and replenished by suppliers that can meet agreed lead times *and* are able to respond if stock target penetration happens more quickly than expected.

Supply chain complexity, variability and smart metrics

This section describes how poorly designed supply chain metrics interact with variability (that well-known destroyer of supply chain performance) to create forms of (damaging) behaviour common to complex adaptive systems. It goes on to demonstrate how supply chain variability can be minimized and smart metrics introduced that, together, will eliminate those behaviour patterns and drive significant, sustained and predictable supply chain performance improvements.

Variability

Supply chains are really just flows of materials that, as they travel through multiple 'constraints' (eg manufacturing machines, warehouses) on their way to customers, are prone to develop into stationary queues. These queues develop not because of inadequate processing capacities (if capacity were insufficient the queues would grow without limit) but because of the impact of variability (ie unevenness of arrivals and processing-rate fluctuations such as breakdowns and changeovers – particularly unplanned changeovers such as those caused by service-saving schedule 'hotlists' and expedites). In fact, the average queue length is directly proportional to the level of variability for any given level of capacity utilization but, as that utilization increases, so the queue grows exponentially, as demonstrated in Figure 4.5.

With an understanding of supply chains and basic queuing theory it becomes possible to understand why most supply chains have significant room for improvement in terms of their service levels, inventory turn and cost-efficiency. Most ex-stock supply chains are driven by SKU-level time-phased forecasts through an MPS/MRP engine. Such forecasts, of course, are always wrong,[5] and MRP therefore blows the forecast error up the supply chain, resulting in too little or too much being supplied. The consequent generation of MRP exception messages, whenever safety stock consumption is predicted, inevitably results in schedules being changed to avoid service threats and these cause the variability that creates cost-generating buffers – time, capacity and inventory.[6] And if long time fences are used to try

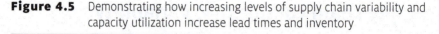

Figure 4.5   Demonstrating how increasing levels of supply chain variability and capacity utilization increase lead times and inventory

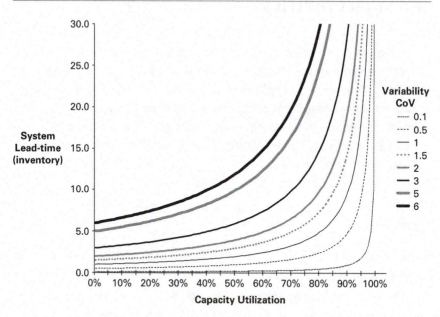

to prevent such schedule amendments then we have responsiveness degrading and inventory-rich time buffer in place instead – and still service issues occur![7]

And to make matters much worse, MRP's erroneous use of fixed lead times and dependent demand[8] propagates and amplifies any source of variability (be it demand or supply side) up and down the supply chain through the impact of batching and latency.[9]

In multistage, dependent-demand supply chains the delays caused by variability always accumulate, whereas the gains do not,[10] which explains why 'forecast push MRP' supply chains always suffer from excessive lead times (usually with a value-add ratio[11] of just around 5 per cent), excessive and unbalanced stock levels, and have to rely upon spare capacity as the means to minimize service issues.

Complexity

The propensity of supply chains to generate unplanned buffer in response to flow variability also causes them to behave like complex adaptive systems (CASs).

CASs are those that manifest chaotic or non-linear behaviour that, like the weather, makes them very difficult to predict as outcomes are subject to significant latency, often involve circular/amplifying feedback loops and are heavily dependent upon the minutiae of original conditions.[12] Unlike pure 'chaos', however, a CAS also involves the concept of 'agency' that really just translates into the fact that they are composed of many players, or groups of players, with interdependent objectives and who have the ability to internalize information, to learn, and to modify their behaviour as they adapt to changes in their environments. The upshot is that a CAS demonstrates an 'emergent' type of system behaviour that, while it can be described in general terms, cannot be accurately predicted, extrapolated from the behaviour of its component parts or in any way optimized, because any apparent linear relationships are constantly in flux. Examples of CAS can be recognized in the behaviour of an economy, an ant colony, the brain/consciousness and genes/evolution.

That supply chains are also CASs is now well documented.[13]

Examples of CAS phenomena in supply chains are:

- Virtually all supply chain managers fail to realize that the linear assumptions behind their S&OP process are utterly confounded by variability when replenishment execution using 'forecast push MPS/MRP' is undertaken. The impact of this variability is such that reality significantly diverges from the seemingly good plans that were defined and (assuming the existence of a reasonable review process) everyone ends up confused ('What really happened?!!!') and frustrated ('Why don't we get the results if everything looked good?'). And this happens month after month after month and, across industry, millions of dollars continue to be spent with consultants on trying to establish the chimera of an effective and accurate S&OP process.

- The contrast between the commonly articulated desire of supply chain participants to 'optimize' or maximize performance and the common emergent behaviour of a continuous oscillation between focus upon 'conflicting' objectives (eg service and inventory reduction) and consistently very poor performance.

- Similar to the above, the development of upstream bullwhip volatility that is a phenomenon in supply chain networks, which emerges due to delays in the arrival of materials and information: latency.[14]

Metrics

One of the most powerful causes of CAS behaviour in a supply chain is that of the interaction between supply chain managers' frequent lack of knowledge about the effect of variability on supply chain performance (ie the unplanned buffers) and the most commonly used SCM measures – including those of financial management, particularly that of generally accepted accounting principles (GAAP) financial reporting.

Some examples of how variability generates destructive CAS behaviour through traditional supply chain measures are:

- The conflict between the desire for finished product inventory reductions and high service levels that cannot be reconciled when variability is high and that therefore results in an oscillation between the two in response to the latest corporate requirements.

- The desire by procurement to achieve material price reductions that lead them to select a new supplier that then quickly demonstrates an inability to deliver against desired lead times because of their focus upon high-capacity utilization and 'sweating their assets' to achieve high efficiencies. The consequence is delayed supplies and lost throughput, which costs the customer far more than the procurement saving could ever have delivered. A new round of supplier selection then follows.

- The continuous tension between the supply chain's desire for responsiveness and low inventories and the need for operations to achieve GAAP-driven overhead/labour recoveries. The latter often results in excessively large production batches that drive up variability, inventory levels and lead times. In addition, the financial recoveries objective often causes operations to produce unnecessary, and cost-generating, inventory, simply to achieve a recoveries number that is in danger of being missed because of past production hold-ups or because demand is lower than expected. In both cases some form of inventory rebalancing action is then inevitable at a later date.

A common trait inherent with these examples, and many similar, is not that the objectives are necessarily misguided in themselves (eg high service, low inventory, low costs). But they tend to be distributed across the company with poorly designed KPIs that lead the various functions to undertake activities to achieve them, which actually conflict with each other and any overarching performance objective – such as high return on investment (ROI) – and thereby lead to overall continuous poor performance that oscillates between alternating forms of inadequacy.

For example, it is important of course that companies operate with low levels of cost, but using a backward-looking GAAP reporting measure such as recoveries is a totally inadequate way of monitoring progress on this all-important metric. It leads to completely the wrong behaviours as companies try to chase recoveries in a manner that is often decoupled from service requirements and thereby serves only to increase costs through excessive inventory building. It fails utterly to deliver lower costs because it does not recognize that assets are sunk costs and labour, in the short term, is a fixed cost.

Instead, the thought process should be:

1 Based on the aggregate forecast what capacities do we need and where?

2 Set up those capacities.

3 Respond to demand.

If overall capacity utilization is poor the reasons could be as follows:

1 Not enough product was made and service therefore suffered.

2 The forecast was grossly overstated.

3 The capacity calculations are wrong.

In each case, making product that is not required to achieve a recoveries target can only add to costs and inventories. In the first case, and assuming current labour capacity is correctly sized for current demand levels, it would of course be commercially perverse to catch up on the lost volumes using overtime (though I have seen it happen). In the second and third cases, the aggregate planning process has gone badly wrong and that is where urgent improvement activity should be focused. Making product now, just for a recoveries number, will simply incur cash-flow and inventory costs and will have to be rebalanced in the next accounting period. So unless, in the next accounting period, the right mix of demand picks up, or capacities are downsized, the recoveries 'day of reckoning' is just being expensively delayed.

The way forward

The way forward for companies that recognize they are suffering from excessive supply chain variability and these destructive aspects of CAS behaviour is threefold:

1 Ensure all supply chain leaders and employees have an understanding of how supply chain variability impacts performance,[15] how 'forecast push MPS/MRP' generates that destructive variability and how the Demand-Driven SCM approach minimizes its impact.[16]

2 Minimize supply chain variability and generate flow by becoming Demand-Driven.[16]

3 Implement 'smart metrics' that support and encourage a flow-orientated supply chain, which by its very nature delivers high service levels with right-sized inventories and high/level-loaded capacity utilization.[17]

Demand-Driven SCM

The Demand-Driven supply chain that is, in effect, 'enterprise(s)-wide pull', can be defined as:

A segmented multi-echelon supply chain execution process featuring multiple deliberately positioned and planned, but independent, inventory locations that are replenished, in an efficient and stable sequence, to a calculated stock target in line with real demand – not the forecast. (NB But forecasts <u>are</u> used for S&OP, event management (see below) and buffer sizing.)

To learn about how to operate a Demand-Driven SCM see the section 'Demand-Driven SCM: agility thru' stability' in Chapter 2; for why it works so effectively to deliver the results given below, see the section 'Why pull?' in Chapter 3.

The typical benefits, compared to 'forecast push MPS/MRP', to companies that adopt Demand-Driven SCM are:

- achievement of consistently high planned service levels;

- reductions in average inventory of 30–50 per cent;

- reduction in unplanned overtime, or increase in capacity utilization, enabling cost reductions of around 20 per cent;

- lead-time reductions of up to 85 per cent;

- without expediting or firefighting and any focus upon achieving high levels of forecast accuracy.

The reason that Demand-Driven SCM is so effective is that it enables the supply chain to flow by eliminating the forecast error-induced variability and minimizing any that is residual – thereby also minimizing the unplanned cost-generating buffers of stock, time and capacity.

Smart metrics[17]

Given that the Demand-Driven supply chain suffers minimal levels of variability, other than that generated by market demand, natural process variation and batching (all of which are adequately buffered), it is the role of SCM to further reduce variability, maximize cash-generating throughput, manage the buffers in line with demand and protect end-to-end flow. And it is essential that supply chain metrics do not themselves generate behaviours that create variability.

The authoritative smart metrics taxonomy is that provided by Debra Smith and Chad Smith in *Demand-Driven Performance using Smart Metrics* (2014), as shown in Table 4.1.[17]

Table 4.1   Summary of the six objectives for a Demand-Driven performance system

Strategic Decision making	Day to Day Operations Control	The Six Metric Objectives	Measurement Objectives & Examples
	Yes	Reliability	Consistent execution to the plan / schedule / market expectations
	Yes	Stability	Pass on as little variation as possible
	Yes	Speed/Velocity	Pass the right work on as fast as possible
Yes	Yes	System Improvement	Identify, prioritize and implement ROI improvement opportunities
Yes		Local Operating Expense	What is the minimum spend necessary to achieve the above
Yes		Strategic Contribution	Maximize throughput cash rate and volume according to relevant factors

Examples of pertinent measures that contribute to coherent supply chain system performance in line with flow and corporate objectives (ie ROI) include:

- Aggregate forecast bias for accurate capacity planning.

- Actual cycle times versus planned-for capacity planning – if they are trending up or down, appropriate capacity adjustments might be necessary.

- Actual lead times versus planned, including through 'strategic control points', for accurate buffer sizing and process control.

- Buffers penetration:

  - Frequency of supply orders being placed too early/late versus buffer penetration.

- Frequency and degree of on-hand 'variability buffer' penetration/ non-penetration.

- Frequency of stock outs with/without demand.

• Progress on continuous improvement (eg reductions in changeover times, MOQs versus average demand percentage, unplanned downtimes, quality release failures and delays, etc).

Remarkably these are the few key performance measures that are needed to ensure that the appropriate root-cause investigations and actions are taken to maintain planned service meeting flow with the correctly sized inventory buffers and consistent achievement of those recovery numbers.

The nature of a CAS and flow is such that management and control of a few critical or primary 'leverage' points is all that is necessary to successfully manage non-linear system performance. And it will be found that actions taken to deliver improvement against these measures will deliver ever-improving flow and the primary performance measures (eg service, inventory and capacity utilization/cost) will all, by definition, also continuously improve. And performance improvement can be continuous.[18] As Hopp and Spearman have said:

> Lean is fundamentally about minimizing the cost of buffering variability.[4]

And, as is clear from the taxonomy, the companies that excel in implementing continuous improvement will gain competitive advantage. Lean activities such as TPM, TQM, SMED/batch-size reduction, poke-yoke, DFM, standard work, 5S etc, in a Demand-Driven SCM environment supported by smart metrics, will reap reward in the form of further minimized inventories and improved capacity utilization (plus capex avoidance), while delighting customers and shareholders with ever-improving value and service excellence, plus the capability to adapt and respond to the ever-changing and increasingly volatile marketplace.

The organizational impact of Demand-Driven SCM

As manufacturing companies seek competitive advantage, adoption of centralized or regionalized organizational structures have become the norm across many business functions as a means to reduce costs. To a large extent this trend has been facilitated by use of integrated ERP systems that support a 'shared services' approach to, for instance, finance and human resources (HR) that significantly reduces much labour-intensive transactional activity and supports centralized decision making through faster access to relevant data (and located in the right territory, of course, these centralized organizations can be very tax efficient).

Similar approaches have also been sought in SCM but results have been disappointing. Centralization of order management and demand planning has occurred with varying levels of success, but all too frequently the supply planning activity is still disconnected, and factory-centred, despite significant expenditure upon ever more tecŸologically sophisticated and integrated software systems such as ERP and APS.

The key reason for such lack of organizational progress and, indeed, supply chain performance as a whole, is not the increasing volatility, uncertainty, complexity and ambiguity (VUCA) of the competitive business environment. It is the widespread continued use of an ineffective 'forecast push MRP' process that becomes significantly less effective in the presence of this *VUCA*, especially when supply chains become more complex, larger and more global (eg outsourcing, emerging market penetration, SKU proliferation, etc) because of the inevitable growth of forecast inaccuracy.

'Forecast push MPS/MRP' (which is the basis of nearly all ERP/APS systems used in ex-stock supply chains) actually amplifies forecast error-induced supply chain variability through its dependent demand network thereby creating increasingly high levels of cost-generating buffer (inventory, capacity, lead time). This explains why so many companies can only achieve good service levels with inexplicably high inventories, and find it impossible to sustainably reduce them (and desired operational costs) without negatively impacting service. So supply planning continues to be dispersed and largely factory-based to help operations to prioritize and cope with the volatile demands upon them.

Companies that are in the 'early adopter' phase of Demand-Driven SCM, however, are quickly having it confirmed that, even in a VUCA world, the following SCM performance improvements are possible:

1 achievement of consistently high planned service levels;

2 reductions in average inventory of up to 50 per cent;

3 reduction in unplanned overtime, or increase in capacity utilization, enabling cost reductions of around 20 per cent;

4 planning lead-time reductions of up to 85 per cent;

5 without expediting and firefighting or focus upon high levels of forecast accuracy.

(Readers not familiar with the practice, rationale and evidence for Demand-Driven SCM, or Demand-Driven Materials Requirements Planning (DDMRP), might now like to refer to the section 'Demand-Driven SCM: agility thru' stability' in Chapter 2.)

Such companies are also discovering that adoption of Demand-Driven SCM can support significantly increased levels of SCM headcount efficiency and functional regionalization/centralization. The reason for the former is, of course, elimination of the continuous non-value-add firefighting/expediting that is the main activity driver in 'forecast push' supply chain organizations (because the forecasts are all so wrong[5]) – not to mention the reduction in focus upon item-level, time-phased forecast accuracy. And the reason that genuine full SCM centralization/regionalization becomes feasible is both because of the character of the new planning and how it is facilitated through functionality-rich Demand-Driven (SaaS) systems.

The new planning

Demand-Driven SCM is effectively composed of two key, but (in contrast to forecast push MRP) decoupled, activities: planning and execution, as follows:

Planning

- *Strategic*: positioning and review of the independent inventory buffers up and down the supply chain and selection/review of the most appropriate replenishment tecŸique at an item/echelon level. Also, of course, evaluation of capacity requirements over the medium and long term.

- *Buffer sizing*: initial sizing of the planned but independent inventory buffers at each echelon using an estimate of average demand (ie a naive forecast) over the local lead time plus something for variability and rounded for MOQs.

- *Buffer maintenance*: in line with significant demand changes (trend, seasonality etc) – sometimes called 'conditioning'.

Execution

- *Replenishment*: the actual replenishment process, through work-to list generation, in the appropriate time buckets (eg daily, weekly, two-weekly etc, with/without offsets) in line with demand and including, by exception, advance builds (or MTO/ATO) for events such as significant promotions, seasonality, holiday shutdowns, etc.

- *Monitoring*: checking that materials are flowing as planned within the supply chain via on-hand inventory alerts and, by exception, expediting if there have been delays or unexpected demands that threaten service levels.

A key feature of Demand-Driven SCM is that, assuming an effective planning process, execution becomes almost autonomous requiring minimal intervention. Thus the supply planner's role switches from the typical 'forecast push MPS/MRP' focus upon execution expediting/firefighting to that of strategic planning and exceptional event management – both of which become part of a far more useful and effective S&OP process. It is this switch in focus that allows the Demand-Driven planning process to become so much more efficient because parameter change alerts and calculations/recommendations up and down the supply chain are all managed by exception. The software also supports 'what if' simulation functionality across the end-to-end supply chain allowing evaluation of multiple forecast scenarios upon inventory and capacity requirements – in line with a 'best practice' S&OP process but all too difficult to achieve with the most common current form of S&OP software – XLS!

The new SCM organization

Because Demand-Driven software is effectively a single instance, albeit linking multiple ERP instances (see the example of a global chemical company in Figure 4.6), it supports centralized and end-to-end value stream planning.

As a result, the planner can have visibility of item-level inventories and in-transits, versus target across their network and adjust parameters/monitor material flows, as necessary, across the entire value stream.

In fact, such end-to-end management is recommended because adjustments to downstream stock buffer targets should be synchronized with upstream parameter changes in order to avoid the impact of supply chain latency or bullwhip,[14] and this can be achieved best by one person with end-to-end visibility and responsibility.

Different companies adopting Demand-Driven SCM will, of course, adopt different supply chain structures depending upon the nature of their business but, in general, the greater the extent of cross-regional or global supply and demand, the greater the extent to which supply planning can be centralized – be it of demand, distribution or the factory. The latter might appear a little difficult to believe by those for whom the everyday experience is the recurrent instability of typical factory schedules, for which local 'forecast push' planners are essential to identify the continuously shifting priorities. But with Demand-Driven SCM (and its elimination of 'forecast error-induced' variability), the schedule stability and autonomous response to demand largely eliminates the need for significant localized factory planning resource.

None of this is to suggest that the planning role should become isolated. Another important consequence of Demand-Driven stability is that planners can focus far more effectively upon genuine event management, be it seasonality or abnormal demands. For this, of course, they need to maintain excellent communications with operations regarding capacity availabilities, and with demand planners/

Figure 4.6 Example of how a single-instance Demand-Driven supply chain SaaS system can be used to enable a Demand-Driven global network

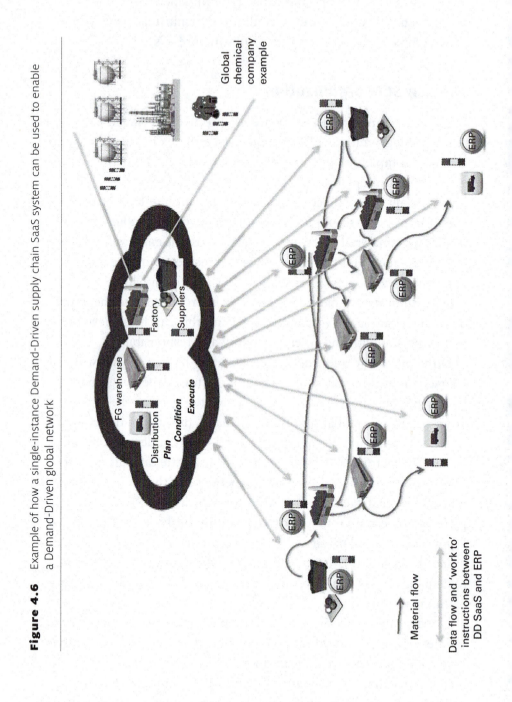

Global chemical company example

FG warehouse

Distribution

Factory

Suppliers

Plan

Condition

Execute

Material flow

Data flow and 'work to' instructions between DD SaaS and ERP

sales teams regarding the timing and the extent of such events. These events, however, are now genuine exceptions (and branded CPG manufacturers are often surprised at how little promotions planning is actually needed due to the high resilience of the Demand-Driven buffers) and their significance and impact becomes far more visible to everyone, which is very encouraging of genuinely effective internal collaboration.

And as is well known, one of the most common causes of abnormal demands upon a business is being on the receiving end of another company's bullwhip despite end-customer demand being relatively stable. This is often seen between contract manufacturers and their customers and between affiliates (eg in emerging markets) of the same company. It frequently involves an MTO replenishment process with all the detrimental impacts upon factory flow volatility that this involves. In these circumstances, the use of Demand-Driven collaboration between such trading partners can be of extremely high value. It allows the supplier to have visibility of downstream inventories versus target and thereby allows them to replace their customer's previously erratic and lumpy order pattern with something far more stable and in line with consumer demand. Figure 4.7 demonstrates such a set-up.

Figure 4.7   The application of Demand-Driven collaboration – reducing the unplanned buffers and providing two-way visibility

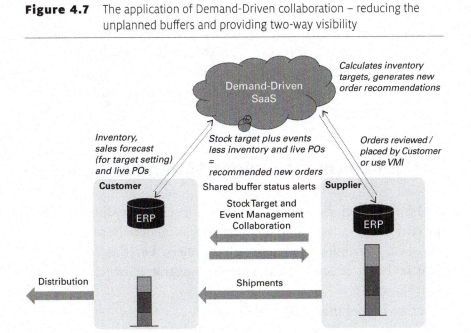

And there are significant benefits to both the customer and the supplier: inbound and outbound service excellence and responsiveness; lower levels of average inventory at both locations; smoother, more predictable demand upon factories and warehouses; shared visibility of inventories and in-transits versus target across the supply chain; and lower transactional costs due to elimination of firefighting and expediting.

Summary

As companies seek to improve competitiveness, their supply chain performance becomes increasingly important as efforts are made to reduce costs and minimize inventory levels. If supply chain variability can be reduced then both can be achieved to a significant degree and the quickest route forward is to adopt Demand-Driven SCM replenishment in place of 'forecast push MPS/MRP'. And, to adapt the words of Alfred Chandler, who famously said that 'structure follows strategy', so 'structure follows process follows strategy'. Adoption of Demand-Driven SCM, facilitated by the end-to-end visibility and functionality provided by the new wave of Demand-Driven SaaS system vendors, allows companies to stabilize their material flow (with immense service, cost and inventory benefits), significantly improve the efficiency and effectiveness of their planning processes and adopt a far higher degree of process standardization through centralization. Such systems can now be quickly and inexpensively piloted and implemented across multiple ERP instances – be they within the walls of a single company or across the extended enterprise.

Just how integrated does SCM have to be?

SCM is very much a cross-functional activity encompassing sales and marketing, operations and procurement as materials are sourced, processed, distributed and sold to customers. For this reason it is often said that effective SCM must be 'integrated' or 'end to end', even 'holistic'.

But what does this really mean?

It is certainly not an organizational aspiration as all businesses need functional expertise and, in fact, the only place where all the functions actually come together, from an organizational perspective, is the CEO's office!

And if SCM is just a cross-functional activity why is there a supply chain function at all? What do those working in SCM actually do?

Leaving aside logistics (which is arguably an operation anyway), the main role of SCM seems to be to coordinate the activities of all the other functions: to ensure that the right quantities of material are delivered on time to support the planned manufacturing schedules that deliver the right amount of product, at the right time, into distribution channels that take them to customers when and where they want them. And all this has to be achieved without the business holding 'too much' stock (especially at year end!) and using only the planned levels of available manufacturing capacity.

In order to do all of this, most ex-stock businesses generate monthly SKU-level sales forecasts that are used for:

- S&OP: planning required supply capacities, inventories, financials;
- execution: driving replenishment through DRP/MRP/APS calculations that tell purchasing, operations and logistics what quantities of what needs to be sourced/made/shipped where and when.

Of course, because all the forecasts are wrong,[5] the wrong quantities of everything are sourced, made and shipped at the wrong time to the wrong places and the supply chain function often has to spend an enormous amount of time expediting particular products through the schedules to prevent service issues occurring. This is often called 'firefighting' – is a fairly thankless task and actually costs the business significant money in the form of unplanned machine 'downtime' and emergency shipments.

To help harassed supply chain people, huge sums have been spent over the years on 'supportive' enterprise-wide IT systems with functionalities as benign as simple transactions through to forecasting/demand planning, inventory optimization, advanced planning and scheduling and, latterly, demand sensing and shaping with 'real-time' visibility and response.

To what avail?

These companies still struggle to achieve their planned service levels, have excessive and unbalanced inventories and are still looking for the 'magic' piece of software that will give them accurate forecasts in today's increasingly volatile and competitive marketplaces.

If tecŸology cannot help (and, to be fair, marginal improvement might be possible at enormous cost) then maybe better 'integration' between the functions *is* required? Maybe a more 'holistic', 'end-to-end' and 'strategic' approach to SCM **is** a necessity?

Or maybe not!

In fact, I would argue that the various functions that SCM is attempting to coordinate should focus more, not less, upon practising, and improving, their area of expertise with significantly less coordination (read interference!) from planners, expediters and schedulers!

In reality, the desired end-to-end 'integration' of the various value-add processes in the supply chain (aimed at achieving the desired service levels with lower inventories and lower costs) can best be achieved just through changing the replenishment process. And what is more, the new process allows those various functions to operate extremely effectively, in their own 'silos', with minimal interference just so long as they follow some very simple and basic 'rules'.

The 'new' process is that of the Demand-Driven SCM and understanding of its rationale and practice can be gained from reading 'Demand-Driven SCM: agility thru' stability' in Chapter 2.

The evidence that Demand-Driven SCM delivers effective 'integration' is through its performance. Typical supply chain performance improvements are:

- achievement of consistently high planned service levels;

- reductions in average inventory of 30–50 per cent;

- reduction in unplanned overtime, or increase in capacity utilization, enabling cost reductions of around 20 per cent;

- lead-time reductions of up to 85 per cent;

- without expediting and firefighting or any focus upon achieving high levels of forecast accuracy.

The reason that Demand-Driven SCM is so effective is that it supports material flow through the supply chain by eliminating forecast error-induced variability, and minimizing any that is residual – thereby also minimizing the cost-generating buffers of excessive stock, excessive lead times and use of unplanned capacity.

As was mentioned earlier, the reason that all the billions of dollars of spend on supply chain IT systems (ie ERP and APS) had no discernible impact upon business performance is that they have all been focused on supporting/optimizing the wrong supply chain replenishment process – 'forecast push MPS/MRP/APS'! No amount of so-called 'optimization' can get near the supply chain performance achievable by simply eliminating forecast error-induced variability.

And funnily enough, the Demand-Driven supply chain actually allows and encourages the value-add operations to 'do their own thing' without explicit coordination from SCM. Just so long as the various replenishment tecŸiques are operated at roughly the correct rate, sequence and cycle, to the roughly correct stock targets, the end-to-end supply chain (and that includes across business boundaries) will achieve these performance improvements with an absolute minimum of so-called 'holistic strategic integration' – or forecast error-induced interruption from well-meaning supply chain planners! In my experience, the greatest supporters of a Demand-Driven replenishment execution initiative are those who work in operations, because they immediately recognize the benefits that it will deliver for them – and their company.

Demand-Driven supply *change* management

Introduction

As increasing numbers of companies adopt Demand-Driven SCM to enable them to make a step-change improvement in their supply chain and operations performance, so we are quickly learning about the factors that contribute to a smooth and rapid implementation.

To a large extent the lessons learnt strongly validate what we already know about significant change management programmes such as Kotter's 'eight-step process for leading change' (which is based upon four decades of observation and research by one of the world's foremost academics on business and leadership)[19].

Kotter's eight steps are:

1 *Create a sense of urgency*: craft and use a significant opportunity as a means for exciting people to sign up to change in their organization.

2 *Build the guiding coalition*: assemble a group with the power and energy to lead and support a collaborative change effort.

3 *Form a strategic vision and initiatives*: shape a vision to help steer the change effort and develop strategic initiatives to achieve that vision.

4 *Enlist a volunteer army*: raise a large force of people who are ready and willing to drive change.

5 *Generate short-term wins*: consistently produce, track, evaluate and celebrate small and large accomplishments – and correlate them to results.

6 *Enable action by removing barriers:* remove obstacles to change: policies, systems or structures that pose threats to the achievement of the vision.

7 *Sustain acceleration*: use increasing credibility to change systems, structures and policies that do not align with the vision; hire, promote and develop employees who can implement the vision; reinvigorate the process with new projects, themes and volunteers.

8 *Institute change*: articulate the connections between the new behaviours and organizational success, and develop the means to ensure supportive leadership development and succession.

The challenge

There is no doubt that replacing forecast push MPS/MRP with Demand-Driven SCM is a major change in the way that a company operates its entire supply activity – from procurement through operations and distribution and, potentially, beyond into suppliers and customers.

Ironically, the change challenge is not made any easier by the fact that, although the evidence and rationale for its superiority as a replenishment execution and planning process is incontrovertible, the process itself is incredibly simple and straightforward. It is almost as if some in SCM are so used to the daily challenge and complexity of creating/amending/expediting/recutting inaccurate replenishment plans, based upon inaccurate forecasts in highly expensive software systems that they cannot accept or don't want to, and that a far easier and more successful process can be undertaken in relatively simple software that they have never heard of.

Assessing the challenge

In fact, planners at the coal face are usually very receptive to Demand-Driven SCM (as are most operations and procurement people – they love its delivery of schedule and sequence stability). It is sometimes their leaders who are more reluctant to get involved because, maybe, they have forgotten about the awful reality of daily planning, they have just led the installation of a new APS, they are frankly embarrassed that they have never heard of it (after all Demand-Driven SCM is nothing more revolutionary than multilevel reorder point/cycle or enterprise-wide pull), or they cannot visualize a future in which daily crisis management doesn't keep them fully occupied.

So, if you work in SCM and know about the Demand-Driven SCM approach but your company has just installed/is installing a new and expensive forecast push ERP/APS/optimization/demand-sensing system or your leadership is predominately reactive and/or lacking in expertise and/or there is no real desire to implement radical improvement, it is maybe best you keep quiet and, perhaps, leave (get out of the millpond) and join a more enlightened and progressive organization. Because, as that other expert on political leadership observed: 'There is nothing more difficult to take in hand, more perilous to conduct, or more uncertain in its success, than to take the lead in the introduction of a new order of things' (Nicolo Machiavelli, *The Prince*).

However, if you have some influence and a boss who is motivated to make improvements, or a new boss who wants to make an impact and, maybe your legacy IT systems are up for review or, simply, your company is facing an existential crisis that requires quick and dramatic performance improvement to overcome, then Demand-Driven SCM is something you should have every confidence in proposing.

The key enabler

Fortunately, Demand-Driven SCM is usually delivered, via SaaS so the initiative doesn't face the hurdle of a large financial investment and all the perceived risk that goes with it. And, because Demand-Driven SCM involves the decoupling of MRP's dependent demand network with independent inventory positions, it can be implemented in a piecemeal fashion across the supply chain as fast as is comfortable, in a manner that both pays for itself and attracts support and momentum as the performance improvements are actively communicated across the organization – and can convert even the most die hard of sceptics.

Approaches to change

There are effectively two organizational approaches to the implementation of Demand-Driven SCM: bottom up and top down.

Bottom up

Bottom up is the approach that has been most common up to now because Demand-Driven SCM has been a very low-profile alternative to the traditional forecast push MRP juggernaut. It has usually involved innovative mid-level SCM managers, sometimes quite surreptitiously, conducting a quantified assessment (eg comparing historical service/inventory performance with that which Demand-Driven SCM would have delivered using the same parameters: service level targets, MOQs, lead times, cycles), then trying Demand-Driven SCM via an inexpensive small-scale pilot (sometimes with software, sometimes simply via XLS) and, finally, instigation of a wider roll out.

Such an approach, when allowed to proceed, has indeed resulted in astonishing results and continued success (particularly, it has to be said, when associated with software support because the functionality is far richer, there is no risk of data/formula errors and the infrastructure is simply far more robust), but all too often they fail as some other 'bigger and better' initiative (eg a ERP/APS implementation) comes along and flattens it.

On other occasions this approach, while sustaining some level of success, often fails to deliver the full potential of Demand-Driven SCM because its implementation across the full end-to-end internal supply chain is prevented. This happens because vested interest groups are powerful enough to prevent such a mid-management-driven initiative from encroaching upon their territory – for whatever reason!

Top down

Now that Demand-Driven SCM has started to become higher profile as more people have become aware of its benefits and through the impact of the Demand Driven Institute (eg conferences, books, white papers, webinars, training courses – Certified Demand Driven Planner (CDDP), Certified Demand Driven Leader (CDDL) – see www.demanddriveninstitute.com), senior management (although the initial idea may still come from a mid-level manager) are becoming interested and supportive from the offset and helping to drive a top-down implementation. Referring back to Kotter's eight steps (above), it is clear that implementing the first four steps is far easier to meaningfully accomplish with overt support from top management than being tried by someone from a mid-level position, no matter how intelligent (both intellectually and emotionally) and determined.

And, when a top-down approach is implemented, certain critically important elements of the last three steps of the change process can be achieved:

KPIs and metrics[17]

If SCM and operations managers continue to be measured using simplistic and misleading KPIs that incentivize short-term behaviours that are contrary to supporting flow (which, by definition, always leads to desired service levels, minimized inventories and high OEEs that maximize ROI) such as backward-looking GAAP recoveries, period-end discounting and arbitrary stock-level reductions then Demand-Driven SCM will be severely undermined and its transformational performance impact diminished. So it is very important that financial and supply-side KPIs and metrics become 'flow centric' so that real flow is encouraged and the business fundamentals (service, cash flow, costs → ROI) can be allowed to benefit: only top management can undertake such changes to a company's metrics and performance management system.

Organization

There is no doubt that Demand-Driven SCM dramatically improves the efficiency of many SCM processes, not least that of planning. In addition to eliminating the time-consuming firefighting/expediting activity and management of the external XLS systems (that always proliferate around 'forecast push MRP' systems), the process also facilitates real end-to-end supply chain management because the software provides a genuine 'single instance' view of the supply chain.

For instance, the maintenance of inventory targets, which is one of Demand-Driven SCM's most important activities, is actually best accomplished if done by someone who has visibility right across the supply chain. This is because end-to-end inventory targets should be changed in an aligned manner to prevent, say, downstream targets being raised, to reflect increased demand levels without relevant upstream targets being amended, which otherwise results in latency/bullwhip as the upstream inventories get quickly emptied and then overcompensated to prevent a repetition.

Another example of the benefit of end-to-end supply chain visibility is that it becomes possible for a fully informed centralized manager to see the status of all inventory actuals versus targets, see immediately where there might be flow disruptions (eg supply delays, unexpected demand surges), make the necessary checks with the relevant people and, if necessary, advise on the best course of action.

Clearly, with centralized end-to-end supply chain visibility, transparency and management the Demand-Driven supply chain can be managed with fewer people and it is sometimes only senior management who can both visualize this and make it happen. And in doing so, of course, the application of Demand-Driven SCM becomes very embedded into the organization, as without it such an organizational structure, and its benefits, is impossible to achieve.

Possible IT obstacles

Another possible requirement for early top management involvement in the implementation of Demand-Driven SCM is that posed by the need to manage the potential adverse influence of vested interest groups that might seek to prevent its progress – either directly or via deliberate stalling. Some IT groups, and most IT suppliers, have built their existence on the back of highly complex ERP implementations, their maintenance/upgrades and 'improvement' with ever more 'sophisticated', and expensive, 'enhancements'. And then along comes Demand-Driven SCM that delivers transformational performance improvement without the need for additional 'on premises' software, and, because it is SaaS, requires negligible in-house support. Unsurprisingly, some IT teams and people can be a little less than enthusiastic about this 'new kid on the block' and, on occasion, can be downright obstructive. Top management might need to ensure that any obfuscating and empty tecŸobabble about data infrastructure compliance and 'bla bla bla' is kept in check and not allowed to interfere with the speed of its adoption and implementation. Having said that, of course, most IT leaders are very constructive and their active support and involvement will help both to validate the initiative and accelerate its progress.

Summary

The adoption of Demand-Driven SCM is one of the most important innovations that a company can undertake to transform its competitive performance, and even achieve competitive advantage – for a short time at least, before others implement it too when its absence will become a positive competitive disadvantage.

Demand-Driven SCM is, tecŸically, quite a simple process and the IT requirements are very straightforward, but it is this very simplicity that can be its Achilles heel as vested interest groups seek to put up barriers as a means to protect the 'old ways of working' – for various reasons, including fear of the future, job preservation, maintenance of influence, lack of understanding and sheer embarrassment.

The degree and speed with which your company will benefit from Demand-Driven SCM is heavily dependent upon how overtly supportive are top management and the actions they take, in addition to the words they write in mails or articulate in presentations. Demand-Driven SCM is not a complex process and it really helps if top management play their part in being involved in, and supporting, a well-managed change programme such as Kotter's eight-step process.

Notes

1 The planned safety stocks of fast-moving items are often excessive if they also have long lead times. This is because the commonly used safety stock calculation (z factor for service level x standard deviation of demand x square root of lead time) is an approximation of the actual safety stock requirement (which is calculated using the variability of demand over multiple historical lead time buckets) and its positive error grows in line with the lead time

2 The item-level average volume and CoV data can be usefully converted into a scatter graph and you can also, of course, use the data to check the veracity of the 20:80 rule in terms of item numbers and sales volumes

3 Another factor is use of forecast error to calculate safety stock, which is always far higher than actual demand variability, and therefore leads to excessive safety stock

4 Hopp and Spearman (2004) To pull or not to pull: what is the question?, *Manufacturing & Service Operations Management*, 6 (2), pp 133–48

5 When one considers that world-class portfolio mix forecast accuracy is just 80 per cent (ie 20 per cent wrong) and hiding the fact that the majority of SKUs – those with medium to small volumes and medium to high variability – will be achieving errors of 40 per cent+, it is not surprising that FG inventories tend to be severely unbalanced and prone to service threats

6 Service-saving production schedule changes cause expensive unplanned machine changeovers, schedule congestion and increased lead times with knock-on effects upon other schedules up and down the factory routings. In consequence, average lead times increase and become volatile (contrary to the DRP/MRP assumption of fixed lead times, therefore causing a further service risk) and stock becomes both excessive and unbalanced, with service issues often continuing to occur

7 Using 'forecast push MRP' planners should ignore exception messages and focus upon sizing their safety stock correctly and, of course, event management. But this will be significantly less inventory efficient than Demand-Driven SCM due to the magnitude of the forecast error

8 In any MRP environment in which there is no WIP control mechanism, the lead times will never be constant as confirmed by Little's Law (Ave. LT = Throughput/WIP) and VUT. This is one of the most critical and fundamental flaws of traditional MRP

9 Latency is when changes in the rate of downstream demand fail to be matched further upstream, leading to shortages, in the case of accelerations, of materials and the late and unexpected need for catch-up activities, which are often then exaggerated, leading to the well-known bullwhip phenomenon

10 Readers may have noticed this working on the factory floor: while there is no limit to how far you can fall behind schedule (despite the attentions of your manager!), you are limited in how far you can get ahead by the availability of upstream supply. It also explains why railway operators are often reluctant to hold trains for late connections as they know such delays accumulate across the network

11 Perfect flow is achieved when value-add time/lead time = 100 per cent

12 Often known as the 'butterfly effect'

13 See for instance: Choi *et al* (2001) Supply networks and complex adaptive systems: control versus emergence, *Journal of Operations Management*, **19** (3), pp 351–66; and C Wycisk, B Mckelvey and M Hülsmann (2008) Smart parts – supply networks as complex adaptive systems: analysis and implications, *International Journal of Physical Distribution and Logistics Management*, **38** (2), pp 108–25

14 HL Lee, V Padmanabham and S Whang (1997) The bullwhip effect in supply chains, *Sloan Management Review*, **38** (3), pp 93–102

15 ES Pound, JH Bell and ML Spearman (2014) *Factory Physics for Managers*, McGraw Hill, New York; WJ Hopp (2013) *Supply Chain Physics*, McGraw Hill, New York

16 C Ptak and C Smith (2016) *Demand Driven Material Requirements Planning*, Industrial Press, Connecticut

17 D Smith and C Smith (2014) *Demand-Driven Performance Using Smart Metrics*, McGraw Hill, New York. This book also provides an excellent summary of CAS and how it applies to supply chains

18 It is important to note that a CAS, even one with minimized variability and subject to 'smart' management, cannot be optimized in a static sense, as some software providers seek to misleadingly suggest. A CAS can only respond, improve and adapt to its dynamic environment

19 JP Kotter (2012) *Leading Change,* Harvard Business Review Press, Boston

Demand-Driven SCM and Lean

05

Some reassurance and some counter-intuitive facts

Demand-Driven SCM is essentially enterprise-wide pull and, therefore, effectively part of the Lean tool set. A key difference between the traditional approach to Lean pull, which uses visual management systems on a factory floor such as kanbans, and Demand-Driven SCM is that the latter is supported by software. This enables the pull process to be operated across complex networks and seamlessly with legacy transaction systems, both for supporting planning decisions (eg S&OP and buffer sizing) and execution (eg works orders, purchase orders and transport orders).

Of particular importance is that, because such systems use transaction data, the replenishment orders can respect forms of inventory consumption that visual systems do not recognize. Examples include overdue customer orders and large future orders, both of which can otherwise undermine the effectiveness of a visual management pull system. Using a visual replenishment system, in these circumstances, can lead to delayed supply orders and subsequent service issues. Use of Demand-Driven SCM software support, therefore, allows businesses to operate pull replenishment execution successfully across complex and relatively volatile demand environments (whereas visual systems can only work effectively in relatively simple, stable demand environments upstream of a TPS/heijunka-style level schedule) and to plan their resources effectively through S&OP – with a forecast.

Being part of the Lean tool set might, in the mind of some operations people struggling to achieve overhead/labour recovery targets, cause concern that Demand-Driven SCM requires batch sizes to be reduced. This is emphatically untrue. Demand-Driven SCM simply changes the replenishment signal from that which is wrong (ie the forecast) to that which is correct (ie demand). This ensures that production capacity is used to make what will sell, instead of wasting capacity making the wrong stuff at the wrong time in the wrong quantities and running production cycles and sequences in a sub-optimal pattern, with unplanned service-saving schedule amendments and changeovers. In fact, implementation of Demand-Driven SCM actually increases OEEs by stabilizing production cycles, eliminating the unplanned downtime and allowing operations to focus upon improving productivity. Productivity increases of up to 30 per cent have been recorded by companies that stabilize production in this way. Thus Demand-Driven SCM allows companies to use their capacity more effectively, reduce their inventories, maximize service levels and sales and, thereby, improve ROI – and achieve their recoveries!

Another misapprehension about 'pull' or Demand-Driven SCM is that it requires very flexible production machinery that can be used for multiple products with quick changeovers and is not, therefore, appropriate where high-speed production facilities are in use. Again, this is emphatically not the case. Demand-Driven SCM simply ensures that such high-speed productive capacity is used to its best advantage by making product that will sell quickly instead of making stock that won't, and maximizes its up-time by preventing the need for service-saving schedule interruptions.

In summary, Demand-Driven SCM does not require batch-size reduction or highly flexible manufacturing resource. It is about ensuring that the production capacity available is used more effectively by ensuring that it is used to make the right product at the right time in a stable, predictive and efficient manner so that levels of productivity can rise. As a consequence, inventories fall, service levels rise, OEEs increase and unplanned service-retrieving overtime is eliminated. These improvements can be profound – sometimes companies find that their inventory position, before switching to Demand-Driven

SCM, is such that very little production is required for a short time while the excess inventories are rebalanced. And other companies find that they actually have far more capacity available than required to maintain planned service levels when using Demand-Driven SCM, in contrast to when they were using 'forecast push MPS/MRP'.

It is the case, however, that if excessively large batch sizes (ie relative to average demand) can be reduced in size (without losing required productive capacity) supply chain performance *will* improve: lead times will be reduced, average inventory levels will fall and capacity utilization *can* actually rise. Similarly, the acquisition of expensive super-fast production machinery, as a means to achieve low costs, can be very misguided unless the relevant product portfolio is appropriate in terms of demand volumes and stability.

The following discusses why and how smaller batches and less high-speed production machinery can sometimes deliver lower costs and better supply chain performance.

Can smaller batches reduce costs? Yes – really!

The use of SMED to justify the reduction of batch size was possibly one of the true original innovations that came from Lean. After all, haven't activities such as waste reduction always been with us, in one name or another, as part of basic cost management?

Surely, however, smaller batches can only be contemplated if the potential lost throughput, due to the more frequent changeovers, is balanced by those changeovers being proportionately quicker? And, of course, the answer is 'yes' – if production output is reduced by an increase in changeover frequency then service issues may result and costs increase as asset and labour costs are spread over a smaller volume.

But why bother at all to reduce excessive batch sizes? After all, don't bigger batches mean less lost capacity through those changeovers and, therefore, lower costs?

Actually that is wrong, but to appreciate why we need to understand something about what really drives costs in factories and supply chains.

Factory Physics

At the heart of Hopp and Spearman's 1996 book *Factory Physics* are two fundamental equations that explain the cost behaviour of factories and supply chains.

One is the VUT equation, a simplified version of which is:

Average time in **Queue** = Variability x 1/(1 – capacity **Utilization**)
x average processing **Time**

This tells us, effectively, that queue length at a constraint (such as at a work centre) is proportional to the flow variability at the constraint (ie variability of both the timings of arrivals – eg batches – and the constraint's rate of processing) but is exponentially related to the level of capacity utilization – especially when utilization or variability is high.

The other equation is Little's Law:

Average System Inventory = System Lead Time
x System Throughput

This simply tells us what we already know: that inventory levels are directly related to lead time.

So, variability in supply chains causes queues and longer lead times; longer lead times represent stock, and the higher the capacity utilization the longer will be the queues and the queue length will increase exponentially as utilization rises. Conversely, of course, queues and stock can be minimized by reducing variability or increasing capacity. We have all experienced queues that behave in this way when waiting for service at supermarket counters and in high-density motorway traffic at rush hour when queues seem to appear out of nowhere for no apparent reason (they are caused by the inability of drivers to all drive at exactly the same high speed, and unexpected speed-adjustment braking cascades back into queues – it doesn't happen if traffic is light or moving more slowly, aka: low-capacity utilization).

Cost generators

We all understand that inventory is a cost driver in the sense that it represents tied-up cash and requires space to hold it – let alone all the risks associated with holding stock such as deterioration, shelf-life expiry, damage, etc.

And, in a sense, we can grasp the fact that long lead times are a form of cost in that they represent inventory (through Little's Law) and poor responsiveness, and cause service issues/lost sales when they fluctuate wildly in line with load when capacity utilization is high – MRP assumes that lead times are stable. And in an MTO businesses, of course, lead-time length can be an order winner – or loser.

We also know that high-capacity utilization is good as it spreads fixed and labour costs across more output, thereby lowering unit allocation. It is this form of cost reduction that tends to really interest finance and operations people and, as will be explained (in the section below: How smaller batches increase capacity utilization!), smaller batches can reduce these costs as well.

To summarize: variability creates queue time and inventory, the levels of which can only be ameliorated through reducing that variability or using expensive spare capacity. Let's call queue time, inventory and capacity 'unplanned buffers' created by variability and recognize that they all generate cost.

Another way of recognizing how costs are associated with variability is to consider its opposite: flow. Perfect flow, in a supply chain context, is when material moves non-stop through value-add processes to the customer. Any stopping (ie as stock) is a symptom of flow variability and is caused by flow constraints – sometimes planned such as finished goods, but often not (eg stock queuing up to be processed). Clearly, if the constraint is 100 per cent the queue grows without limit but most queues don't, they are finite in average length and are caused, as we saw from the VUT equation, by flow variability at the constraint.[1]

The relationship between flow and cost is demonstrated simply as follows, and perfect flow is when the PCE is 100 per cent:

Process Cycle Efficiency = Value Add Time/Lead Time per cent

Few companies find, when they do this sort of an analysis as part of a value stream mapping exercise, that their PCE exceeds 5 per cent!

The impact of flexibility

Materials that have 100 per cent flexibility, such as water, can obviously be blocked from flowing and a queue created – think of a dam blocking a river and causing a lake.

But with rapids, a form of partial constraint in the path of a river, the water will simply run around the rocks and no upstream queue will be created.

Similarly, imagine a narrow street with cars parked alternately on either side. A small car will definitely slow down a little but will not have much difficulty weaving its way through the constraint. But a large lorry will find it extremely difficult, though maybe not impossible, to negotiate its way through and will do so very slowly – thereby causing quite a queue of waiting traffic behind it on busy days (ie when there is high-capacity utilization).

The lesson of these two examples, of course, is that small batches pass through supply chain constraints more easily and quickly than big batches, thereby causing less delay upstream.

In other words, bigger batches cause more variability than smaller batches and, therefore, create greater cost-generating buffers. Smaller batches are better than big batches, given no consequent losses in throughput capacity, as they allow the supply chain to be more responsive, hold less inventory and they actually enable higher levels of capacity utilization.

How smaller batches increase capacity utilization!

The last six words of the above section might appear somewhat surprising but it's true...

Excessively big batches on shared work centres mean that it takes far longer to make the portfolio sequenced through the production line. A bizarre consequence is that the factory often ends up using scarce capacity to make stock which is not needed in order to save time on changeovers to make the products they really do need, which of course they will often end up doing anyway, in an unplanned manner, due to chasing consequent service failures.

So factories with smaller batches prove to be more responsive/inventory efficient *and* have lower costs (or higher overhead/labour recovery) than those with unnecessarily big batches because, though they may *plan* to use more capacity on changeovers, they actually use less because they don't have all the *unplanned* service-saving changeovers.

And supply chains that are driven by forecasts suffer this unwanted 'real' cost from big batches with even greater severity because their schedules have to be changed with particularly high frequency. This is because, inevitably, inaccurate forecasts lead to the building of unbalanced stocks, service risks and, therefore, much expediting/schedule changing as planners respond to exception messages to prevent service issues.

The responsive, low-inventory, low-cost supply chain

Putting it all together should now be clear. Supply chains with low levels of variability and high levels of flexibility will have minimal cost-generating buffers (ie time, inventory, capacity) and will therefore be responsive with low costs and low inventory levels. Companies that adopt Demand-Driven SCM find that their effective capacity and service levels rise as lead times and average inventories fall. And if they reduce excessively sized batches, further improvements will accrue.

The key contributors to variability, and how to address them, in most supply chains today are:

1 Driving replenishment execution with inaccurate forecasts that cause schedules to be frequently changed to prevent service issues. This increases lead times, wastes capacity and causes excessive inventory levels to develop. Demand-Driven SCM eliminates this source of variability.

2 Excessively large batches, relative to demand, that increase lead times and average inventory levels and lead to more frequent unplanned service-saving, capacity-wasting changeovers. Very often a simple revisit, analysis and rebalancing of batch sizes versus demand, will enable a reduction in inventories and in unplanned lost capacities. A focus upon changeover speed will enable further such improvements by enabling smaller batch sizes without loss of capacity.

3 Losses in productive capacity due to supply variability, quality failures or machine breakdowns should be addressed through such Lean tools as standard work, poke-yoke, TQM and TPM.

High-speed machines – do they always pay?

I once joined a company that had, not that recently, installed what they called 'the high-speed machine' (HSM) – and very proud of it they were too. Senior management took great pride in showing it to visitors, telling them it was the fastest such machine in the world.

On the shop floor, however, it was regarded as a joke. The assumptions justifying its acquisition, such as average run speed and up-time, had nowhere near been achieved. Changeovers took hours, if not days, due to the sensitivity of the machine to set-up accuracy and the high, and growing, number of relatively low-volume SKUs run through it ensured it was unproductive far more than it actually ran. And the fact that the headcount needed to run the HSM was less than the machines it had replaced paled into insignificance compared to the level of lost sales and the high costs of the various engineers who spent their working hours dedicated to helping it run. It was only after around seven years, and some tender loving care from extraordinary, but overworked, operations professionals, that the HSM started to run in anything like the manner that had been intended.

Of course, the story of the HSM is not typical of all companies and their acquisition of 'better' manufacturing machinery. It does demonstrate, however, many of the issues that need honest appraisal before such investments are made. But let's assume a high-quality investment appraisal is made and a 'super-fast' machine is projected to genuinely deliver the labour cost savings necessary to justify its acquisition – has anything been missed?

Before addressing this question, let's ask what 'super-fast' in this context actually means. If a number of 'manned' machines, all making a standard product, are to be replaced by one machine that has equivalent, or superior, output with less labour content, then subject to the lessons learnt from the HSM above (and the discounted cash-flow criteria, etc, have been met), the investment should go ahead. But if many different products are to be run on the machine, they require complex, time-consuming changeovers, the market is fragmenting and more variants are expected, then the issue may not be so straightforward.

The problem with funnelling a large range of products through a single machine is, obviously, the fact that more time will be devoted to changeovers. And, inevitably, the various different WIPs will queue up while waiting to be processed. This means that the rate at which each WIP is processed on the machine has to be far in excess of their demand rate in order to allow the others to be processed before their turn comes around again – and the smaller the volumes sold of particular SKUs the greater will be the excess of the batch size necessary to justify the machine's changeover time. So the upshot is higher levels of WIP, excessively large batch sizes and longer queue/lead times.

Does this matter if the labour cost content has diminished significantly? Clearly the real cost of holding inventory also needs to be considered, as does the cost of losing responsiveness: in an ex-stock supply chain, for instance, the bigger the batches and the longer the lead times the more likely it is that schedules will have to be interrupted to prevent service issues. This firefighting and expediting is, of course, in the form of unplanned downtimes, extremely expensive on 'super-fast' machines. And if the machine is highly utilized (and if not why not? after all it cost a fortune!) the repercussions are significant.

The key point is that supply chain variability, of which excessively big batches are an example, destroys flow. This is important because perfect flow is when supply chains are operating at their most efficient:

Perfect Flow = Value-Add Time/Lead time = 100 per cent

And when one considers that most supply chains operate at below 5 per cent it is clear that there is enormous scope for improvement.

So, before buying a new high-cost 'super-fast' manufacturing machine, ensure that all your assumptions about the impact of the learning curve upon its planned run speed and changeover time are realistic, that you have factored in the additional inventory costs accurately (eg space, cash flow, shelf-life obsolescence, etc) and that you are properly considering the impact of any variability you may be introducing into your supply chain – now and in the future.

Some key questions to consider are:

1 Where in their life cycle are the products to be made on the new machine? As products mature, competition increases and markets fragment: are more and more low-volume products going to have to be squeezed onto the machine, to justify its acquisition, while the big fast sellers decline? And what are the downtime implications of such a trend?

2 Is the product going to be launched into emerging markets? Demand from such markets tends to be extremely volatile/difficult to predict and highly utilized inflexible machines may not be appropriate.

3 How highly capacity utilized does the machine have to be and how realistic is the assumption given the levels of supply and demand variability in the form of maintenance and changeover frequency/complexity?

It is a fact that Toyota refers to 'super-fast' machines as 'Monuments', and when one appreciates that Lean is 'fundamentally about minimizing the cost of variability'[1] it is unsurprising. However, a great deal of variability can be removed from supply chains by adopting Demand-Driven SCM in place of the forecast push MPS/MRP process. Demand-Driven SCM ensures that products are replenished at the right time, thereby allowing achievement of planned service levels. For this reason, even with excessively large batches (due perhaps to the existence of a 'super-fast' machine), unplanned capacity wasting schedule interruptions are far less likely.

Note

1 Hopp and Spearman (2004) To pull or not to pull: what is the question?, *Manufacturing & Service Operations Management*, 6 (2), pp 133–48

Why aren't we already using Demand-Driven SCM?

06

In the beginning there was simple reorder point and reorder cycle

Those with long memories and who worked in SCM (or, as it might have been called, supply management or production planning or production control) before the proliferation of computers in business, will remember how replenishment was managed. In one form or another, manual systems were used to keep a track of inventory levels and to trigger their required replenishment using very simple reorder point systems. There would be such a system for finished goods, perhaps a visual system for factory sub-assemblies (eg when the racking is half-full, make some more) and another manual reorder-point process for raw materials.

Calculating safety stocks and reorder points in those days tended to be very 'rule of thumb' because it was so difficult to collate the necessary data and process it appropriately – let alone keep it regularly reviewed. In those days the replenishment occurred when the level of stock in the warehouse reached the reorder point – there was rarely any desire to have multiple outstanding supply orders and incorporate them into the process. As a result inventory levels were high but, because the focus was upon service, and cash flow tended not to be the concern that it is today, this was not considered a major problem.

And back in the early 1970s manufacturing was very different to today. Many companies sourced materials and components locally, at least within their own national boundaries, so lead times were relatively short. They sold their products locally too and their product range was quite narrow compared to that which is typical today. As a result, demand per item was far higher than in today's world of rampant SKU proliferation and, as we have learnt from the central limit theorem, it was therefore relatively stable and predictable. In consequence, manufacturing companies could, and would, manufacture product in reasonably predictable cycles (which, of course, helps stabilize requirements for materials and components) with, in the absence of major cash-flow pressure, lots of inventory around the place, which ensured that production capacity could always be used to make something, and service levels were adequate.

The supply chain performance achieved back in the 1970s would not possibly satisfy today's aspirations, but back then the tecŸology available (manual records, log tables and slide rules!) was not adequate to even properly measure performance (except at a very aggregated level) let alone support anything significantly more detailed and sophisticated.

The MRP Crusade[1]

The first experiments with materials requirements planning (MRP) began in the 1950s, and the first commercially developed system was written by Dick Ling in 1961 for the Wilmot Castle Company. It had 12kb of memory and four tape drives and it was simply called 'requirements planning'. In the early to mid-1970s its adoption by manufacturing companies really began in earnest. This was the culmination of a highly intensive and effective promotional offensive in the United States by Joseph Orlicky and others (eg Dick Ling, Oliver Wight and George Plossl) to persuade industry to adopt the data-processing power and calculating logic of the computer to displace conventional reorder point and reorder cycle. Orlicky had worked for IBM between 1965 and 1968 and in 1975 published *Materials Requirements Planning*, in which he pointed out that, given a large number of components required to assemble a finished product, the likelihood is quite high, if using an old-style stock reorder process, of at least one item being out of stock when required and thereby preventing production.[2]

More formally this can be put as follows: if the service level for each item is 99 per cent and there are 10 such components, the likelihood of production being delayed is $1 - (0.99$ to the power of $10) = 9.6$ per cent.

Orlicky therefore proposed that manufacturers should, and now could, exactly 'plan requirements for materials' by exploding a master production schedule (MPS) through its bill of materials (BOM) and order in the netted quantities (ie net of any that remain from earlier deliveries) of the materials when they are required using a lead-time offset.

The term 'MRP Crusade' is commonly used to describe how, over the 15 years subsequent to around 1970, the ideas and practice of MRP were promoted to US companies, largely through the American Production and Inventory Control Society (APICS). This was substantiated by the academic community showing an interest in what was a significantly new way of working, such as, in 1973, MRP's first appearance in college text books: *Operations Management: A systems model management approach*, by Thomas Vollman,[3] and in the UK, *Requirements Planning*, by Colin New.[4] This academic interest was no coincidence: Orlicky, Wight and Plossl focused a great deal of effort on encouraging the academic world to investigate MRP and evaluate its benefits versus traditional methodologies. They went as far as positioning MRP as having a potentially similar impact on ways of thinking in the operations community as Copernicus had had in the 15th century on people's view of the universe and the earth's place in it!

As the 1970s merged into the 1980s MRPII arrived – it was a significant step away from materials requirements planning as the acronym stood for 'manufacturing resource planning', a term coined by Oliver Wight in 1979. With the advent, and greater sophistication, of standardized software applications, came rigorous implementation 'best practices' such as the 'proven path': an Oliver Wight template that ranked implementations on a scale from A to D and provided appropriate support and guidelines.

A key difference between MRP and MRPII is that the latter was designed to allow users to use aggregated forecasts to plan future capacity requirements. And the way that these early MRPII systems were used was that the individual item-level time-phased forecasts, with appropriate adjustment for actual orders (called forecast consumption), were also used to drive replenishment through the various stages of production (or routings) and out to the material requirements.

As we know, MRPII was later merged into other IT-enabled company activities such as customer order management, purchasing transactions, finance, distribution, warehousing, etc, and this was called enterprise resource planning.

So today, and helped along by fears about the ability of early-legacy computer systems to survive the year 2000 (or Y2K as it was known), MRPII can now be found, in one form or another, in most manufacturing and distribution companies. The form might be an old-style pure MRPII system, ERP or some other form of advanced planning system that purports to optimize the replenishment schedules around certain constraints (eg capacity bottlenecks) according to certain cost, service and/or revenue criteria. And if companies are not using a formalized MRPII-type software they can usually be found trying to replicate the functionality using some form of spreadsheet system. A key characteristic of all of these systems is the fact that they use the same set of forecast numbers to both plan capacities and, in the short term, to drive item-level replenishment execution.

1961: Forrester, Burbidge, Little, Kingman and bullwhip

At the same time as MRP was being coded, conceived and commercialized during the 1950s, 1960s and 1970s/1980s respectively, there were voices in the 'academic wilderness' who were developing the tools that are now being used to explain why the MRP Crusade turned out to be such a mistake.

Jay Forrester and bullwhip

Nowadays all students of supply chain learn something about the 'bullwhip effect' – the phenomenon in which a small change on downstream demand levels amplifies into a far larger level of variability upstream. Sometimes known simply as 'demand amplification' it was first written about by Professor Jay Forrester of the Michigan Institute of TecŸology (MIT) in a 1958 article in the *Harvard Business Review* and his book *Industrial Dynamics* in 1961.[5] Through computer simulations of simple decision-making rules Forrester was able to demonstrate, and explain in behavioural terms, why and how upstream suppliers tend to suffer far greater levels of demand variability than is apparent downstream, thereby explaining why upstream inventory levels tend to fluctuate wildly, good service is difficult to achieve and capacity availability similarly swings between insufficient and excessive.

Forrester went on to apply his findings in other areas of the social sciences such as business and economic cycles, and is regarded as one of the founders of 'systems theory', which is the study of the non-linear behaviour of complex systems, over time, involving feedback loops, adaptive behaviour, bounded rationality and time delays. Since Forrester's early work on this aspect of supply chain dynamics the MIT, amongst others, have continued to investigate the phenomenon and many supply chain students and managers will have heard of, and probably played, the Beer Game that was developed by MIT's Professor JoŸ Sterman.

Professor Hau Lee from Stanford University popularized the term 'bullwhip' in the 1990s in a *Sloan Management Review* article,[6] in which he explained the increasing variability of orders, as they cascade up the supply chain from the relative stability of consumer demand (he used the example of babies nappies/diapers), in terms of:

1 Demand forecast updating: each echelon within the supply chain generates its own forecasts of future demand based upon recent orders but, when demand changes, there is a propensity for orders to exaggerate the trend as they contain an element for covering both demand and, often, a revised safety stock level. These exaggerated orders amplify as they propagate upstream.

2 Order batching: due to the desire to maximize utilization of transport and production capacity, companies tend to batch their orders into minimum order quantities and, thereby, order relatively infrequently. The consequence is that the orders fluctuate quite considerably due to the size of the batches, which tend to also increase up the supply chain, thereby exaggerating the swings in upstream forecasts and subsequent supply chain activity.

3 Price fluctuations: anticipated price changes and promotions encourage buying companies to fluctuate their purchase quantities to avoid, or take advantage, of them. This demand variability can, again, be misinterpreted and exaggerated upstream through the forecasting process.

4 Rationing and shortage gaming: this occurs when upstream short-term capacity constraints are anticipated, which lead to suppliers rationing supplies to their customers. In response, or in advance, customers attempt to circumnavigate the restrictions by exaggerating their orders, which feeds into upstream demand forecasts, leading to capacity and supply increase decisions that turn out to be far in excess of what is really required.

Jack Burbidge

In the UK, in the same year that Forrester's *Industrial Dynamics* was published, 1961, Jack Burbidge, then an industrial engineering and management consultant (after working for many years in various engineering company production roles) published 'The new approach to production', which he started with these words:[7]

> To production historians of the future, the 20th century will be known as the 'Age of Waste'. An age when much of the wealth invested in production was stored away unused in the form of stock; an age when a large part of the labour force was wasted on the unproductive processing of administrative paperwork; and an age in which most of the production capacity was left unused for long periods, due to our failure to control the demand cycle.

In that paper Burbidge advocates what he calls 'high batch frequency line flow' for all types of product and for all levels of output (effectively heijunka-style level schedule) and goes on to justify the approach by explaining how traditional 'economic batch quantity' decision making through the various machines in a factory causes underutilization of capacity, and excessive and unbalanced stocks through the impact of consequent material flow phasing and dynamics:

> The adoption of single-phase, high-batch frequency line flow can reduce stock and capital tie-up; release factory floor area; reduce data processing; reduce total cost; simplify and increase the flexibility of control; and, finally, by smoothing the demand variation, can increase effective capacity and output.

He explains how it can be achieved through:

1 The line flow system: whereby all the components made on a multiprocess factory floor are classified into families of similar parts so that they can each be made by similar operations in the same sequence on the same plant.

2 Plant layout: the various manufacturing machines should be laid out, not in functional groups, but in the sequence dictated by the standard process layout for each 'family'. And components should, as far as possible, be standardized to enable a minimum number of such families.

3 Tooling: every machine should be equipped with jigs and tools, preferably through inexpensive adjustable tooling, so that all the components in the family can be easily processed consecutively.

4 Machine set-ups: should be designed and practised so that change downtime can be measured in minutes, not hours, to facilitate the desired high frequency batch flow without losing capacity.

5 The demand cycle: high-frequency material flow should be matched by high-frequency demand or order flow: companies should avoid batching orders but should pass on customer orders as quickly as feasible: 'The final demand at the consumer level is generally a high-frequency demand, calling for single items rather than batches. Any reduction in this frequency of order issue, by

accumulation into large batches, tends to multiply the demand variation. The ideal system for minimum demand variation would be one in which each sale to a customer caused an equivalent order to be issued to all production units in the flow system.'

Readers familiar with the principles of Lean manufacturing will recognize that many of its attributes are exactly those being recommended by Burbidge, and the fifth point is a very succinct description and rationale for 'pull'.

Burbidge describes the benefits of the 'new production' in both hard operational performance terms (eg lower costs, lower inventories and better service) and he also mentions very relevant qualitative benefits such as operator satisfaction, higher morale levels and data-processing simplicity due to the repetitive and predictable batch cycles through the line-flow layout.

In 1984 Burbidge, by that time a professor at Cranfield University in the UK, published another short and, in academic circles, famous paper called 'Five golden rules to avoid bankruptcy',[8] which starts:

In recent years there has been a number of engineering company failures in Britain, for which the trade unions, high interest rates, the high (or low) value of the pound, or Mrs Thatcher could not reasonably be blamed. These were 'crashes', which can only be listed under 'pilot error'.

They were liquidity failures caused by an excessive and avoidable investment in stocks and work-in-progress, financed in many cases by borrowing at very high rates of interest. It was obvious that some boards of directors had no idea how to reduce stocks, or how to design a production system that could then operate efficiently at high rates of stock turnover.

The five golden rules, which are a summarized form of his 1961 'New production' paper, are:

1 Only make products that you can quickly despatch and invoice to customers.

2 Only make in this period those components you need for assembly in the next period.

3 Minimize the material throughput time.

4 Use the shortest planning period (ie smallest run quantity) that you can manage efficiently.

5 Only take deliveries from suppliers in small batches, when they are needed for processing or assembly.

Burbidge explicitly advises readers not to use MRP as it: 'generates excessive stocks because it is based on sales forecasts for long periods into the future, which are always inaccurate' and:

> There is no possible way of avoiding the fact that production based on long-term sales forecasts with large run quantities and long throughput times inevitably causes a heavy investment in stocks and work-in-progress.

He goes on to provide evidence for the veracity of what he is recommending by saying:

> The best proof that it is profitable to operate at high rates of stock turnover can be found in Japan. The average rate of stock turnover in Britain is two times per year. In the United States it is between three and four times per year. In Japan it is over eight times per year. We have no company in the engineering industry in Britain that comes anywhere near Toyota, which turns its stocks over 72 times per year!
>
> Two of the main reasons the Japanese can make products, ship them half-way around the world, pay our customs duties and still sell at lower prices than we can make the products, are firstly that most of their capital is invested in plant and methods of improvement, and secondly they do not suffer the very heavy costs of holding high stocks and work-in- progress.

John Little

Also in 1961, the same year as Burbidge's 'New production' paper and Forrester's publication of *Industrial Dynamics*, JoŸ Little mathematically proved the law that is named after him:[9]

> Little's Law: Average Lead-time = Average Inventory in System/
> Average Throughput

The law might seem intuitively obvious but Little was able to prove that there was no possible situation (eg any throughput pattern) for which the relationship did not hold.

Little's Law is used in SCM to demonstrate the 'obvious' relationship between the level of inventory in production and the length of time it will take for newly manufactured product to pass through the supply pipeline and into the warehouse (ie the supply lead time). It clearly tells us that the greater the level of 'work in progress' the longer that lead time will inevitably be. It also tells us, of course, that speed of cash-flow throughput from when materials are purchased to when they are sold as finished goods is similarly related to the amount of inventory on order, in WIP and in the finished goods warehouse(s).

John Kingman

The lesson from Little's Law is that shorter, more responsive lead times can be achieved by increasing the rate of throughput relative to system inventory. How can companies do it? The answer, also provided in 1961, came from a mathematician with an interest in queuing theory, a discipline within probability theory. JoŸ Kingman derived the equation, named after him, which tells us that in a system with a single processing constraint and an arbitrary, but different, distribution of both arrival times and process times, the average waiting time in the consequent queue is directly related to the average processing time and the level of variability of arrivals and processing times, and is exponentially related to the level of the constraint's capacity utilization.[10] Although the formula is an approximation, it is known to be generally very accurate, especially at higher levels of capacity utilization.

Kingman's formula tells us that, in factories and supply chains, if we wish to increase throughput, shorten lead times and reduce stock levels we have two choices. We can either put on more capacity (which is intuitively obvious and expensive) or reduce the level of variability, which tends not to be obvious and is perhaps difficult to accomplish. Actually, however, it is not too difficult and most companies have been doing it for many years – it is called Lean.

During the 1950s and 1960s, while MRP was in the early stages of its development in the United States, in Japan the Toyota Production System was well on its way to being developed. It was brought to the attention of the West in the early 1980s when MRP was being commercialized. At around the same time, Eli Goldratt was developing another very influential and valuable approach that became known as the Theory of Constraints (ToC) and then, in the mid 1990s, Wallace Hopp and Mark Spearman published *Factory Physics*, which was able to explain, using fundamental principles, the behaviour of supply chains and factories and why some replenishment tecŸiques, such as Lean and ToC, work very effectively and forecast-driven MPS/MRP execution doesn't.

Lean, Theory of Constraints and Factory Physics

Lean

One of the first books to describe what we now know as Lean was Richard Schonberger's *Japanese Manufacturing TecŸiques: Nine hidden lessons in simplicity*, first published in 1982.[11] Schonberger described the heart of Japanese manufacturing success as being 'just in time' (JIT) production and 'total quality control'. He introduced readers to the concepts of mura, muri and muda (unevenness, excess and waste), described the use of kanban cards for facilitating JIT or 'pull' and revealed the extent to which factory-floor operatives were trained and empowered to contribute ideas on how to improve processes and ways of working. In subsequent years of that decade English translations of books by the Toyota Production System pathbreakers such as Shigeo Shingo[12] and Taiichi OŸo[13] arrived in the West.

Then, in 1990, the world was introduced to the word 'Lean' in *The Machine that Changed the World*, by Womack, Jones and Roos,[14] a book that comprehensively and rigorously described how the Toyota Production System operated, and contrasted its performance with automobile manufacturing practices in other parts of the world – mainly Germany and the United States. Later, in the 1990s, Womack and Jones further published *Lean Thinking: Banish waste and create wealth in your corporation*,[15] in which they identified the five key attributes of Lean as being:

1 Identify and specify what the customer values.

2 Configure and design the appropriate value-adding stream.

3 Configure the value stream to flow.

4 Use pull to drive the rate of flow.

5 Continuous improvement – empower and motivate those who are adding value to continuously improve their processes and techniques in support of flow.

Ironically, the Japanese had learnt a great deal about a major component of the Lean system, total quality management, from Americans who had failed to get a hearing in their own home country – Deming and Juran.

Theory of Constraints (ToC)

Eli Goldratt published his famous book *The Goal* in 1984[16] and it has had immense influence on supply-chain thinking ever since. The underlying premise of the ToC is that organizations can be measured and controlled by variations on three measures: throughput, operational expense and inventory. Inventory is all the money that the system has invested in purchasing things that it intends to sell. Operational expense is all the money the system spends in order to turn inventory into throughput. Throughput is the rate at which the system generates money through sales. This model has spawned what is known as throughput accounting that, effectively, demonstrates that 'to make money now and in the future' a company should, unsurprisingly, maximize manufacturing and sales throughput. Unfortunately this is often not the objective of many operations leaders, not because they are stupid but because they get measured using labour and overhead recoveries that reward 'production of anything' – whether it sells or not. In consequence, there is all too frequently, in many manufacturing companies, a bias towards excessively large batch sizes and a disconnect between service and cash-flow aspirations and what gets made on the factory floor.

Given the objective of maximizing throughput, a strong focus of the ToC is identifying and unblocking anything that is a constraint and prevents achievement of this goal. Constraints can be internal or external, are generally few in number (always at least one) and can be reduced, or eliminated, by a disciplined and iterative approach as follows:

1 Identify the system's constraint(s): these are where management attention must be focused to achieve the goal of making money now and in the future. Focusing anywhere that is not a system constraint is wasted resource as it will not improve system throughput.

2 Decide how to exploit the system's constraint(s): learn how to maximize the efficiency of the constraint and increase its throughput capability. This might include improving the quality of the output, reducing changeover times, preventative maintenance, etc – all those activities that can expand the constraints capacity other than actually buying more capacity per se.

3 Subordinate everything else to the above decision(s): this means that all the non-constraints should be operated at a rate that does not exceed that of the constraint. This is to prevent bloating inventories, elongating lead times and the frequently seen firefighting/expediting that commonly accompanies unbalanced production environments. Subordination also includes ensuring that the rest of the system supports the work of the constraint at all times. The system constraint must never be starved of materials to process, or supplied with poor-quality materials. The former is achieved by maintaining a buffer of appropriate inventory in front of it. Buffers are also allowed behind the constraint to prevent downstream failure from blocking the constraint's output. Used in this way, buffers protect the constraint from variability in the rest of the system and help stabilize processing rates both upstream and downstream of the constraint.

Buffer management is a key aspect of the Theory of Constraints and the most often used method is a visual system of designating the buffer in three colours: green (okay), yellow (caution) and red (action required). Creating this kind of visibility enables the entire system to be aligned and thus subordinated to the need of the constraint. The term 'drum, buffer, rope' is often used to describe this process of aligning a system's throughput with that of its constraint.

4 Elevate the system's constraint(s): once the potential capacity of the system has been fully exploited it can, if necessary, be expanded by investing in additional equipment and/or, hiring people. This is deliberately the fourth step because the first three effectively cost nothing and can typically, and very quickly, expose a minimum of 30 per cent of hidden capacity.

5 Do not allow inertia to cause a system's constraint: if, in the previous steps, the constraint has been broken, go back to step one and start again and follow this cycle of improvement continuously.

Between them the practices of Lean and the Theory of Constraints are delivering immense benefits to those businesses that are managing their supply chains and factories with them. But it took another new approach to definitively explain exactly why they work and it employed much of the conceptual framework that had been developed back in 1961 by Forrester, Burbidge, Kingman and Little.

Factory Physics[17]

The new approach was that of Factory Physics, which first appeared in the book of that name by Wallace Hopp and Mark Spearman in 1995. At the heart of Factory Physics is Little's Law and Kingman's formula, the latter of which they refer to as the VUT equation. In essence, Factory Physics treats supply chains and factories as what they really are: flows of materials that turn into queues at constraints due to variability. Based upon this, mathematical modelling and simulations, various laws of Factory Physics have been derived such as:

1 Increasing variability always degrades the performance of a production system.

2 In a line where releases are independent of completions, variability early in a routing increases cycle time more than variability later in the routing.

3 Variability in a production system will be buffered by some combination of inventory, capacity and time.

4 Flexibility reduces the amount of variability buffering required in a production system.

5 In a steady state all plants will release work at an average rate that is strictly less than the average capacity.

6 If a work station increases utilization without making any other changes, average WIP and cycle time will increase in a highly non-linear fashion.

7 The manufacturing lead time for a routing that yields a given service level is an increasing function of both the mean and standard deviation of the cycle time of the routing.

Using the principles expounded in *Factory Physics*, Hopp and Spearman have defined Lean as: 'fundamentally about minimizing the costs of buffering variability'[18] and they define pull, in contrast to push, as any replenishment methodology that caps inventory.

Summary

Forrester, Burbidge, Little and Kingman all developed the conceptual framework in the early 1960s that is now being used to explain why supply chains, driven by forecasts through MPS/MRP calculations, deliver appalling performance. Ironically this was at the very same time as MRP was in the early stages of its development but, as we have seen, the MRP Crusade proved unstoppable as computer technology became commonplace and it appeared so very suitable for supporting what intuitively appears to be a sensible replenishment process: forecast what you are going to sell and make the necessary quantities at the right time to meet the demand, and use a planned safety stock to buffer against the forecast errors.

As we have learnt, however, while the forecast-driven approach might work reasonably well for driving execution when demand volumes are large and stable, and the forecasts are reasonably accurate, it proves impossible to manage efficiently when forecast error is large, MRP exception messages become legion and planners respond by trying to avoid service issues by interrupting production schedules, thereby generating variability and its three unplanned buffers – capacity, time and inventory.

Forecast error tends to be higher for lower-volume/medium- to higher-variability demand volumes because of the central limit theorem (ie relative or percentage variability increases as the average declines). Forecast error also tends to increase with distance upstream from where the forecasts are generated: the bullwhip effect. It is the impact of this forecast error-induced variability upon flow that generates the excessive and unpredictable queues of inventory that confound MRP's assumption of known and fixed lead times, which causes the vicious circle of further service risks, further schedule interventions and more variability.

Of course, if there were no capacity constraints then lead times would be known, stable and planned, and service levels would be reliably achieved. Unfortunately, capacity is not infinite, which is the key weakness in the entire MRP framework. And there is nothing in the design structure of MRP that can absorb the variability – in fact the entire logic of MRP replenishment is built upon 100 per cent dependent demand, so any variability – be it forecast-induced or natural process variation – is transmitted and amplified up the supply chain, so the delays always accumulate and there is no scope for catchback unless additional capacity can be found.

Why has it taken until the second decade of the 21st century for the fundamental weaknesses of forecast-driven MRP – as a replenishment execution process – to be identified and something done about it? To the first part of the question, of course, the answer is that MRP's problems have been known about for some time in academia, certainly as far back as Burbidge's 1983 article. In fact, there is evidence that Orlicky himself was aware of a problem when he wrote:

> Stock replenishment is a concept forcibly grafted onto a manufacturing inventory. It is in conflict with basic management objectives of low inventories and high return on investment.[2]

And in today's standard texts on planning and inventory control management there is usually some mention of what is called 'MRP nervousness' – the propensity for calculated MRP material requirements to change dramatically and quickly through the various multilevel batching calculations as demand and forecast go out of alignment or as supply schedules diverge from plan.

With respect to the second part of the question, until recently companies have had little option than to use the MRP embedded in ERP systems because there has been no viable alternative. Companies and supply chains are complex and use of MPS and MRP logic for forecast-driven planning for materials and capacities is eminently sensible. And although some of the larger ERP systems do have two parallel versions of MRP – one for execution and one for planning simulation – very few companies make use of this separation. And why should they? As previously mentioned, forecast-driven replenishment execution seems intuitively sensible and few supply chain leaders, except perhaps those with a deep understanding of Lean, are familiar with the queuing theory and Factory Physics principles that explain why forecast push MPS/MRP cannot possibly operate effectively in an environment (be it a factory or a supply chain) without infinite capacity (and even if there were minimal capacity constraint, use of inaccurate forecasts for driving execution will quickly lead to its misuse and the creation of real constraints).

And anyway, what alternative replenishment method could possibly be adopted by ERP users? One option has been the very simplistic single echelon reorder point functionality available from most ERP systems, with no supporting functionality for the critically important inventory target-sizing activity; another is level schedule, which works very well for high-volume/low-variability demand patterns but is extremely costly in terms of inventory, and usually service, for items of lower volume and higher variability.

It can be argued that markets tend to be served by the products that they demand, or deserve, and in the case of the supply chain planning marketplace there has been little demand for an alternative to MRP. One reason has been mentioned – lack of knowledge about supply chain dynamics and its negative impact upon flow variability. Another might be lack of awareness amongst MRP users that their performance is so poor – after all, if everyone else is using it and 'benchmarking' is telling you that your performance is 'in the right ball park' versus your peers, then why worry?

In the absence of an alternative to MRP/ERP it would take a brave executive to declare that he/she 'knows' that the millions spent on their APS/ERP systems was not well spent and that he/she is going to decouple the company's replenishment activities from the MRP system and use spreadsheet-supported reorder point mechanisms instead (though, ironically, most MRP planning people are very heavy users of spreadsheet systems for replenishment calculations as they find pure MRP totally ineffective).

If, however, there is a recognition by some CEOs and senior supply chain executives that APS/MRP/ERP has not delivered much in the way of the promised performance improvements (eg due to persistent service and inventory issues and decline in ROI), despite its very high investment costs, the life of that investment is coming to an end and another expensive investment is required for the next upgrade, then maybe they would be receptive to an alternative? Especially if that alternative was credible, could be demonstrated to be transformational upon performance and was inexpensive, low risk and quick to trial and implement? That, of course, is the proposition from Demand-Driven SCM, with its credibility stemming from the fundamentals of queuing theory and the fact that it has been developed using what works from the other key SCM practices, as follows:

- *S&OP/MRP*: although Demand-Driven SCM eliminates forecast-driven MPS/MRP from the replenishment execution activity, it still very much uses the item-level forecasts blown through MRP's BOMs, routings and inventory parameters to provide planners with a view of future capacity and inventory requirements as well as a picture of the company's likely forward financials. This, of course, is the foundation of the S&OP process but, unlike traditional MRP, which uses the forecast-driven MPS and MRP for both replenishment and planning, when execution is Demand-Driven the unplanned forecast error-induced variability-generated buffers are minimized, which means that the forecasts of capacity requirements, inventory levels and revenue, at an aggregate level, will be far more accurate. So forecast-driven S&OP, using the MRP demand and supply network, continues to play a very important role in a Demand-Driven supply chain – and needs to do so because, as we have seen, constrained capacities cause exponential increases in lead times and service issues, so it is vitally important to plan capacities appropriately in advance.

- *Lean*: Demand-Driven SCM can reasonably be considered a form of enterprise(s)-wide pull – and pull, of course, is a key element in the Lean toolbox. It has, however, been thought by many practitioners that Lean pull is only really suitable for stable demand patterns, maybe because the use of 'pull in the Toyota Production System has been in support of a known and stable heijunka/mixed-model schedule. Heijunka/mixed-model scheduling works very well for the manufacture of cars but it is by no means the only way in which pull can be employed in a supply chain. The use of multiple independent and decoupled, planned and maintained inventory positions in a supply chain that are replenished using a make/ship to replace mechanism, or pull, is a core element of Demand-Driven SCM and a significant contributor to the delivery of that other key component of Lean: flow (or minimization of variability).

- *Theory of Constraints*: an important focus of both ToC and Demand-Driven SCM is their use of planned and independent buffers, which are the subject of regular maintenance and review.

Supply chain leaders who have a desire and opportunity to renew their supply chain planning process need to have an awareness of the Demand-Driven SCM alternative and how it can be implemented. One of the key reasons for that awareness now starting to percolate through industry in the United States, Europe and AsiaPac is the founding of the Demand Driven Institute, its success in promoting Demand-Driven MRP (DDMRP) and its development of the professional certifications: Certified Demand Driven Planner (CDDP) and Certified Demand Driven Leader (CDDL). Such supply chain executives also need to have access to appropriate functionality-rich and robust software support to enable them to manage their complex and, often, dispersed supply networks. Fortunately the rediscovery of enterprise(s)-wide pull or Demand-Driven SCM has coincided with the arrival of SaaS that enables low-cost and low-risk simulations and pilots with Demand-Driven SCM, followed by an incremental full-scale implementation.

The Demand Driven Institute, DDMRP and SaaS are the subjects covered in the next chapter.

Notes

1 VA Mabert (2007) The early road to materials requirements planning, *Journal of Operations Management*, 25, pp 346–56

2 J Orlicky (1975) *Materials Requirements Planning*, McGraw Hill, New York

3 TE Vollman (1973) *Operations Management: A systems model building approach*, Addison-Wesley, Massachusetts

4 CC New (1973) *Requirements Planning*, Gower Press, London

5 JW Forrester (1961) *Industrial Dynamics*, MIT Press, Massachusetts

6 HL Lee, V Padmanabhan and S Whang (1997) The bullwhip effect in supply chains, *Sloan Management Review*, 38 (3), pp 93–102

7 JL Burbidge (1961) The 'new approach' to production, *The Production Engineer*, 40 (12), December, pp 769–84

8 JL Burbidge (1983) Five golden rules to avoid bankruptcy, *The Production Engineer*, 62 (10), October, pp 965–81

9 JDC Little (1961) A proof for the queuing formula: L=$/Lambda$W, *Operations Research*, 9 (3), pp 383–7

10 JFC Kingman (1961) The single server queue in heavy traffic, *Proceeding of the Cambridge Philosophical Society*, 57, pp 902–4

11 R Schonberger (1982) *Japanese Manufacturing TecŸiques*, The Free Press, New York

12 Shigeo Shingo (1992) *The Shingo Production Management System: Improving process functions (manufacturing & production)*, Productivity Press, Cambridge, USA

13 Taiicho OŸo (1988) *Toyota Production System*, Productivity Inc.

14 JP Womack, DT Jones and D Roos (1991) *The machine that Changed the World*, Productivity Press, Cambridge USA

15 JP Womack and DT Jones (1996) *Lean Thinking*, Simon & Schuster, New York

16 EM Goldratt 'The Goal' 1984, Productivity Press

17 WJ Hopp and ML Spearman (1995) Factory Physics, McGraw Hill Intl, New York

18 Wallace J Hopp and Mark L Spearman (2004) To pull or not to pull: what is the question?, *Manufacturing and Service Operations Management*, 6 (2), pp 133–48

The Demand Driven Institute, Demand-Driven MRP and SaaS

07

The Demand Driven Institute

The Demand Driven Institute (DDI) was founded in 2011 by Carol Ptak and Chad Smith.

Carol has considerable practical supply chain and operations experience from the factory floor through to the boardroom, she has authored several books on MRP, ERP, Lean and the Theory of Constraints and, in the past, has been a president of APICS and an executive at PeopleSoft where, before their acquisition, she developed Demand-Driven Manufacturing.

Chad was a co-founder and managing partner of the Constraints Management Group, a services and tecŸology company specializing in pull-based manufacturing, materials and project management systems. He is an internationally acknowledged expert on the Theory of Constraints and worked closely for many years with Eli Goldratt.

In 2011 Chad and Carol wrote the third edition of *Orlicky's Material Requirements Planning*, Orlicky's seminal text on the subject, which had not been revised since George Plossl's update in 1994. In that book they describe the detailed operation of Demand-Driven MRP, which has since been significantly expanded upon in their 2016 book, *DDMRP: Demand Driven Material Requirements Planning*.[1]

The Demand Driven Institute is, in its own words:

Dedicated to proliferating consistent Demand-Driven methods and approaches through education, training and certification. The Demand Driven Institute has a global presence through its partnership with the International Supply Chain Education Alliance (ISCEA) and its global network of affiliates. DDI's Certified Demand Driven Planner (CDDP) and Certified Demand Driven Leader (CDDL) programmes are quickly becoming the world standard for the emerging Demand-Driven methodology in planning, scheduling and execution.

(www.demanddriveninstitute.com)

They have affiliate organizations across the world and a growing number of endorsed instructors for their CDDP programme; in 2016 the CDDL qualification was launched. Both programmes are listed in Gartner's 'Market guide for supply-chain certification programmes'.

Demand-Driven MRP

The methodology that is the primary subject of the CDDP, and an important component in the CDDL certification, is called Demand-Driven MRP (DDMRP) and is entirely consistent with what has been described in this book as Demand-Driven SCM.

DDMRP is the disruptive step-change evolution of MRP that enables it to perform effectively in the 'new normal'. The new normal is today's world of increasingly complex and global supply chains with longer lead times, volatile demand, inaccurate forecasts, short customer tolerance times, product variety proliferation and multiple routes to market. And in parallel with the emergence of the new normal the pressure upon supply chains to deliver ever more competitive service levels has been growing, while at the same time, similar pressure has been exerted from senior management to improve inventory turn and cost performance. DDMRP is positioned as a significant and more appropriate upgrade to the antiquated 1950s MRP logic. It brings supply order generation into the modern era because it doesn't force the use of forecasts that are inevitably inaccurate in the new normal to directly drive replenishment through an MPS.

Figure 7.1   The five stages of Demand-Driven MRP

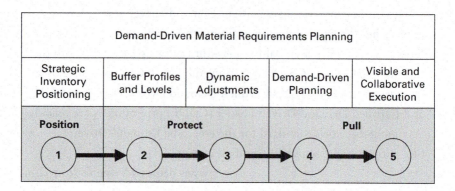

Instead, and in common with Demand-Driven SCM, DDMRP involves the deliberate positioning, sizing and maintenance of multiple independent and decoupled inventory locations in the supply chain. It also involves the Demand-Driven replenishment of these inventories using the net flow equation (instead of the traditional inaccurate MPS/MRP projected available balance calculation by time period) and a series of early warning 'flow' alerts based on penetration of the planned inventory buffer that indicates to planners that some form of expediting action might, in exceptional circumstances, be required. DDMRP can best be summarized as 'position, protect and pull'. This is accomplished through five stages that must be implemented in sequence:

1 Position – Strategic Inventory Positioning (for increasing responsiveness and absorbing variability).

2 Protect – Buffer Profiles and Sizing (according to demand levels and variability).

3 Protect – Dynamic Adjustments to the Buffers (to reflect changing demand levels and variability).

4 Pull – Demand-Driven Planning.

5 Pull – Visible and Collaborative Execution.

Thus DDMRP's processes of *position*, *protect* and *pull* drive supply of what can and will be sold, which is contrasted to the *push* and *promote* mechanism of traditional MRP that results in rigid forward schedules of what will be made and hoped might be sold, ie the MPS, and which results in service issues, an unbalanced bimodal inventory profile, ie items are either overstocked or understocked and swing between those extremes, unplanned service-saving schedule interruptions and costly promotional efforts, sometimes called 'demand shaping', to sell off the excessive inventories.

DDMRP has three significant innovations – decoupled lead time, buffer sizing and the net flow equation – as follows.

Decoupled lead time The supply lead time for replenishing an inventory buffer. It is not the cumulative lead time, which is the total time it takes to supply a finished product from the longest leg of raw-material supply through manufacture and release into stock. Nor is it a part's manufacturing lead time, which is simply how long it takes to make that particular part through a particular process. The decoupled lead time is effectively the supply lead time for a planned stock item that is its longest routing leg back to another buffered stock component. The decoupled lead time is very important because its length is used to size the part's inventory target: the average demand over the decoupled lead time (plus something for variability and the greater of either demand over the order interval and the minimum order quantity). The positioning of any other upstream inventory position should only start to be considered if it reduces a downstream item's decoupled lead time.

Buffer sizing DDMRP uses a very clever methodology for sizing and segmenting the calculated buffers (see Figure 7.2). Depending on whether the item is a distributed item, a manufactured item, a manufactured intermediate item or a purchased part it is classified as, say, D, M, I or P – and this can be useful for allocating them to category planners. The lead time for each part is then classified as long, medium or short and the demand variability as low, medium or high. Each of these lead-time and variability classifications are then allocated a percentage such as follows:

> Lead-time factor (LTF) S = 30 per cent
>
> Lead-time factor M = 50 per cent
>
> Lead-time factor L = 70 per cent
>
> Variability factor (VF) H = 70 per cent
>
> Variability factor M = 50 per cent
>
> Variability factor L = 30 per cent

Of course, these percentages can be adjusted or ranged as the environment changes and dictates.

Part types might therefore be referred to as MLL (manufactured, long lead time, low variability) or PSM (purchased, short lead time, medium variability), etc.

The inventory targets and their segments are then calculated as follows:

> Lead-time segment (yellow zone) = average daily usage x decoupled lead time (ADU x DLT)
>
> Variability segment (red zone) = (ADU x DLT) x LTF + ((ADU x DLT) x LTF) x VF
>
> Order segment (green zone) = larger of minimum order quantity, ADU over the planned reorder cycle or (ADU x DLT) x LTF
>
> Planning buffer = variability segment + lead-time segment + order segment

The reason why the variability factor increases directly in line with variability is obvious but the behaviour of the lead-time factor as it applies to both the variability and order-size segments is less so. With respect to the order quantity, the longer the lead time the smaller should be the desired order quantity, relative to lead-time demand, to avoid having to hold high levels of stock in the warehouse and to maintain supply continuity – delays in smaller, more frequent deliveries have less of an impact than delays in infrequent

Figure 7.2   The DDMRP inventory buffer zones

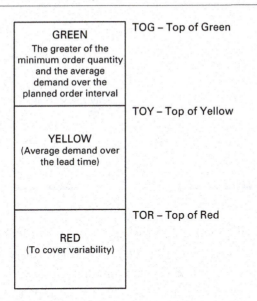

large deliveries. And the impact of the lead time upon the variability segment, while it should be positive, should not increase in a linear manner because, as the lead time increases, so the lead-time volume also increases and the relative error between it and actual decreases due to the central limit theorem (and as demonstrated by the lead-time square root rule in traditional safety stock calculations).

Net flow equation The stock target less the level of the net flow position determines the quantity for ordering to replenish the stock position. If the net flow level is above the variability and lead-time segments combined (Top of Yellow – TOY in Figure 7.2) then no order is required, but when it reaches, or dips below, that level then the calculation is made and the order placed.

Net flow position = physical stock on hand plus stock on order less (back orders and today's orders and qualified spike demands) (Figure 7.3)

Figure 7.3   The components of the net flow position

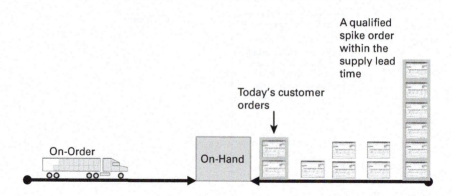

Qualified spike demand is the aggregate of orders on a particular day in the future (usually set as far forward as the decoupled lead time plus the planned replenishment cycle – if there is one) that exceed a percentage (often 50 per cent) of the variability segment. Including this abnormally high-level demand quantity in the net flow equation, at the earliest opportunity, gives the supply chain enough time to make it in addition to the average level of demand. A further refinement of this principle is to include in the net flow equation the future abnormal orders that are above a larger threshold, which therefore require capturing even further ahead.

There is no doubt that the formation of the Demand Driven Institute and the development of Demand-Driven MRP and the Demand-Driven Adaptive Enterprise (which describes how, through DDMRP and Demand-Driven S&OP, enterprises are able to seamlessly adapt to changes in their demand and supply environment without disrupting material flow) are very significant developments in the evolution of SCM (Appendix 1 is a description of how the DDI evolved – in the words of Chad Smith and Carol Ptak). DDMRP is a process that has repeatedly been proven to deliver transformational supply chain performance improvement and the Demand Driven Institute is undoubtedly fulfilling an excellent role in evangelizing the Demand-Driven approach, setting minimum standards for software providers (to ensure that claims from vendors regarding Demand-Driven functionality can be trusted) and running very high-quality global learning programmes to enable supply chain professionals to be informed, trained and certified in Demand-Driven ways of working.

Software as a Service (SaaS)

Large and complex manufacturing and distribution companies almost always use computer systems and software to manage their transactions in the form of ERP. Such companies usually also use the MRPII functionality that is embedded in these ERP systems or they use a 'bolt-on' specialist planning and replenishment system, sometimes termed an advanced planning system.

Mid-size companies often use some form of transaction system as well, perhaps ERP, or interface it with various other specialist supply chain systems such as order processing, stock management and/or MRP. The point is, most companies these days have access to an IT system, or systems, of record that help them to operate efficiently and produce their legally required financial statements. Until recently such systems were almost exclusively bought and managed by the companies on their own premises. However, a new route to accessing software support is opening up and is commonly known as the 'cloud' or 'Software as a Service'(SaaS).

Some Demand-Driven software systems are available to users as purchased 'on premise' systems, but all are also available as SaaS, which makes their trial, evaluation and implementation both relatively inexpensive and low risk. As Demand-Driven SCM is a relatively new concept for many supply chain executives, this 'low entry barrier' is another of its significant advantages.

Already we know that Demand-Driven SCM involves the decoupling of the various levels within the supply chain so it can be implemented at separate discrete stages of the supply chain without affecting the echelons either upstream or downstream (eg finished products might be subject to a Demand-Driven pilot but raw materials still ordered using MRP or, perhaps, the other way around with finished goods replenished using forecast push MRP but the materials ordered using a decoupled reorder point or recycle mechanism). Similarly, an additional benefit of Demand-Driven SaaS is that it is extremely flexible, easy, quick and inexpensive to link with multiple transaction systems to reflect a company's merger, acquisition or divestment activities.

Demand-Driven SCM SaaS lends itself extremely easily to supporting a Demand-Driven 'proof of principle' pilot across a specified range of items at a particular location or locations, for just the cost of the implementation and the monthly SaaS fee – no software acquisition required. Prior to this step it is also possible, and very common, for interested companies to provide their software vendor with some historical demand data and supply chain parameters to allow a simulation of the Demand-Driven SCM process and to compare the output with what actually happened.

Are these simulations and evaluation pilots expensive? The answer is obviously relative but they certainly do not have to involve IT software acquisition costs nor the costs of complex integration with legacy IT systems. The required data can be simply shared using flat files between the SaaS and legacy ERP using the secure file transfer protocol (SFTP). Setting this up is extremely quick and easy; the most common rate-limiting factor is usually the client company accurately identifying the whereabouts of the necessary demand, transactions and supply parameter data (the latter can actually be managed directly in the Demand-Driven SCM system if desired) within its ERP system and getting it extracted!

Note

1 C Ptak and C Smith (2016) *DDMRP: Demand driven materials requirements planning*, Industrial Press, Connecticut

What next – control theory?

08

The bullwhip effect has been studied very thoroughly in academia and one of the most fruitful approaches has been through the lens of control theory. Control theory is an inter-disciplinary branch of mathematics and engineering that deals with dynamic systems involving an input, an output, feedback and a desired level of performance. It is best understood by way of an example such as a thermostat. Given the desire to keep a room at a specified temperature above its surroundings, the thermostat keeps the heating on until that temperature is reached, when it switches off. The room will then cool down, which at some point triggers the thermostat to again switch on the heating. In this case the controller is very 'naive' and the actual temperature will oscillate a great deal around the target. A more sophisticated controller might recognize not only the actual temperature but also the rate at which it is rising or falling and use this information to determine when, and how much, heat should be released to achieve the target more consistently. There are three forms of feedback controller – proportional, integral and derivative – and one or more are used very widely in products and industry; examples include automatic steering systems, car cruise controls and many forms of manufacturing process control such as in the management of chemical reactions.

The behaviour of supply chains in terms of the alignment between actual demand for product and the quantity being made, shipped and available in stock is ideal for analysis using control theory due to the existence of the 'bullwhip' phenomenon. For example, across particular industries we see bullwhip over quite long timescales, such as in mining and commodities, where rising demand, and prices, encourage the opening of new mines and investment in extraction machinery, which of course takes considerable time. And when all the new, and excess, capacity eventually comes on stream, stocks build up and prices plummet. On much shorter timescales we see bullwhip occurring in supply chains where forecast-driven ordering and replenishment decision making amplifies the upstream response to small levels of consumer demand variability. Bullwhip is caused, in this case, by independent participants in the supply chain, misinterpreting each other's demand-and-supply signals (often because there are delays in their communication – latency) and making replenishment decisions, based upon them, that exaggerate any real level of variability. That bullwhip is a source of unnecessary business cost has been calculated by one academic, Professor Richard Metters,[1] to be such that it can reduce company profits by up to 30 per cent through its impact upon inventory levels, generation of excess capacity and sales losses.

Much of the academic work on the application of control theory to dampening bullwhip is aimed at finding an optimal supply-ordering response to demand changes in terms of impact upon production stability and inventory levels. This can be best thought about by thinking of the extremes of the possible supply responses to demand variability. When demand for a single item is very variable, one strategy is a level schedule – very efficient for production but finished-product inventory levels will swing up and down significantly as demand falls and rises respectively. At the other extreme is a forecast-driven replenishment process in which, if the forecasts are accurate and capacity is not an issue, supply is pushed into the supply chain in advance, so supply would track demand as it rises and falls. But, of course, forecasts are not accurate and capacity is constrained so lead times vary with load and, in a multiproduct environment using shared resources, variability-induced chaos ensues as supply schedules are interfered with by planners to save service levels. A third theoretical approach is to pass on all orders – as they arrive – to production, which would result in supply following demand up and down, with maintenance of a stable and low inventory level as the orders are shipped immediately upon receipt.

There are numerous activities that can be undertaken by supply chain participants to dampen the bullwhip effect and there are many academic papers that have analysed and described them. The key activities are twofold:[2]

- *Simplified material flow*: activities that minimize flow variability and reduce lead times; this includes active time-compression tecŸiques, use of the shortest possible planning period, batch-size reduction and pull replenishment systems. In other words: Lean.

- *Supply chain relationships*: collaborative 'partnerships' between key suppliers and customers, involving a key player managing the synchronization and coordination of the supply chain, with a single point of control, and an integrated information/decision support system.

In effect, the actions listed under *simplified material flow* contribute to bullwhip dampening by increasing the frequency and speed of material replenishment up and down the supply chain and, thereby, keeping them better aligned, both in terms of quantity and timing, with actual demand. The *supply chain relationship* activities contribute in a subtle, but no less important manner. When there is a significant step change in the rate of downstream demand, upstream inventories are likely to be drained, perhaps emptied, until upstream replenishment activities can also permanently change their rate of supply and catch up – and the longer the delay in communicating the downstream demand change to upstream participants, the more severe will be the supply misalignment and the greater the risk of overcompensation (ie often known as latency). End-to-end coordination and synchronization of supply rates, in line with actual demand, is of course designed to eliminate the communication delays and ensure that fully aligned and synchronized capacity and throughput decisions are made.

In a Demand-Driven Supply Chain, simplified material flow is of course beneficial and largely the objective of Lean's focus upon 'continuous improvement'. The recommendations from supply chain relationships are fulfilled by a properly designed Demand-Driven Supply Chain process in the form of collaborative inventory buffer sizing and maintenance so that the planned buffers can be sized, maintained and aligned in line with actual downstream demand levels. Trading partners should also have, through information exchange (eg shared SaaS), visibility of inventories and shipments versus the buffer targets so that both parties can be equally informed about the robustness, or otherwise, of their shared material flow and avoid making one-sided and disruptive interventions. If all of these activities are implemented successfully, end-to-end supply chain flow will be assured with minimal bullwhip. This is described in more detail in the section on 'Demand-Driven Collaboration: key to the fight-back against low-cost competition' (Chapter 2).

Control theory, however, has a contribution to make in supply chains that are subject to significantly variable rates of demand and where neither effective simplified materials flow nor supply chain relationships are in place. In these circumstances it is suggested that an upstream supplier uses an 'automatic pipeline inventory and order-based production control system' (APIOBPCS), in which the planned production rate is adjusted by some fixed fraction of the discrepancy between planned and actual stock on hand or scheduled. Alternatively, the production rate for the forthcoming period is the same as that of the former period plus a fraction of the difference between desired and expected inventory at the end of the period, assuming the preceding rate was maintained. In both cases, the closer the control factor is to one the closer will production track sales fluctuations about the forecast and the smaller will be the consequent inventory level. In contrast, controllers of zero result in levelled production and very high average inventories. Depending upon the relative cost of changing production rates versus the inventory impact, a company can manage the control factor accordingly. This process was first described by JoŸ Magee as far back as 1954 in his book *Production Planning and Inventory Control*.[3] In more recent times the process is described by Disney, Towill and Van de Velde as:

> Let the production targets (or replenishment orders) be equal to the sum of: average demand (exponentially smoothed over *Ta* time units), a fraction (1/*Ti*) of the inventory difference in actual net stock compared to target net stock and the same fraction (1/*Tw*) of the difference between target work in progress (WIP) and actual WIP.[4]

In essence, the approach is similar to a standard 'order up to' technique, such as ROP or ROC, but includes only a proportion of any demand change and a proportion of any planned pipeline inventory discrepancy. Depending upon the degree of demand smoothing and the fraction used in the controllers, different replenishment behaviours can be modelled and a large amount of simulation and mathematical analysis has been undertaken to identify optimal solutions. In a 2010 paper by Zhou, Towill and Disney,[5] it is concluded that:

> Organizations (that are neither part of an extended enterprise backed by analytic capability, nor associated with an altruistic supply chain with information and philosophy sharing) can readily exploit the APIOBPCS as a decision support system via simple rules-of-thumb that do not require exactly matching to individual products. The outcome is a *capability* (of matching goals when operating in the expected scenario) and are surprisingly *copable* when surrounded by uncertainty.

Stephen Disney, Professor of Operations Management at Cardiff University, one of the co-authors of this paper, has worked with retailers and manufacturing companies to successfully implement replenishment processes that use this form of control theory methodology.[6]

As Demand-Driven SCM diffuses through industry, its application, in combination with control theory, will certainly be subject to investigation and the latter will surely find a role in enhancing material control.

Notes

1 R Metters (1997) Quantifying the bullwhip effect in supply chains, *Journal of Operations Management*, **15**, pp 89–100

2 S Geary, SM Disney and DR Towill (2006) On bullwhip in supply chains – historical review, present practice and expected future impact, *International Journal of Production Economics*, **101**, pp 2–18

3 JF Magee (1954) *Production Planning and Inventory Control*, McGraw Hill, New York

4 SM Disney, DR Towill and W Van de Velde (2004) Variance amplification and the golden ratio in production and inventory control, *International Journal of Production Economics*, **90** (3), pp 295–309

5 L Zhou, DR Towill and SM Disney (2010) A pragmatic approach to the design of bullwhip controllers, *International Journal of Production Economics*, **128**, pp 556–8

6 SM Disney, L Hoshiko, L Polley and C Weigel (2013) Removing bullwhip from Lexmark's toner operations, in *Proceedings from Production and Operations Management Society Annual Conference*, Denver, CO, USA, 3–6 May; also A Potter and SM Disney (2010) Removing bullwhip from the Tesco supply chain, *Production and Operations Management Society Annual Conference*, 7–10 May, Vancouver

POSTSCRIPT
From supply chain – an apology to our commercial colleagues

Over the years you may have gained the impression that we thought you hadn't a clue about the complexity of SCM and how it operates. You might have felt that nearly every time there was a stock out it was your fault because the sales forecasts were inaccurate; we might have appeared less than enthusiastic when you suggested we launch another line extension and, when you suggested we should be more agile, flexible and cost-efficient to meet increasing demand volatility and market competitiveness, we might even have suggested you had gone completely bonkers!

We now realize that you were right all along. It was always unreasonable for us to expect anyone to generate accurate time-phased item-level forecasts; of course, line extensions are essential in today's fast-fragmenting markets and, yes, we should indeed be far more efficient, agile and flexible to meet the demands of an ever more volatile and competitive marketplace (that's what Lean is really all about, but we got that one wrong too, by thinking it was about waste reduction and thinking that it needed stable demand to work effectively)… and the idea that we should try to stick to firm supply schedules for any more than a week, at absolute maximum, is complete nonsense.

Not only have we been in the wrong but it is totally our fault – for some reason, around 35 years ago we decided to follow the MRP Crusade and have been spending millions ever since trying to make a broken replenishment process work – along the way calling it MRPII, APS, optimization, real-time enabled or demand sensing. We were told by some, back then, that MRP couldn't work and only now have we begun to recognize where we went wrong and, with the emergence of Demand-Driven SCM, we can start to get back to real business.

So, please forget about accurate item-level forecasts – they are not important. In future we will be able to handle *any* level of consistent and high-demand volatility, such as that caused by all those promotions, without needing lots of detailed forecasts and planning and, believe it or not, we will be able to do so with much less average inventory. All we ask is that you let us know in advance of any really exceptional and extreme demand events for which we should plan a stock build.

And now that we have rediscovered how to drive our supply chain and operations properly, we are not going to use nearly as much capacity as we have needed in the past, so our costs will indeed come down and we can easily fit in more product launches. In fact, we are going to spend so much less time firefighting and expediting supply that we're going to have far more time to focus on new product launches and other value-add activities such as process improvements, supplier/customer collaboration, design for manufacture, network design, risk management and, even, how we can design our supply chain to provide competitive advantage such as postponement in support of mass customization. Even our S&OP meetings will become far more accurate and strategic in nature as we will eliminate the unplanned levels of inventory we create and capacity we use, and move on from just focusing upon service/inventory crisis reviews.

So, sincere apologies and we look forward to a far more constructive working relationship, based upon managing real commercial issues and opportunities without being held back by our inability to manage supply and operations in an effective manner.

PS If you're interested in Demand-Driven SCM take a look at the section 'Demand-Driven SCM: agility thru' stability' in Chapter 2.

PPS IT are quite active in tabling proposals to the board to invest millions in upgrading our current forecasting and advanced planning systems, and we would appreciate some support in blocking it on the grounds that Demand-Driven SCM is far more effective, far less expensive and can be piloted without risk using 'Software as a Service'.

PPPS Martin Christopher, Professor of Marketing and Logistics at Cranfield University, is very positive about Demand-Driven SCM. He says 'it is powerful and practical' and hopes it 'continues to gain traction in industry and… quickly becomes the norm.'

THE STORY BEHIND DDMRP

CONTRIBUTION BY CHAD SMITH AND CAROL PTAK, CO-FOUNDERS OF THE DEMAND DRIVEN INSTITUTE

The journey to discover and articulate Demand-Driven Materials Requirements Planning (DDMRP) is one of two very different paths that crossed. Each path was able to bring crucial knowledge and articulation to make DDMRP what it is today; one about the extent and depth of the MRP problem, the other about the extent and depth of what to do about it. Both were necessary conditions to get where we are today. First, we need to talk about the paths before they crossed.

Chad Smith

I got my start working for Eli Goldratt (bestselling author of the book *The Goal*) at the Goldratt Institute in New Haven, Connecticut in 1995. Dr Goldratt had an amazing analytical mind – I have never met anyone like him. I learned a set of very powerful thinking processes that allowed me to look at companies and supply chains as systems. Over the next 20 years we used this set of powerful tools to develop and articulate DDMRP and the Demand-Driven Adaptive Enterprise model. When I left the Goldratt Institute I co-founded, with Debra Smith, a consulting company called Constraints Management Group. I served as Managing Partner from 1997 to 2015.

We did a lot of pioneering work in the Theory of Constraints field in large complex manufacturers. We had to constantly fight against the native systems in order to implement common sense in planning and on the floor. In many cases we were working directly with several IT departments, coding new functionality within their ERP products.

It led us to get into software planning, scheduling and execution systems in 2003. Writing software specifications really forces you to understand and articulate desired inputs and outputs as well as cause and effect. We developed a product called Replenishment+®. It seemed to have an enormous amount of promise.

In 2008 I scheduled an online meeting with a senior account executive at Infor. I had known him for years and felt comfortable getting his opinion on what we had developed, from a solution and software perspective. That meeting convinced me we were on the right track. After taking him through the basics of the method and showing how that method could be achieved in software, he said, 'I don't know if you have any idea how big this is. I sell five different major ERP platforms and none of our MRP or SCM modules can come close to this.'

This convinced me and my partners to reach out to Carol Ptak. I had known Carol for several years and she was living and working close to my home in the Tacoma, Washington area. I knew we had something big but I simply didn't know what I didn't know. That meeting proved to be a watershed event.

Carol Ptak

My start was very different. In college I got my bachelor's degree in Biology with a specialty in genetics! I expected to be in the research lab for the rest of my career but I ended up in a company that manufactured biologicals for the medical market. It was there that I discovered that manufacturing was far more interesting than biology. I stayed in operations and project management for the next almost 20 years – biotech, aerospace, machine shops. Fortunately for me I had a mentor who urged me to join my professional society and get involved. That started my association with APICS for the next 40 years and resulted in my serving as APICS President and CEO in 2000. I was the first and still remain the only female to ever serve in that role. I was hired by IBM in 1999 into executive sales and moved around the company, ending up in a position responsible for analysing ERP companies and how IBM could support their offerings.

Moving to Washington State and doing a green-field start-up in aerospace led to my first book *MRP and Beyond*, because of discussions with the chief financial officer on how the MRP system should be set up. His favourite way to end the conversation was 'you didn't write the book on it' – so I did. After that I was encouraged to write one of the first two books ever published on ERP. That book came out in 1999, and during the presentation summary at the APICS conference that year, Eli Goldratt walked in. We had a cup of coffee with Eli Schragenheim and the result of that meeting was the collaboration that produced *Necessary but not Sufficient* in 2000. Quickly that new knowledge was incorporated into the ERP book and the second edition of that book came out in 2002.

When a headhunter called me at IBM and told me he had the perfect job for me, I decided to go and have a chat, since this company kept popping up on my analysis at work. After a full day of interviews at PeopleSoft I accepted the position of Vice President of Manufacturing, Distribution and Retail industries. It was there that the term 'Demand-Driven Manufacturing' was coined, after PeopleSoft purchased the software assets from JCIT. I knew the direction that manufacturing had to go in, but did not have a good idea how to get there. I knew it had something to do with leveraging Lean, TOC, Six Sigma and MRP. So during my tenure there I had the opportunity to work with the CEO of JCIT to rewrite *Quantum Leap: the next generation*, as well as to write a book with Harold Cavallaro called *Theory H.O.W.: How organizations could work*.

After the hostile takeover by Oracle was lost I was invited to be the Distinguished Executive in Residence at Pacific Lutheran University in Parkland, Washington. It was there that Chad came to visit me to ask for feedback on some innovation that he and his team at Constraints Management Group had been doing. As Chad said, it was a watershed event.

The collaboration begins

It only took about one hour for both of us to get very excited about the future. Carol demonstrating and explaining the magnitude of the problem and Chad demonstrating and explaining the extent of a practical solution. The immediate problem became how to get the word out, since these ideas were truly breakthrough concepts. Articulating the new concepts and critical differences between the new Demand-Driven approach to planning and the standard and insufficient approaches was the next big obstacle.

We wrote a white paper called 'Beyond MRP'. On a whim we sent it off to APICS to see if they had any interest in it. The response was almost immediate. APICS asked us to condense the article for their magazine. APICS not only put it in the magazine but made it the cover article under the title 'Brilliant Vision' (July/August 2008 edition). Shortly after that APICS sponsored a webinar with us in August 2008 on the subject of the article. Over 200 companies signed up! Then, in September 2008, Carol spoke on the topic at the APICS International Conference in Kansas City. The response was standing room only! In short, within a few short months, these responses were enough to convince the authors that they had struck a chord with the mainstream world's difficulty in trying to plan materials in a volatile and complex world using antiquated approaches.

With this encouragement we began to further articulate the solution. We initially gave the solution the name 'actively synchronized replenishment' (ASR). Chad spoke on the topic in November 2008 at the TOCICO Conference in Las Vegas. At that conference we were approached by Dr Jim Cox to continue writing on this topic. Dr Cox is well known in both the ToC and APICS worlds. He was to be the co-editor with JoŸ Schleier of a new book to be published that was to be called *The Theory of Constraints Handbook*. Dr Cox asked the authors to contribute a chapter to the book. The chapter was submitted about nine months later. Jim and JoŸ were very enthusiastic about the chapter content and sent it to the publisher, telling them that there should be a whole book dedicated to this. Below is what JoŸ had to say:

> 'Wow! What a chapter. My head is spinning around networks of interconnected buffers pulling production from the market side of the supply chain through multilevels in a shop with other buffers protecting its supply side. This is really an exciting story about a very creative piece of work. I wrote the first MRP system for JoÚ Deere's Ottumwa, Iowa plant in

the late 1950s; automated the BOMs, routings, inventory records, MRP, shop floor scheduling, and the purchasing system. Then in the early 1960s I then headed the development team that built the complement of logistics systems for the IBM Rochester Plant, later implemented at the IBM plants in Boulder and Boca Raton, with elements in IBM European plants. I only mention this to frame my appreciation for the incredible progress reflected in your work on actively synchronized replenishment (ASR). Congratulations! I wish we had some of these solutions back then… I am really blown away by the calibre and scope of this work.' John Schleier

In the spring of 2010, McGraw-Hill, acting on JoŸ's recommendation, offered Chad and Carol a contract to write the third revised edition of *Orlicky's Material Requirements Planning*. In 1975 Joe Orlicky wrote the first book on MRP, called *Material Requirements Planning*. This first MRP book is still seen today as the 'bible' and the genesis of standardized MRP to which every software company coded their product. In 1994, Joe's close friend, George Plossl, revised the book and it was called *Orlicky's Material Requirements Planning (Second Edition)*. George was one of the thought leaders at the time in the implementation of these concepts with Joe Orlicky, Oliver (Ollie) Wight and Richard (Dick) Ling. These two book editions have sold over 175,000 copies combined – clearly demonstrating this significant impact.

Through 542 pages the third edition not only allowed us to thoroughly describe the conventional MPS–MRP approach and its challenges but also offered an alternative that we now called 'Demand-Driven MRP' and its benefits. The name Demand-Driven MRP came to us at Carol's kitchen table preparing for the book. We knew that 'actively synchronized replenishment' (ASR) would not work – we were writing a definitive work on MRP! Carol explained the story of how they came up with the name Demand-Driven Manufacturing at PeopleSoft. Then it hit us; the method still incorporates elements of MRP yet it utilizes a different element of **demand** to **drive** supply order generation – it is Demand-Driven MRP! The name fitted like a glove in the context of the Orlicky book, and being in the book would also quickly bring DDMRP into the mainstream.

Based on initial reaction and the release of Orlicky's third edition we knew that people would want to know more. Where and how could that happen? We also knew that there would need to be consistent and standardized education and training around the method. Furthermore, the method could not be dominated by one brand of consulting and tecYology – that was precisely the path that would severely constrain its growth.

In 2011 we founded the Demand Driven Institute. Its mission was to focus on education and certification for the method – to get the world to say, 'Yes!' to DDMRP. In 2012 the Demand Driven Institute partnered with the International Supply Chain Education Alliance (ISCEA) to offer the Certified Demand Driven Planner (CDDP) programme. The CDDP programme was designed to provide consistent global standards for the DDMRP approach and to teach and certify practitioners in those standards. From 2012 to 2015 over 1,000 people, across six continents, took the CDDP programme. By the end of 2016 that number will be well over 2,000. At the time of this writing it is the fastest-growing supply chain certificate programme in the world.

In July 2016 we released *Demand Driven Material Requirements Planning* (Industrial Press), which is the authoritative work on the DDMRP, with 343 pages of content.

But DDMRP is just the engine of a Demand-Driven operating model (DDOM) and the DDOM is just part of becoming a Demand-Driven Adaptive Enterprise. The Demand Driven Institute is continuing to drive research and articulation in order to help organizations transform and sustain in the new normal.

We are very excited about books like this one by Simon and look forward to many more! It shows the proliferation of and hunger for a new breed of organizational management based on common sense and properly applied mathematics, physics and economics.

The Demand Driven Institute has published several white papers and case studies on DDMRP and the Demand-Driven operating model. A repository of case studies and white papers is available at www.demanddrivenworld.com.

FURTHER READING

The following are a selection of books and articles that are relevant to Demand-Driven Supply Chain Management, grouped according to their theme.

Supply chain dynamics and bullwhip

Burbidge, JL (1961) The new approach to production, *The Production Engineer*, **40** (12), December

Burbidge, JL (1983) 5 golden rules to avoid bankruptcy, *The Production Engineer*, **62** (10), October

Forrester, JW (1961) Industrial Dynamics, MIT Press, Massachusetts

Geary, S, Disney, SM and Towill, DR (2003) Bullwhip in supply chains: past, present and future, 17th International Conference on Production Research, Virginia, USA, 3–7 August

Lee, HL, Padmanabham, V and Whang, S (1997) The bullwhip effect in supply chains, *Sloan Management Review*, **38** (3), pp 93–102

Towill, DR (1994) 1961 and all that: the influence of Jay Forrester and JoŸ Burbidge on the design of modern manufacturing systems, *Proceedings of the Systems Dynamics Conference on Business Decision Making*, pp 105–15

Lean

Balle, F and Balle, M (2006) *The Goldmine*, Lean Enterprise Institute

Balle, F and Balle, M (2011) *The Lean Manager*, Lean Enterprise Institute

Bicheno, J and Holweg, M (2016) *The Lean Toolbox*, 5th edn, Picsie Books, Buckingham

Liker, JK and Meier, D (2006) *The Toyota Way Field Book*, McGraw Hill, New York

OŸo, T (1988) *Toyota Production System*, Productivity Press, New York

Schonberger, R (1982) *Japanese Manufacturing TecŸiques*, The Free Press, New York

Shingo, S (1992) *The Shingo Production Management System: Improving process functions (manufacturing & production)*, Productivity Press, New York

Womack, JP, Jones, DT and Roos, D (1991) *The Machine that Changed the World*, Productivity Press, New York

Womack, JP and Jones, DT (1996) *Lean Thinking*, Simon & Schuster, New York

Theory of Constraints

Goldratt, EM (1984) *The Goal*, Productivity Press, New York

Goldratt, E (1990) *Theory of Constraints*, North River Press, New York

Goldratt, E (1996) *The Race*, North River Press, New York

Goldratt, E, Ptak, C and Schragenheim, E (2000) *Necessary but not Sufficient*, North River Press, New York

Hepstinall, I and Bolton, R (2016) *Breakthrough Project Management*, Denehurst Publishing

Leach, LP (2000) *Critical Chain Project Management'*, Artech House

Factory Physics

Hopp, WJ and Spearman, ML (1995) *Factory Physics*, McGraw Hill, New York

Hopp, WJ and Spearman, ML (2004) To pull or not to pull: what is the question? *Manufacturing & Service Operations Management*, 6 (2), pp 133–48

Pound, ES, Bell, JH and Spearman, ML (2014) *Factory Physics for Managers*, McGraw Hill, New York

Spearman, ML and Hopp, WJ (1998) Teaching operations management from a science of manufacturing, *Production & Operations Management*, 7 (2), Summer

Standard, C and Davis, D (1999) *Running Today's Factory: A proven strategy for Lean manufacturing*, Hanser Gardner Publications, Ohio

Demand-Driven Materials Requirements Planning

Mondon, C (2016) The Missing Links, a Demand Driven Supply Chain Detective Novel, Industrial Press, Connecticut

Ptak, C and Smith, C (2016) *Demand Driven Materials Requirements Planning*, Industrial Press, Connecticut

Smith, D and Smith, C (2014) *Demand Driven Performance using Smart Metrics*, McGraw Hill, New York

Sook, LJ and Yong, JS (2014) *A Case Study of the System Dynamics Model to Evaluate the Performance of MRP and Demand Driven MRP*, Seoul National University of Science and TecŸology

Supply chain segmentation

Christopher, M and Towill, D (2001) An integrated model for the design of agile supply chains, *International Journal of Physical Distribution and Logistics Management*, 31 (4), pp 235–46

Christopher, M, Peck, H and Towill, D (2006) A taxonomy for selecting global supply chain strategies, *International Journal of Logistics Management*, 17 (2), pp 277–87

Fisher, ML (1997) What is the right supply chain for your product?, *Harvard Business Review*, March–April, pp 105–16

Godsell, J *et al*, Enabling supply chain segmentation through demand profiling, *International Journal of Physical Distribution and Logistics Management*, 41 (3)

Vitasek, KL, Manrodt, KB and Kelly, M (2003) Solving the supply – demand mismatch, *Supply Chain Management Review*, September/October, pp 58–64

INDEX

Note: The index is filed in alphabetical, word-by-word order. Within main headings, numbers are filed as spelt out in full and acronyms filed as presented. Page locators in *italics* denote information contained within a Figure or Table.

DATE DUE

GAYLORD   PRINTED IN U.S.A.

CPSIA information can be obtained
at www.ICGtesting.com
Printed in the USA
LVOW13s2008070518
576285LV00022B/244/P